The social work supervisor

Supervision in community, day care and residential settings

Allan Brown and
Iain Bourne

Open University Press
Buckingham · Philadelphia

Open University Press
Celtic Court
22 Ballmoor
Buckingham
MK18 1XW

email: enquiries@openup.co.uk
world wide web: www.openup.co.uk

and
325 Chestnut Street
Philadelphia, PA 19106, USA

First Published 1996
Reprinted 1998, 1999, 2002

A catalogue record of this book is available from the British Library

ISBN 0 335 19458 3 (pb)   0 335 19459 1 (hb)

Library of Congress Cataloging-in-Publication Data
Brown, Allan G.
   The social work supervisor: supervision in community, day care,
and residential settings / Allan Brown & Iain Bourne.
      p. cm. — (Supervision in context)
   Includes bibliographical references and index.
   ISBN 0–335–19459–1. — ISBN 0–335–19458–3 (pbk.)
   1. Social workers—Supervision of. 2. Home care services—
Management. 3. Day care centers—Management. 4. Group homes—
Management. I. Bourne, Iain, 1955– . II. Title. III. Series.
HV40.54.B76 1995
361.3'2'0683—dc20   95–14730
                                                                      CIP

Typeset by Graphicraft Limited, Hong Kong
Printed and bound in Great Britain by
Biddles Limited, Guildford and King's Lynn, www.biddles.co.uk

Contents

Series editors' preface

As an introduction to this series we would like to start with a story about the legendary Sufi 'wise fool' Mulla Nasrudin that concerns the time he was asked why he had never married and if he had ever come close to doing so:

> 'Indeed yes,' he replied, 'When I was young I was very keen to marry the perfect wife. I travelled through many lands looking for her. In France I met a beautiful dancer, who was joyful and carefree, but alas had no sense of the spiritual. In Egypt I met a princess who was both beautiful and wise, but sadly we could not communicate.
> Then finally in India after much searching I found her. She was beautiful, wise and her charm captured the hearts of everybody she met. I felt that I had found the perfect wife.'
> The Mulla paused with a long sigh. So one of the audience eagerly asked: 'Then did you not marry her, Mulla?'
> 'Alas,' sighed the Mulla, 'she was waiting for the perfect husband.'

In all the helping professions there are many who are waiting for the perfect supervisor. The person who will make the confusion clear, the complex understandable, absolve the guilt, rebuild our self-worth and magically remove the pain and distress. Inevitably there is much disappointment, for such supervisors do not exist. Instead it is necessary that all helping organisations are clear about the nature of 'good-enough supervision' and the training necessary to achieve it. To train, equip and support good-enough supervisors, there is a real need for well constructed books written by those from within each of the helping professions. It is with that need in mind that we are launching this new series, of which this is the first book.

The series

This is a series about supervision in a variety of professional contexts. Therefore this preface is both an introduction to the whole series, as well as to this particular book.

Before we wrote our own book on supervision in 1989 we had already carried out a good deal of supervision training in the fields of psychotherapy, counselling and social work; but since 1989 we have been invited into other professional worlds such as nursing, psychology, psychiatry, general practice, education, probation, organisational development and marriage guidance.

At one level the issues of and needs for supervision are very similar across all these helping professions; but we became aware of the differences between each profession, both in organisational structure and culture and the particular pressures that front-line workers and those that supervise and manage them, have to face.

While discovering that the principles outlined in our book can be widely applied, we also discovered an unmet need for much more detailed models and information which were profession specific. At the same time we became more aware of many individuals who were opening up new territory in different professional fields of supervision.

This gave us to the idea of a supervision series in which each book would address the particular contexts and issues of one of the major helping professions, whilst avoiding professional insularity by being part of a series in which each book relates to the ideas and concerns of the other professional fields. We are striving to establish a series which combines specificity with interconnection: a series where each book is written very much in the authors' own style and from their point of view, but which relates to wider concerns both within their own profession and in the growing field of supervision.

This book on the social work supervisor is to be followed by books on supervision in the professions of psychotherapy, counselling, nursing and medicine. It is also planned to add a book that will look at the role of mentoring for managers, in both the helping professions and in general management in all types of organisation.

The social work profession

Social work has been caught in a storm of change in the last two decades. At times the winds have eased, but the periods of calm have been short lived, before once again the profession has been battered and tossed about by new currents and political winds. This climate of change can be divided into six areas, with the acronym PESTLE, which stands for: Political, Economic, Social, Technological, Legal and Environmental, and in all six areas, social work has had to cope at times with severe pressures.

In the United Kingdom the Conservative ideology of market forces has pushed local government and health services into the areas of competitive tendering and a mixed market of provision based on a purchasing 'enabling' authority and a whole range of providers – statutory, voluntary and private. Many social workers entered the profession because of a vocation and an interest in working with individuals in need. Many now find themselves having little or no time to develop in-depth relationships with clients or carry out traditional 'casework', but instead are making assessments and brokering scarce resources. Often their job is no longer to understand the individual, but to decide who gets what help. Probation officers also experience their role as having moved away from work to help individuals and groups of offenders change their behaviour and ways of being in the world, to carrying out 'containment in the community'.

Political influences on social work are also affected by wider economic and social changes in society. The average life expectancy in 'first world' countries is continuing to grow at the same time as are the numbers of unemployed and students in higher education. These demographic and social trends radically affect the balance between the percentage of the population which is in employment and those who need to be supported by the state, voluntary organisations or their families. Handling this changing balance by large scale increases in taxes seems to be politically unpalatable. Technology can only provide limited savings through increased efficiency, in what is of necessity a very labour intensive profession. The inevitable result is the need for greater rationing of social welfare and help.

In addition social work has constantly had to realign its services, policies, structures and systems to respond to the new legal requirements of Child Care, Mental Health, Criminal Justice and Care in the Community legislation. On top of all these, local government reorganisation has brought an additional tidal wave of both uncertainty and restructuring. One Director of Social Services commented: 'You have not won your spurs as a Director until you have done at least two reorganisations of your department!'

The stresses on the profession continue to grow. In one social work office we saw the phrase: 'If you see light at the end of the tunnel, it is probably a train coming in the opposite direction!' and in another office, on the other side of the country: 'Owing to the need to economise, the light at the end of the tunnel has had to be extinguished!' These light-hearted slogans are the more humorous symptoms of a profession reeling from change.

Many people argue that there are stresses in all walks of life and every organisation is having to learn to manage constant and accelerating rates of change. Rossabeth Moss Kanter, the eminent writer on organisational dynamics, believes we all have to stop complaining about the carpet being pulled out from under our feet, and learn to dance on the flying carpet. However, the helping professions do differ from commercial companies or other professions. This we believe is due to the fact that social work, probation and health services are daily importing distress, disturbance and dis-ease through the process of empathically identifying with their clients. This response can not just be one of rational business management, but involves those working in the field forming relationships with those in distress. This distress not only affects the worker directly involved, but flows back into the team and management levels of the organisation (Hawkins and Shohet 1989, Chapter 10). Many in these organisations are then caught at the confluence of the individual distress flowing upwards and the political, economic and social stressors flowing down.

This scenario sounds very depressing and yet our experience of working with many social work organisations is that despite the pressures there is much creativity, and pockets of excellent new practice. But this is only sustained where there is effective supervision for the individuals and the teams involved, so that they can process the personal distress, disturbance and dis-ease which they have been affected by, and also understand and respond adequately to the waves of change.

The social work supervisor

This book both argues and demonstrates how supervision can no longer be seen as something for just new or front-line workers, but is a necessity for all those involved in the profession, whether they are junior receptionists or chief probation officers; and whether they are providers or purchasers of services. Without supervision you might just about stay riding the waves of change, but in the present climate it is doubtful that you will continue to develop your personal and collective effectiveness to help clients in difficult circumstances.

Allan Brown and Iain Bourne provide the reader with a model that brings together the various elements of supervision. This model shows how supervision needs to focus on the supervisee, their professional practice, the dynamics of the team and the requirements of the agency. They show how the process develops over time as the supervisory relationship matures through the phases of 'induction, connection and integration'. They show how the model works in practice in all types of social work settings and supervisory arrangements, from individual sessions, through to pairs, groups and team supervision.

So often books such as this can provide powerful models that are elegant on the page but fail to address the complexity of difficult everyday situations at work. This book overcomes that danger by using the direct research of the authors, in a wide variety of different social establishments, to present a number of detailed case examples of difficult supervisory challenges. It then shows how the theories and models can help both the supervisor and supervisee understand what is happening and be more selective in their responses.

The authors

Allan Brown and Iain Bourne are very well qualified to write such a book. Allan has many years experience as a practitioner and supervisor in probation and groupwork, as well as many more years as a lecturer, senior lecturer and head of department in Social Work at the University of Bristol. He has also been widely published, including key books on *Groupwork* (1992) and *Consultation* (1984).

For his PhD Iain carried out original research in the area of group super-vision. He worked in and managed several therapeutic communities, and later he became the Principal Training Consultant for the Richmond Fellow-ship College. In 1994 he set up IMPACT Training and Consultation as a specialist agency concentrating on 'responding to violence, suicide and self-harm, psychosis and trauma'. In addition to his training work, Iain works with staff following traumatic incidents, and continues to provide both individual and group supervision.

Together they use all of this rich diversity of experience, sharing their own successes and failures and also draw upon the experiences of those they have taught, supervised or for whom they have been consultants. The strength of their approach is the centrality of clearly articulated values to the supervision process. Their chapter on anti-oppressive practice in supervision provides a much needed perspective which has been missing for too long from super-vision literature. One drawback to their writing partnership is that they are both white and male, but this is an issue that they have clearly addressed from the beginning of both their book and of their writing partnership. They have enlisted help and elicited challenge from colleagues and students who have other perspectives, to balance the limitations in their joint experience. Their work also upholds the importance of the personal relationship in supervision, even in the midst of the market economy and the measurement of social work by tangible outcomes.

This book brings together both theories, maps, models, approaches and useful techniques for all aspects of the supervision process across different settings, and the needs of different supervisees at all stages of their develop-ment. As such we are confident that after having read it, you will want to return and consult it throughout your supervisory career. We hope you will not only enjoy reading it but it will become a supportive companion to you in the difficult but enriching work of supervision.

Peter Hawkins and Robin Shohet

Acknowledgements

In the process of writing this book we have inevitably drawn on our experiences over many years of working with, and learning from, numerous others. Whatever insight and understanding we have subsequently developed, and been able to share in these pages, owes an enormous debt to these anonymous contributors. Thank you.

We are most grateful to Celia Brown, Jac Mathews and Tara Mistry for looking at chapters in draft – particularly Chapter 3 – and for giving us very helpful feedback that enabled us to make improvements. Nonetheless we remain entirely responsible for what we have written. We are also indebted to the five staff teams that were involved in the research that forms the basis of Chapter 9 on group supervision. The five teams were drawn from the following organisations: Wiltshire Social Services Department, The Richmond Fellowship, and Avon Council on Alcohol and Drugs.

We are especially grateful also to our 'link' series co-editor, Peter Hawkins, for his insightful and stimulating feedback and ideas for making the book more attractive and user-friendly.

Lastly, we are both acutely aware that the process of writing a book of this kind has direct consequences for others who share the lives of those who are doing the writing. Thank you Carmen and Celia for not only putting up with the stress and hassle, but for being actively supportive, far beyond the call of duty.

Introduction

When invited to write a book about supervision, we agreed without hesitation, but with some apprehension about the task that lay ahead. The lack of hesitation was because we are both aware of the increasing stress and complexity of the work social workers and social welfare staff are expected to undertake, and the crucial role of supervision in helping them to work at their optimum levels. We are also aware that these work pressures impinge on supervisors doubly – firstly on their role as part of a management team that is expected to deliver improved services with declining resources, and secondly in their role as supervisors of front-line staff who are increasingly put under stress by the demands made on them in a sometimes less than supportive climate of public opinion. Supervisors need all the help they can get, and we hope this book will go some way to assisting them in both reflecting on their task, and getting ideas about how to become even better supervisors than they already are!

Another reason why we decided to write the book was our passionate belief in the importance of the relationship between the supervisor and the supervisee. We wanted to take this opportunity to demonstrate and assert this belief at a time when the *process* of the work in the personal social services tends to be downgraded, and regarded as less important than the *product* – in our view a false antithesis. We also wanted to underline the centrality of values in supervision, viewing the supervision relationship in terms of the wider agency and the socio-political contexts.

Our apprehension came from the daunting challenge of trying to produce a book that is interesting and stimulating to read, considered and informative, conceptually clear and of practical use. Just like supervisors, we have our particular styles and characteristics, our strengths and weaknesses, and we had to try and deploy these as effectively as possible. Readers will notice some variation in style and approach in different chapters. Part of this stems from our differences as two authors, but it is perhaps more a reflection of the variety of subject matter, and our recognition that different readers will be looking for different things in a book on supervision. Equally importantly, different people learn in different ways. Some may read the book systematically from cover to cover; others will select first those parts they are most interested in or which they need immediate help with.

Who this book is for

Our expectation is that this book will be useful for all social work supervisors, whatever stage they have reached in their supervisory career. It will serve as a text book on supervision for those who are entering first-line or front-line management for the first time, or who are expecting to do so in the near future. This includes those supervisors who carry supervisory responsibility, but not yet a full management role: a pattern that occurs quite commonly in day and residential settings. We are not, however, writing for novices because all new staff supervisors already have much relevant experience. This may be of a directly related kind as, for example, in student supervision and as a supervisee; or less obviously but equally relevantly, it may be drawn from the wealth of their personal life and relationship experience.

Some more experienced supervisors, perhaps with many years of supervision behind them, have quite probably had to learn their supervisory skills on the job with very little training. This hands-on experience is invaluable, but inevitably both good and bad habits are likely to have developed along the way. For those in this position, we hope that selective use of this book can offer an opportunity to take stock and reassess skills and approaches to the highly skilled task of supervision. A further point of relevance is that the state of the art moves on, and there is new material here: for example, on anti-oppressive supervision, group supervision and supervision in circum-stances of post-traumatic stress.

Those that have special responsibility for the training of staff supervisors in social work and social welfare agencies are likely to find this book a useful resource. Chapter 10 is entirely on training, but many other sections, for example the model developed in Chapter 5 and the case studies in Chapter 6, could be of immediate practical use to trainers when planning supervisor courses.

We also hope that senior managers, directors, and chief officers will read this book. We say this partly because we think that supervision is a resource that should be available at all levels of management, including the most senior; but most importantly we think it is essential that agencies give high priority to supervision, with clearly developed plans and strategies. Chief officers, directors and senior managers are the ones best placed to make this happen.

Another group of staff whose work may be enhanced by reading this book are practice teachers; those who supervise the work of students on practice placements. There is a considerable overlap between the skills of staff and student supervision, as well as important differences. This is an issue we discuss in Chapter 2.

The approach to supervision taken in this book is one that can be applied widely to the full range of social work and social welfare agencies, settings and staff groups. Supervision is an integral part of quality assurance and staff development, whether in statutory agencies, large voluntary organisations, small community-based voluntary agencies, or the growing number of independent and private agencies. Supervision is needed equally whether in fieldwork, community, day or residential settings, although the form and emphasis will vary according to task, size of organisation and value base.

We think much of the content can be applied, suitably adapted, to supervision across the whole range of staff posts in the personal social services. Thus whilst we have written with the needs of supervisors of front-line social work staff particularly in mind, much applies to the supervision of those in other posts, for example, senior managers and administrative staff. Supervisee needs will vary greatly according to several factors, including whether they are completely new to social work and social welfare, or if they are not new, how much experience they have, or whether their job involves direct work with service users. Furthermore, new staff roles keep emerging, one of the most recent being that of care manager (Orme and Glastonbury 1993); each needs suitably adapted supervision arrangements.

How this book is organised

The chapters in the book are organised so that whilst any one chapter can be seen as standing alone, it relies in varying degrees on what has gone before, and what follows. Thus Chapter 3 discusses issues of power, discrimination and oppression, and the ways in which these have a profound effect on the supervisory relationship and activity. This understanding is of fundamental importance to all that is developed in the chapters that follow. By contrast, two of the later chapters – on stress and trauma (Chapter 7), and on group supervision (Chapter 9) – each cover more specialised aspects of supervision. However, for a fuller appreciation of what they have to say, the reader needs to link them with the main themes of the book.

The overall sequence starts in Chapter 1 with a baseline framework for considering supervision. We try to clarify what supervision is and to establish its basic underpinning values. We go on in Chapter 2 to examine the significance that the new supervisor's previous personal and professional life will have for their perspective and approach to their role. This includes their internalised model of supervision and how they typically learn. The framework is completed with the material on anti-oppressive supervision in Chapter 3.

Chapters 4 and 5 take us to the starting point for supervision work, with considerations of contract and boundaries (Chapter 4), and a model for thinking about the four primary systems that influence supervision (*practice, worker, team* and *agency*). Attention is also given to the importance of taking into account the developmental stages of supervisee and supervisor respectively.

Chapter 6 is a full and very practical chapter based on a series of case studies of common situations that can arouse concern in the supervision relationship. Each scenario is analysed and suggestions made to stimulate thinking about some of the ways in which the difficulties might be resolved.

Chapter 7 concentrates on the critical areas of worker stress and trauma, offering supervisors a framework for thinking about ways in which they can respond whilst managing their own stress at the same time.

The first seven chapters having concentrated mostly on one-to-one supervision, the balance is restored in Chapters 8 and 9, which focus on the group dimension. The former looks at the team as a group, the dynamics of which have a profound effect on the quality of the supervision relationship with individual team members. The latter concentrates on group supervision, with ideas drawn from field research on why this method is mostly underused, and what factors are likely to increase its success as a method of supervision.

Chapter 10 is specifically on the training and professional development of supervisors, both in general, and when working in particular settings. The (brief) Chapter 11 attempts to draw together the main strands and key themes of the book, set in the context of the rapidly changing social work and social welfare scene in Britain.

Setting the scene

1

In this first chapter we set the scene for the rest of the book. It seems to us appropriate to start by considering the various factors that convince us that there is a need for a new textbook on staff supervision at the present time. After that we offer our own working definition of supervision, and discuss the different elements in some detail. We then go on to identify the main components of the value base we regard as fundamental to the whole approach taken to supervision. Finally, we examine the very important issues surrounding the choice of language and terminology.

The need for this book

There are several reasons for writing this book at this time:

- the expressed need of supervisors themselves
- the widespread dissatisfaction with supervision standards overall
- the intrinsic importance of supervision in the maintenance of high morale and quality service delivery
- the rapidly changing context of social work and community care services
- an apparent gap in the literature currently available to supervisors
- the need to establish a clear value base for supervision
- affirmation of the centrality of the relationship between supervisor and supervisee.

The needs expressed by supervisors themselves

The first and arguably the most important evidence of the need for this book comes from supervisors themselves, particularly from those who are quite new to the task. Many of these are also first-line managers in statutory or quasi-statutory agencies, in posts that carry great responsibility at the sharp end of social work and social welfare services.

In the course of our work, supervisors repeatedly tell us how ill-equipped they feel themselves to be for carrying out what they know to be a task of great importance. They point out the extraordinary contrast between the two full-time years rightly deemed to be the absolute minimum necessary for social work training, and the occasional short course of a few days duration for learning to be a supervisor. On promotion to supervisor/manager for the first time they are expected to be proficient virtually overnight. This expectation probably stems from the social work tradition that supervisors are primarily super social workers, thus blurring the distinctions between what – especially for those who are also team managers – are two very different tasks.

As we shall see in Chapter 2, most new supervisors are left with no alternative but to draw on their own internalised models based on their experiences as supervisee, bolstered for some by experience of supervising students on placement. One of the central aims of this book is to demonstrate that there is knowledge and skills that are specific to the role of supervisor, at whatever level and in whichever setting they are working.

Dissatisfaction with standards of supervision

Given the wholly inadequate preparation for this skilled task of supervisor, it is hardly surprising that there is unfortunately evidence from a range of research studies (for example Stevenson *et al.* 1978; Satyamurti 1981; NALGO 1989; Kadushin 1992) of widespread dissatisfaction with supervision – from both supervisors and supervisees. There is also substantial evidence from child care research and enquiries into child care tragedies (Brent Borough Council 1985; DHSS 1985; DHSS/SSI 1986; Lambeth Borough Council 1987) of serious flaws in supervision practice in some social services departments (hereafter SSDs). There are of course also many instances of excellent quality supervision and satisfied customers; these provide fine examples for others to emulate, and for a book like this to try and capture and make available as widely as possible.

Some of the dissatisfaction with supervision is structural and inevitable, stemming from the dynamics of a relationship in which power is not distributed equally and which also provides a focus for the wider frustrations and anxieties that arise in the daily, often stressful and demanding, work of practitioners in social work and community care services. We believe, however, that there is considerable scope for raising the overall standard and quality of supervision:

1 by agencies and senior managers giving it increased priority and higher profile in agency policies
2 by identifying the relevant knowledge, skills and values
3 by creating the space for the necessary training to be undertaken
4 by ensuring that all staff – whatever their role in an organisation – are offered regular supervision, suitably adapted to their task and their particular needs and stage of professional development.

*The intrinsic importance of supervision in the maintenance of high
morale and quality service delivery*

We have no doubt that the quality of personal social service available to
users of social work and related activities is significantly affected by the
quality of supervision available to staff. As will become clear throughout this
book, we are thinking not only about the quality of the actual service provided,
but equally about the morale and well-being of the workers whose task it is
to offer those services. A central theme of our approach is that staff who are
empowered by the agency context and culture in which they work are more
likely to provide services that are both empowering and effective for those
who need them.

*The rapidly changing context of social work and social welfare
services*

Another reason for a new text on supervision is the new circumstances
emerging from the rapidly changing context of supervision and community
care. The whole shape and nature of the personal social services is being
radically altered by major new pieces of legislation for the 1990s: the Children
Act (Department of Health 1989), the Criminal Justice Acts (Home Office
1991; 1993), the National Health Service and Community Care Act (Department of Health 1990).

A common feature of all these Acts is the shift in service provision from the
statutory sector to the voluntary and private sectors. This has implications for
new types of posts, for example care managers, with new patterns of supervisor and supervisee arrangements. It also creates a starker contrast between
the caring and controlling aspects of statutory work. In child care, there is
on the one hand a requirement to establish partnerships with parents, and
on the other a clear imperative to have prior regard for the protection and
welfare of the child. The emphasis in probation has been significantly changed
by the new legislation with a more controlling role for the probation officer,
who is expected to supervise community sentences or penalties, raising the
question whether the task can still be considered to be social work (Parsloe
1991). Whether still social work – as defined hitherto – or not, one thing is
clear: the need for good supervision is greater than ever before, not only for
carrying out different tasks in different ways, but also as an essential place to
hold the increased anxiety felt by all levels of staff at times of major change.

The changes alluded to above are not just organisational and in task, they
are also part of a changing ethos about the very nature of social work,
community care and the role of those who work in these services. Some of
this is potentially a positive step forward, for example, the emphasis on
needs-led services in adult care (although there are fears that in practice they
may become resource led), the partnership principle in children's services
(but with recognition of the fact that a true partnership is between people
with equal power), and the need to be much more focused in probation
work with offenders (though with more emphasis on control). On the other
hand there are some real grounds for concern. These stem from the market-

led managerial approach to the provision of services. Budgetary considerations are in danger of becoming the paramount criteria for judging the worth of a service and, even more worryingly, determining the methods of carrying it out. Quantitative considerations are in danger of taking priority over qualitative, with a contract culture predominating over a person-centred approach to people, their needs, feelings and problems.

The supervision literature

Turning to the general supervision literature, an examination of the existing texts on supervision reveals some useful sources (which will be drawn on and referenced) but also confirms that relatively few British texts have been published, other than on student supervision. There are several publications on the latter (see, for example, Pettes 1979; Butler and Elliott 1985; Danbury 1986; Ford and Jones 1987; Gardiner 1989; Humphries *et al.* 1993) that have many useful pointers for supervision generally. But because they are writing about the practice teaching/learning context, they are significantly different in orientation and focus from supervision in an agency employee context.

It is interesting to speculate about the potential impact that the introduction of accreditation for practice teachers (CCETSW 1989), based on a quite substantial training programme, may have on staff supervision. Accreditation is undoubtedly gradually raising the standard of practice teaching of social work students, and accredited practice teachers will have some transferable skills for use in staff supervision in social work and community care.

There are two recent books on staff supervision published in the USA that we would recommend for reference purposes. These are the classic text by Kadushin, now in its third edition (1992) and probably the most comprehensive text available, and a book by Shulman (1993) that develops the notion of supervision as an interactive process. The strengths of the latter book are the emphasis placed by the author on the skills of supervision, and the centrality of the supervisory relationship.

Earlier British books on staff supervision include Westheimer (1977), Pettes (1979), and Brown (1984) on consultation. More recently there has been Davies (1988), based on a survey in probation, and Hawkins and Shohet (1989), a sort of parent text to this one and a major influence on our own thinking, but which is orientated primarily to supervision in psychotherapeutic/counselling settings. Houston (1990a) again concentrates on psychotherapeutic settings and voluntary supervision more akin to consultation, while Richards *et al.* (1990) is a very useful text specifically addressing supervision in child protection and with some important points of wider application. Morrison (1993) is a supervision manual with checklists and some exercises and Pritchard (1994) has chapters by a range of authors, each taking a specific supervision theme or setting, right across the social work spectrum.

The need to establish a clear value-base for supervision

We attach great importance to the centrality of values in all aspects of social work and social welfare, and therefore in supervision. One of our motivations in writing this book is to assert a person-centred anti-oppressive value base for supervision, at whatever level. Like many others we are concerned about the hard-nosed ethos referred to above that is emerging throughout the personal social services, in which targets, monitoring and competition are in danger of taking precedence over feelings, relationships and attitudes.

Later in this introductory chapter we outline the core values we believe should underpin all supervision. These are reflected throughout the book, and are the central consideration of Chapter 3 which outlines an anti-oppressive perspective on power and supervision. Most books on supervision give attention to the power issues that stem from the delegated authority of the supervisor over the supervisee, but relatively little attention has been given to the unequal power and complexities arising from structural and personal oppressions and discrimination. These complexities include, for example, the sex, race, ethnicity, (dis)ability, class, sexual orientation, age and culture of the participants in the supervisory relationship.

What is supervision?

In a book on supervision the reader is entitled to know what the authors mean when they use the term! However this is not a simple matter as the term is defined and used in different ways by different people. For example, it is used by some interchangeably with consultation, and by others with management. In our view, whilst supervision has both consultative and managerial aspects, it needs to be clearly distinguished from both these related functions. Most authors use as their starting point Kadushin's concept of supervision as having the three principal functions of administration, education and support (Kadushin 1992). Some add on other functions, for example, mediation (Richards *et al.* 1990), while others differentiate managerial functions from administrative. Rather than proceed any further with the terminological and related struggles of other authors we offer our own attempt at a definition, or description, as a starting point for a discussion of the concept and its core aspects.

> *Supervision is the primary means by which an agency-designated supervisor enables staff, individually, and collectively; and ensures standards of practice. The aim is to enable the supervisee(s) to carry out their work, as stated in their job specification, as effectively as possible. Regular arranged meetings between supervisor and supervisee(s) form the core of the process by which the supervisory task is carried out. The supervisee is an active participant in this interactional process.*

There are several points arising from our definition that we think merit further discussion:

1 When we refer to *supervision* we are talking about a relationship between one person, a supervisor, and another, a supervisee. The supervisor has been given authority by their employer to supervise one or more supervisees

who are employees accountable to her or him for their agency work. The concept of *accountability* is less straightforward and presents some possible difficulties. Some would argue – with a degree of support from the new community care legislation – that the worker's first accountability is to the service user or 'client'. Others would say that the first accountability of a professional worker is to their profession, and yet others would say that the first accountability is to oneself. We do not disagree with any of these points about the multifaceted nature of accountability; we only confirm that the above statement is referring to agency accountability.

2 In our use of the terms *enable* and *ensure* we are attempting to capture the dual nature of supervision, which carries the responsibility both to *ensure* that agency policy is implemented – which implies a controlling function – and a parallel responsibility to *enable* supervisees to work to the best of their ability, implying a person-centred caring function. We consider both these functions to be equally important and inextricably related to one another in supervision. As in the parallel process of work with service users in a statutory setting, there are often pressures to be either the agency controller who pays scant attention to caring and empowering, or the caring consultant/counsellor who abdicates the authority vested in the role of supervisor. In a task-orientated, budget-dominated climate, we think the greater risk is the downplaying of the enabling, caring function of supervision.

3 The reference to *individually and collectively* is included to emphasise the centrality of the team or staff group in social work and community care. Whilst much of the discussion here will refer to the one-to-one relationship of supervisor and supervisee, this almost always takes place in, and needs to take account of, a team or work group context. In residential and day care settings this team dimension is an ever-present reality, and in fieldwork the days of private individualised relationships, whether with users or colleagues, are becoming a thing of the past. Thus an essential task of a supervisor is to develop a team and group ethos. This may be achieved directly through various group events, including for example team meetings, away days and group supervision (see Chapters 8 and 9), and indirectly through taking a contextual approach in supervision to the work undertaken by each individual.

4 Arguably the most important point to emphasise is the overall aim of supervision as being the provision of the best possible service to the users of personal social services. This apparently obvious fact needs stressing because it so often gets lost sight of in supervision when agency politics, interpersonal conflicts, personal ambition, games playing, supervisor and supervisee preoccupations and other diversions become the main part of supervision sessions. These dynamics are all normal and ubiquitous, and will be examined in some detail later in the book. The point to hold on to from the beginning, and continuously, when thinking about supervision is that the whole rationale for the agency and its organisational apparatus is to provide a first-class service for people who need it (or in some cases are required to have it, in order that they or others may be protected from harm).

5 We need to state right from the beginning that we regard supervision as an interactional process in which the supervisee is an active participant. In Chapter 5 we look at the developmental stages in supervision and the changing needs and relationship according to the supervisee's level of experience and expertise. However, even the most inexperienced supervisee needs to develop – and be helped to develop – the skills and confidence to be proactive in their approach to supervision.

6 The final point arising from our statement on supervision refers to super-vision taking place primarily in formally arranged regular meetings. The issue here is whether supervision is a specific event, namely the supervi-sion session, or a process, where something occurs continuously between supervisor and supervisee(s) in their day-to-day work – or both. We have had some protracted discussions between us on this issue and, in particu-lar, where to put the boundary around supervision; there have also been discussions about setting the parameters of this book. It would clearly be absurd to restrict our notion of supervision to the single event of the formal supervision session, when so much of the agenda in supervision overlaps with other events and contacts between supervisor and supervisee, many of an informal or crisis nature, and we have no wish to do so. On the other hand it seems important, as stated earlier, to distinguish super-vision from other aspects of management and from the multifarious tasks of those who have supervisory responsibilities.

Our approach, therefore, is that supervision is both an event AND a process, and this duality will be reflected in the perspective of this book. However, we do intend to try to keep a fairly clearly defined boundary around the notion of supervision. We think that having this clarity of focus is likely to be helpful to readers. To cast the net more widely, for example by virtually equating it with management, would be to run the risk of downplaying the importance of supervision *per se*, the very thing we wish to avoid. There are many useful books available on related topics: for example, on management both in the social work and community care context (Bamford 1982; Coulshed 1990; Orme and Glastonbury 1993); in the wider field of organisation theory (Handy 1991); on counselling (Proctor 1978; Houston 1990a; Dryden and Thorne 1991); on consultation (Kadushin 1977; Gallessich 1982; Brown 1984); and on workload management (Vickery 1977).

When thinking about one-to-one supervision it is not too difficult to have some clarity about a defined domain, whilst recognising that, systemically, everything in the work of a staff group relates to everything else. When we move on, as we do later in the book, to consider group supervision it gets much more complicated as we have to try and disentangle the various other functions that may be undertaken in staff groups, such as work allocation, policy discussions, sensitivity training, socialising and so on.

By now you may be saying to yourself, with some justification, why all this fuss about what is and what is not supervision? Perhaps the most important reason of all is that we believe the formal space allocated for supervision sessions is a very precious resource to be protected at all costs, and that this protection is more likely to occur when the function is clearly distinguished from other activities. It is the place and time that the supervisee knows is theirs as of right, an entitlement to seek help with the many stresses of a demanding and often stressful job. It also defines a very clear place where the agency can expect the supervisor and supervisee constantly to check that agency policies, standards, and where relevant, statutory requirements, are being carried out.

In our view it is a sign of strength, not of weakness, to be able to be open and honest about difficulties faced. This applies to both severely difficult work situations that anyone would struggle with, and the more subjective difficulties that impinge on personal feelings or experiences particular to that supervisee. Of course, whether or not a supervisee feels sufficiently trusting and confident in their supervisor to use this space to which they are entitled in the best possible way is another matter, and one we shall be addressing constantly throughout the book. But first we need to examine the core values of supervision.

A value base for supervision

Several fundamental principles and theoretical perspectives form the value base underlying the approach to supervision taken throughout this book.

Supervision needs to be considered in the structural context of the agency and the wider society

To consider the supervisory relationship in isolation from the social and organisational forces that shape it is to take only a very partial view of what is occurring. Putting it another way, both the supervisor and supervisee(s) will be profoundly affected in how they interact with one another, and what they discuss, by the policy and culture of their agency, and by wider social and political forces. For example, in a probation hostel setting, if black offenders are refusing to go there because there are no black staff and previous black residents have reported racism, or if there is a current dispute between probation officers and management about staffing levels, or if there is a threat that the hostel may be closed down because of some new Home Office policy, these contextual pressures will undoubtedly and quite properly influence the supervision agenda, covertly if not overtly.

Social work and community care are essentially collective team-based activities with a high level of interdependence between staff

Whether or not staff and supervisor share an ideological view about the desirability in principle of working collectively, the sheer complexity of many of the tasks in social work and social welfare requires workers to function collectively as a team. This has obvious implications for the approach taken to both the format and the content of supervision. On format, it will be essential that team members and their leader/manager meet together on a regular basis, whether or not this is for group supervision (see Chapter 9) or for other kinds of meetings concerned with, for example, policy, work allocation or relations with other agencies in the locality.

A team approach also has implications for one-to-one supervision sessions. For example, if a supervisee confides to his supervisor that he is facing extra stresses at home because his partner has to go into hospital soon for a major operation and he needs to spend more time with their children, any rearrangement of workloads and schedules will immediately affect colleagues and service users. Similarly, if a supervisee in a family centre trying to attract more fathers to the centre is experiencing sexist comments from one of these fathers and shares this with her supervisor, whatever action is taken needs to be agreed and carried out on a consistent basis by all the centre staff.

Supervision is a person-centred activity that places as much importance on the supervisory relationship, feelings and staff development as on task implementation, regulation and control functions

There is some evidence (NALGO 1989) that the personal social services are becoming more routinised and depersonalised in the way services are delivered and that this bureaucratic ethos is being replicated in supervision. In our view this is not only an undesirable development in principle, but it is also likely to be self-defeating in practical outcome. Social work and related tasks are by definition concerned with people's personal and social pain, disability, oppression, poverty, stress, violence, deprivation and conflict. If the worker is to be an effective helper, she or he must share some of this pain, despair and anger and be affected in their personal feelings. It is essential that the feelings arising from the personal impact of the work can be on the supervision agenda, as well as the practical considerations and the requirements of agency policy and regulations.

If feelings and the personal impact of the work are not legitimised as supervision business, they do not just go away, they stay underneath the surface with at least two possible consequences. One is that the supervisee gets the message that feelings are to be suppressed, and they start to work more bureaucratically and less empathically, and so less effectively; and secondly, stress levels build because they have no outlet in supervision, and the worker begins to take time off work with stress-related physical symptoms (see Chapters 5 and 7). Thus if the primary aim of supervision is to ensure and enable the best possible service to users, a bureaucratic approach will inevitably be self-defeating. A person-centred approach is not a luxury to be dispensed with when the going gets tough; it is integral to the whole purpose and process of supervision.

The content and the process of supervision are to be anti-oppressive and anti-discriminatory, with a commitment to empower both service users and staff

This whole issue and the meaning of the terminology used is discussed in much more detail in Chapter 3. It refers to the inequality of power and of treatment that runs right through society and is reflected in the unequal experience of people according to their structural position and personal identity, for example, as male or female, white or black, middle or working class, young or old, heterosexual or gay, physically able or disabled.

Our value stance is that in supervision – as throughout social work and community care practice – all participants need to work actively to counteract the destructive effects of social oppression on the chances and opportunities of those who are disempowered by the social context in which they live. Whilst some general attention – not always accompanied by commensurate action – has been given to this subject in recent years, little has been said directly about the implications for supervision and the supervisory relationship. The evidence available from the experience of supervisees and supervisors (see Chapter 3) indicates that issues of race and gender and other oppressions are of profound importance in supervision.

The practical application of this anti-oppressive principle is placing empowerment at the heart of good practice and good supervision. The term 'empowerment' is now widely used, and sometimes abused, as it trips easily off the end of the tongue and looks good in policy statements. This is not necessarily a reason for abandoning the term (and we shall use it in this book), because it does communicate in a straightforward way both a fundamental principle and a process, a method of working with people. The principle is that interaction between people, particularly when one is in a more powerful structural and personal position than the other, should be governed by an approach that decreases rather than increases the power differential between them, and that enhances the personal strengths and resources of those who are disempowered. The empowering method of working is the use of practical skills to implement the principle. One of the most detailed and useful accounts of empowerment as a practical method of working can be found in Mullender and Ward's book on *Self-Directed Groupwork* (1991, Chapter 1).

In their text on *Community Care and Empowerment* (1993) Stevenson and Parsloe state that 'we see supervision as a major process in the development of staff towards empowering practice' (p. 57), and 'if users are to be empowered they need empowered staff' (p. 48). In support of this they quote from two supervisors. One was a (female) manager of a residential home for older people who were mentally infirm, who said her task was 'to make the staff feel great so that rubs off onto the client' (p. 40); and the other was the (male) manager of a day centre for older people who said, 'It is really useless to try to empower users before you have a management team and an empowered staff group' (p. 40).

Supervisees and supervisors are adults who learn best when their learning is self-directed, and a proactive approach is taken to supervision

It may seem an obvious point to stress that supervisees – and supervisors – are adults, but it is one often forgotten when a quasi-parental relationship develops in supervision. It is also crucial that the way supervision is approached takes account of the evidence (Gardiner 1989; Burgess 1992; and see Chapter 2) that adults learn best under certain conditions, including being in control of their own learning. This involves, among other things, taking a proactive approach to supervision. For the supervisee this means being prepared to shape supervision sessions and agendas to make sure of getting the maximum benefit from them (see Brown 1984). For the supervisor it means taking an imaginative and creative approach to supervision in both its form and content.

The combination of a directive supervisor and a dependent supervisee may limit the longer term professional development of the supervisee. There are many unanticipated situations that confront staff in social work and social welfare settings, when there is no time or opportunity for consultation, and immediate decisions and actions have to be taken. The overly dependent supervisee is likely to flounder because he or she has been programmed to rely on others rather than exercise their own judgement; whereas the active learner and thinker is able to draw on learning from one situation and apply it to another.

The level of experience of the worker and the nature of the problem faced will be factors affecting the extent to which this particular principle can be applied in a given situation. However, the general idea that supervisors foster an active learning approach in their supervisees still applies; by the same token supervisors need to be proactive in their own approach to their supervision with their line manager when they are in the role of supervisee. In the latter case, the first proactive step may well be to insist on regular supervision (which becomes increasingly less likely as you proceed into senior management), and to establish that to seek help when needed is a strength rather than a weakness in a manager at any level. This is not a contradiction in the principle of self-directed learning: one of the skills the active learner develops is knowing when and where to seek the help needed in a particular situation.

Regular supervision is a resource to which every staff member is entitled

The available evidence (Davies 1988; NALGO 1989) suggests that the general pattern of supervision in different agencies and settings is patchy and uneven. Some staff do not get any at all, for others it is minimal and routinised, and for many it is irregular and given low priority. For those more fortunate it is a regular highly valued resource that is greatly appreciated. In our view, good supervision is an entitlement for all staff and should be enshrined in every agency as a policy priority, with a well-resourced and comprehensive training programme for all supervisors (see Chapter 10).

When first-line managers are under pressure, as they often are (it is one of the most stressful jobs in social work because of the pivotal position between practitioners and senior management), arranged supervision sessions need only be abandoned – and rearranged – when serious crises or indispositions occur. Protecting the importance of supervision in this way is seen to be possible because in some teams, including those where the workloads and stress levels are very great, the supervisor nevertheless manages to organise things so that supervision is protected as far as possible. This committed approach communicates itself to the team, who appreciate that the entitlement to supervision is being applied and taken very seriously by their manager. This in turn will probably have positive spin-off because the supervisees are likely to respond by taking supervision very seriously themselves, preparing for it properly, and thus gaining the greatest advantage. Conversely, supervisors who are casual about supervision sessions, frequently changing the arrangements for relatively unimportant reasons, and making it clear that they give supervision very low priority, communicate a very different message to their staff. They in turn may well become disillusioned and start treating supervision as unimportant and of little value. Some may of necessity seek assistance from other sources, but this should complement not replace supervision.

Use of language and terminology

We are acutely aware that, having established the above value base for supervision, we need to be consistent in applying these values not only in the content of what we write, but also in the language we use and the way we write. As we are two white middle-class men, this is particularly important and potentially problematic.

The most obvious language issue is the use of gender pronouns, and we propose to refer to 'them', 'their', 'he or she', 'she or he', except when there are specific reasons for referring to one sex rather than the other. However, the use of language goes much deeper and is much subtler than gender pronouns. In most large personal social service organisations, there is a very clear pattern of women predominating as service users, carers and practitioners, with senior management dominated by white men (see, for example, Allan *et al.* 1992). We examine the implications of this phenomenon for supervision elsewhere in the book (and particularly in Chapter 3), but we need to note here that one major consequence of this gender pattern is that the language and culture of management – which impinges on supervision – is male and masculine and white. One way this shows is in the prevalence of terminology from military, sporting, financial and industrial origins that has found its way into social work and community care language and communication. Examples of this language include targets, bullet points, level playing fields, killing off, packages of care, selling points, front loading, and so on.

The significance of this kind of language is that it constitutes a culture that can be alienating to women and black people as well as to some men who do not identify with the macho image. We therefore will avoid it as far as possible in what we write, because we are aware that the organisational culture it creates and fosters is inimical to some of the values and principles we have outlined. It can also have significant consequences, for example, for the numbers of women and black people who apply for, and are appointed to, senior positions, and for the kind of experience they have in management (see Allan *et al.* 1992; Grimwood and Popplestone 1993).

One further point on terminology: readers will have noticed that we are using the term 'black' in the inclusive sense to refer collectively to those people in Britain who experience racism because of the colour of their skin. When talking about racism this is satisfactory – although we recognise that others who are white, for example, Irish and Jewish people, also experience racism in Britain. However, it does of course mask fundamental ethnic and religious differences, for example, between those of Indian, Chinese and African-Caribbean origin. Therefore, when discussing cultural factors in the supervision process and content, and elsewhere as relevant, we shall refer to ethnic origin rather than the black/white distinction.

Another language issue is how to refer to the people in the various roles in the social work and community care arena. Those in receipt of services are mostly referred to interchangeably as either 'service users' or 'clients'. No wholly satisfactory term has as yet emerged. The participants in supervision are referred to as 'supervisor' and 'supervisee'.

Finally, we hope that the rest of the book proves as stimulating and as challenging to read as it has been for us to write.

2 ▷ The making of a supervisor

Far from beginning with a clean slate, the new supervisor will be a blend of all that has gone before in their personal and professional lives. In this chapter we discuss how these formative experiences can shape the supervisor's style and its subsequent development. While theoretical models (Chapter 5), and training (Chapter 10) may be important influences on the supervisor's style, their internalised model, or picture of what being a supervisor is, what a supervisor does, and how a supervisor relates to their supervisees, is likely to be at least equally influential.

The relevance to supervision of the following formative influences will be discussed in this chapter:

- personal experiences at home and school
- professional practitioner experience
- experiences as supervisee
- experiences as practice teacher/supervisor of students
- development of work and learning styles.

We shall also touch briefly on the contextual factors of agency, service users and team that will influence a new staff supervision experience.

Personal formative experiences

Family influences

It does not require a detailed knowledge of developmental psychology to appreciate that much of the new supervisor was formed in the first few years of life. The basic characteristics of ethnicity, sex, physique – not to mention many other characteristics that are inherited through the genes – are determined before birth, as are the social class origins of the young child. These 'givens' are followed by the early formative experiences of being parented and family life. Of particular significance for the perspective of supervisors and supervisees is the kind of authority and power which, as a young child, they experienced at the hands of their parent(s) or carers. Was it an experience in which they were given freedom and encouragement to explore the world around them, or were they tightly controlled in all that they did? Were their parent(s) consistent in their use of authority, doing what they had said they would do, or was the message implanted that authority figures are unpredictable and not to be trusted? Was the power of the parent(s) over the child experienced as gentle and loving or violent and abusive?

An example of the significance for supervision of this last point on abuse are research findings that indicate large numbers of professionals who work with children have been sexually and/or physically abused themselves as children. Some surveys suggest about 20 per cent had been sexually abused, with a higher percentage for women than men (Dale 1986; Finkel 1987; Wilson 1987; all mentioned in Richards *et al.* 1990). Thus many supervisees and many first-line supervisors will have experienced abuse personally. This will often be a most significant factor in their work, particularly when their task includes work with abused children and their families, with adult survivors and in the mental health field. Many practice advantages can arise from this personal experience, not least in the increased level of empathy and understanding of others who are experiencing, or have experienced, abuse. On the other side of the coin are the painful emotional stresses that arise from the triggering and resonance of these personal experiences.

There are at least two ways in which this experience of child abuse can impact on the supervisory relationship. The first arises out of the potential difficulties that develop in communication when one, but not the other, participant in the supervision relationship has been abused. This is likely to be particularly significant when work with an abused person is on the supervision agenda and the supervisee is a survivor (most often a woman, but many men are survivors too) and the supervisor is the one without that experience.

The other effect arises when the supervisor's personal experience – in their family, at school or elsewhere – has been of important adults in their life abusing the power they had over them. This may make it difficult for them to use the power that they have in the supervision relationship positively. On the one hand they may 'follow the model' and replicate the abuse; or they may avoid and deny the power that they have.

Schooling

Next comes the impact of schooling, where two factors may be particularly significant. The first is the model of teaching and learning (which we discuss later in this chapter), and the second is the experience of the authority and power of the teachers, and how it was exercised. What feelings did the latter engender in the prospective supervisor/supervisee about powerful non-familial authority figures and how to deal with them? Can they be trusted? Are they consistent? Are they caring? Do they abuse their power? Are challenges to their ideas and views squashed as impertinent, or welcomed as a search for meaning and understanding? If you do not conform is it held against you later? This too can contribute to adult expectations of how the authority of the supervisor may be (mis)used, sometimes evoking self-protective strategies by the supervisee.

There are of course many different forms of abuse that may have been experienced in the formative years, as well as in adulthood. In the next chapter we examine the impact of different kinds of oppression and discrimination, personally and institutionally, and how these structurally determined factors impact on the supervision relationship.

Parenting

Many supervisors will have experience of parenthood, central to which is the supervision of children. Whilst certainly not suggesting too close a comparison between parent–child and supervisor–supervisee relationships, it is interesting to note some similarities that arise from the power one person has over the other. The new supervisor who has learned, as parent, to create safe boundaries and to confront difficult and sometimes taboo issues, has these skills to draw on – suitably adapted – in the supervision relationship.

It is worth noting that another parallel is with foster caring, and that with the growth of foster care schemes an increasing number of supervisors will have entered social work through that route.

Professional experience as a social work practitioner

Most new supervisors are transferring from the role of practitioner to the very different one of first-line manager or team leader. Their accumulated expertise is likely to be in roles other than manager or supervisor. How much does this practitioner expertise count for in their new role?

In some settings, notably residential and day care, the supervisor is likely to have some continuing direct work with service users. This provides an opportunity not only to keep in touch with direct practice, but also to demonstrate their practice expertise directly to supervisees. There is, however, also a risk that this may blur their transition into the very different role of supervisor. Alternatively, in fieldwork, as in a probation or SSD locality team, the transition may be sudden and complete. The role change is clear enough, but to what extent does their practice expertise remain useful in their new role?

For those supervisors who get promotion in their own field of expertise – and this is becoming more likely with the increase in specialisation – their previous experience and knowledge is of immediate and obvious value. For those becoming managers in different fields of work where, for example, some supervisees may have the greater expertise in some areas, or where the task being supervised is a new one, as in care management, there may be more of an apparent problem. We say apparent, because the supervisor who takes a reciprocal participatory approach to supervision, and who is a deep learner, will not expect to have to be the expert on everything. Rather, they will be very open to viewing the resources of the whole team as being available to each supervisee.

Many practitioner skills are directly transferable to those needed in a supervisor, including, amongst others:

• relationship skills
• working with people in groups
• advocacy
• contracting
• giving feedback (challenging as well as positive).

What is needed is the adaptation of those skills to the new role, plus learning new skills to do with the authority and responsibilities of being a manager/ supervisor.

Being supervised

The beginning supervisor will normally have had some experiences of being supervised: quite likely in some non-social work jobs earlier in their career; possibly as an unqualified social worker or care worker; for many as a student on a qualifying course; and probably in at least one post-qualification personal social services post prior to the recent promotion. As indicated in the previous chapter, and as readers will know, the standard of supervision varies greatly both in regularity and quality. A new supervisor's own past supervisee experience, as employee, is therefore likely to have been something of a lottery, with the 'lucky' (in quotes because to some extent supervision is what you make of it) ones having had at least one good quality experience. For those who have been on a social work qualifying course, it is to be hoped that one if not both of their two practice placements offered a good model of supervision.

The experience of student supervision, as student, is likely to have a major impact on future images of supervision, because of its intensity and the formal assessment with pass/fail at stake. Research interviews with students (Gardiner 1989) and our own experience of student behaviour on placements confirm just how powerful the role of practice teacher is felt to be by the student, and how with all but the most confident it can have a profound effect on their behaviour. As one student put it, 'My aim is to pass the course, and if my practice teacher wants me to take on certain cases, or to work in a particular way, so be it.' In another example, there was initially open conflict between a cognitively inclined male student and his psychodynamically orientated female practice teacher, with both requesting the intervention of the student's tutor as mediator. The student decided that given his own weak power position, and all that was at stake for him and his young family in getting qualified, he had no alternative but to adapt to his practice teacher's expectations – which he did.

The significance of these supervisee experiences is the internal picture or model they have created for the new supervisor. This will be highly influential, alongside the other formative experiences outlined above, in how he or she embarks on their new task. The extremes will be the supervisor who had an 'inspirational' supervisor who cannot be emulated, and the supervisor who had a 'dreadful' one, who must not be emulated. To work out your own supervisory style and approach, we suggest the way forward is to be yourself, drawing on lessons learned from the good, bad and indifferent experiences you may have had, and from supervisor training courses you attend. This may be fine in theory, but we appreciate that in practice when the pressure is on, each of us is likely to draw on our internalised role models, whether or not we are conscious that we are doing so.

Being a student supervisor/practice teacher

The experience of having been a student supervisor, or practice teacher (the current term in Britain) will for many new supervisors be the experience closest to their new role and therefore likely to be very influential. There are many positives in this, and one or two caveats arising from the differences in the two roles. The advantages include:

- thinking about the learning needs of a supervisee, and linking these to learning/teaching styles
- making a contract or agreement about how to work together, including sharing of values perspectives, favoured theories and practice approaches
- working to a regular schedule of planned supervision sessions
- taking a position of authority that is both caring and, if necessary, controlling
- making joint assessments of the supervisee's abilities and progress
- working with the different power dimensions of the relationship (see Chapter 3).

Some important differences between student and staff supervision also need to be recognised:

- the student placement has the primary objective of the student's learning and assessment, whereas in staff supervision, the learning of the supervisee comes second to meeting the agency's requirements to provide a good service for service users (though as will be clear throughout this book, we argue that this task cannot be achieved without serious attention being given to the personal/professional development of the supervisee)
- the role relationship is different. In staff supervision, the parties are colleagues who are fellow employees, and in many cases, the supervisee will also be a qualified and experienced professional worker
- in student supervision, the student is often the practice teacher's only supervisee (though since accreditation there has been some clustering of students), whereas a staff supervisor will usually have a team of supervisees. She or he therefore needs to be group-orientated in their thinking, aware of the possible team repercussions of work done with each individual team member
- in student supervision the practice teacher has some accountability to the

training body, whereas in staff supervision it is entirely to the agency via the line manager.

Notwithstanding these and other differences, the experience of student supervision provides invaluable preparation for the role of staff supervisor. Furthermore, student supervision experience, especially if it has been with several different students, provides the novice staff supervisor with an excellent opportunity to learn about their own teaching/learning style. We shall now consider several key components of supervisor style in more detail.

Aspects of supervisor style

'Worker-style' (see Brown 1984: 24–7) is an important concept because we all have one that we need to know about to understand our own – and other people's – ways of working, communicating and learning/teaching. Every one-to-one supervision relationship brings together two different styles, a combination that could mean anything from blissful harmony to complete incompatibility. Not many supervisory relationships will experience either of these extremes, but will vary considerably in degree of compatibility and empathy. Is there anything that a new supervisor can do about their style?

Perhaps the most important thing is to be aware of your own style and repertoire, the latter meaning the degree of flexibility and range you can offer when working with different people with different needs in different contexts. In this chapter we have been discussing some of the fundamental influences on style, and how they determine the orientation of the supervisor – and supervisee. We shall now consider three other core components of style:

- communication mode
- task versus process orientation
- learning/teaching style.

Communication mode

One fundamental aspect of style is mode of communication. Bandler and Grinder (1979) identified the three principal modes of communication or representational systems as visual, auditory and kinaesthetic (communication by seeing, hearing/talking and feeling, respectively), and explained their profound significance for patterns of human interaction. What they found was that whilst each of us – unless our faculties are impaired in some way – uses all three modes of communication, we tend to have one of the three variants as our natural and strongest mode, i.e. each of us has different relative strengths in seeing, hearing/talking and feeling. These communication preferences are likely to have been established since childhood, and if the preferred modes of supervisor and supervisee are different, this may lead to some problems.

The issue can be illustrated by the authors' own experience and behaviour. Iain recalls an occasion when he was a residential manager and was having difficulty in relating to one particular supervisee. Iain noticed that this man used to stare at him but without any real communication occurring. After this had gone on for a number of supervision sessions Iain plucked up courage and asked the supervisee what the problem was. The man replied that he was constantly distracted by Iain's habit of waving his hands about to try to make pictures and diagrams in the air to illustrate discussion points. For Iain, a very visual person, drawing diagrams and pictures in the air was an integral part of his communication style; for the supervisee, an auditory person, the impact was entirely negative. Interestingly, Allan is also a hand waver, but in his case, perhaps due to a kinaesthetic orientation, the communication is simply an expression of animation and may indicate enthusiasm, but it can be an unhelpful distraction to both visual and auditory people. We suspect that the experienced empathic social worker – and supervisor – tunes in quickly and intuitively to the appropriate mode of communication when working with different people, without often being aware that this is what they are doing.

Task versus process orientation

Another style factor, again with roots in past experience, is the relative emphasis supervisor and supervisee give to task and process. Quite a common cause of difficulty in supervision is a clash between a task-orientated supervisor preoccupied with outcomes (the destination); and a process-orientated supervisee concerned with means (the journey). Rather less commonly, the clash is vice versa. There is some evidence that women tend to be more process-orientated than men (see Chapter 3). It is important that both supervisor and supervisee recognise each other's strengths and preferences in this aspect of style, with a particular responsibility on the supervisor to validate the supervisee's orientation, irrespective of their own.

In the early part of this book we have deliberately concentrated on process factors, for reasons already given; but what really matters is that the supervisor has the ability to relate process and task together in supervision. Both are supremely important, and an undue emphasis upon one at the expense of the other is not only likely to skew supervision and reduce its effectiveness, but also to provide an unhelpful role model for the supervisee. The development task therefore, is to work at strengthening the weaker of the two orientations.

Learning/teaching styles

As one of the principal functions of supervision is education/training, it is important that supervisors and supervisees identify and understand their own personal learning styles, and how these affect supervision. How did they learn to learn? Have they been encouraged to be an active learner who takes responsibility for their own learning and search for meaning, or have they been trained to be a largely passive dependent learner who relies on the teacher? Most of us fall somewhere between these two polarised positions on the active/passive learning style continuum. There can, however, be big variations, which will sometimes be a factor needing attention if supervisor–supervisee interaction is to improve. A brief digression into theoretical and philosophical ideas about adult learning may be helpful at this point.

There has been considerable research into the conditions under which adults in general learn most effectively, and Burgess (1992: 2) has summarised five of these as follows:

- when solving problems
- when using previous experience
- when working with others for support and exchange of views
- when being responsible for, and being able to control, one's own learning, using initiative, insight and discovery
- when learning about theory and learning about practice are integrated.

These are factors that constitute what Swedish researchers (Marton and Saljo 1976, discussed in Gardiner 1989) have called deep learning, as distinct from surface learning. Davenport and Davenport (1988) developed and administered an androgogical/pedagogical questionnaire ('androgogical' literally means adult-orientated, and 'pedagogical' child-orientated, but they are roughly equivalent to deep and surface learning respectively). This questionnaire was used to test some research that challenged the then prevalent assumption that younger students necessarily learn best pedagogically, and mature students androgogically. Their results indicated that there is not a clear-cut age/learning style correlation. They did, however, confirm earlier findings that women are more likely to be androgogic learners than men. The Davenports concluded that these results argue for individualising student supervision methods and styles.

The Marton and Saljo research indicated, not surprisingly perhaps, that whereas students exposed to surface learning methods could recall some of an author's ideas, they could not demonstrate the level of understanding of those ideas that another group exposed to deep learning approaches could demonstrate. As Gardiner states, 'This is a very significant finding for all learning in higher education, especially in professional and vocational training, where students are expected not merely to reproduce ideas, but also to reflect on their usefulness, and make use of them in diverse practice situations' (Gardiner 1989: 62).

The implications, for supervision, of this information from adult learning research include:

- a recognition that people's learning styles do vary. Although there are some general differences between women and men, each person's learning style needs to be individually understood rather than assumptions made based on general tendencies
- when we are considering professional judgements, and not confining skills to the routine implementation of agency requirements, the capacity of the supervisee to be an active learner, and of the supervisor to facilitate this approach to learning, is of crucial importance. There are many situations where a practitioner has to make decisions on the spot, without access to their supervisor, for which the capacity to make judgements based on transferability of learning is essential

- the stage of professional development and experience of the supervisee will influence the extent to which the supervisor needs to teach (the developmental stages in supervision are discussed in Chapter 5). Having said that, we would argue that right from the beginning the approach needs to be one that is participatory, interactive and developing the supervisee's own understanding and initiative
- unlike student supervision, the primary purpose of staff supervision is not the learning of the supervisee, but the effective delivery of agency services. This means there will be occasions when the supervisor needs to direct the supervisee to take a certain course of action. When this is necessary it should be accompanied by explanations from which the supervisee can learn for future occasions.

Identifying and sharing styles in the supervision relationship

With all these formative and style variables influencing the supervision relationship, it is not surprising that sometimes blocks and difficulties arise without either participant being able to understand the reason. A good starting point is for the new supervisor, as part of their own training, to do some work on self-assessment, identifying the attributes and style they have developed but perhaps never before made fully conscious. Then when they get into their first supervision relationships, they can discuss with supervisees the latter's own 'learning and supervisory history' (Morrison 1993: 49). This approach could involve encouraging the supervisee to reflect on the nature of their various formative and learning experiences, whilst helping them to identify their style and any ways in which they might develop their learning skills and approach. This is a useful exercise to be undertaken early on in the new supervisory relationship, whether or not there are any obvious difficulties.

In line with our philosophy of supervision as a reciprocal relationship, we would suggest that the supervisor be prepared to share with supervisees, where appropriate, their own learning and supervisory history, as well as other aspects of their work style. They can also share their understanding of how their style affects their own approach as a supervisor. This makes the point that there is no assumption that if difficulties arise the supervisee is 'the problem', but rather that a more likely explanation may lie in the interaction of two different styles and histories. (Chapter 6 uses case studies to look in more depth at some of the difficulties that can arise in the supervision relationship, and possible responses.)

Supervision context: the agency, the service users and the team/group setting

The significance of context is often underestimated. Just as important as style, identity and formative experiences are to the development of the new supervisor, so too will be the agency's expectations and instructions on how supervisors are to carry out their role. At a basic level this can apply, for example, to:

- how much time is allowed to be allocated to formal supervision sessions
- whether there is an official system of staff appraisal
- whether finance is available to arrange consultancy (say for a black colleague in an otherwise white team)
- whether group supervision is encouraged or discouraged.

Throughout the book we try to hold the agency and the personal/professional dimensions in relation to one another, just as the supervisor and supervisee need to in supervision sessions.

The service users

One very powerful influence that we have not yet emphasised is the impact on supervision of the task and the service users with whom the supervisees are working. A random list of just a few of the settings for supervision illustrates the range of clientele and the contrasting demands on workers, which will influence what they bring to supervision:

- a day centre for people with learning difficulties
- a child care locality team
- a prison probation office
- a care manager's team
- a burns unit in a hospital
- a drug advice and counselling service
- a rape crisis agency
- a privately owned residential home for older people, on contract with an SSD.

Each of these settings will have its own characteristics of history, pace, demands, preoccupations, anxieties, challenges, culture, ethos and responsibilities. There will be different racial, age and sex compositions, both of workers and service users. Different kinds of people will probably have been attracted to work in these different settings, associated with their personal history, motivation, experience and interest.

These points, which are rather obvious at one level, will be a recurrent theme in the book as we examine the ways in which the climate as well as the content of supervision is often, and necessarily, influenced by the type of work being done and by the needs and difficulties of the people being worked with. This discussion will include the phenomenon variously referred to as 'the reflection process' (Mattinson 1975), 'the parallel process' (Kadushin 1992), mirroring, or isomorphism, whereby the supervisory relationship and process often replicates that between the supervisee and the service user(s) under discussion.

The team context

The new supervisor will have reached their present position by one of the following routes:

- promotion from within their own team
- promotion within the agency, but into a new team
- appointment from outside the agency.

Each of these alternatives has its own potential advantages and disadvantages. The transition from member to manager of the same team, has the major advantage of familiarity with the work, the relevant networks, and the team members. Making the transition from peer to supervisor can, however, be hazardous. Even when the supervisor is able to be clear about their own changing role, others may find the different role relationship more problematical. If the former peers all support the promotion and recognise the new supervisor's abilities for the post, that will be a great help. Often, however, the picture is complicated by competition in which at least one, and maybe more, of the former peers also applied for the same post and feels bitter about not getting it.

This kind of issue takes time to work through, and we would suggest two essential steps to take. The first is to be clear yourself about your new role and the new role relationships you need to establish with your colleagues. Help should be available for this, not only from training courses and talking with your new supervisor peers who are facing similar issues, but also from your supervision sessions with your own line manager. The second is to have early team meetings specifically to discuss the change, with space for everyone to express what they feel about it, and to discuss how you propose to proceed. This needs to be coupled with frank individual sessions with any team members who are feeling resentful and envious.

The supervisor in a new environment

Here there is the great advantage of being untrammelled either by a past history of peer relationships with the team and each supervisee, or by half-true agency fantasies about what you are like. However the team you are now about to manage will obviously have its own history and tradition, with the thwarted internal candidate issue again quite likely to be part of the dynamic. There could be a wish for a particular type of supervisor who you may or may not be; perhaps a woman, an older person, a black person, a groupwork or family work specialist, a community activist, or an expert in cognitive approaches. There is also the ghost of the previous supervisor. If he or she was very popular, you have the problem of being seen as second best – or worse. If, on the other hand, your predecessor was very unpopular, the team may have idealised unrealistic expectations of what you can offer. Again we recommend early team meetings with full and frank discussions with all members. If there are strong feelings around it is much better to reach for them than to leave them festering under the surface. Also, by adopting this approach early on, you are modelling to new colleagues the kind of open, frank and direct style of working that you intend to use.

When you are promoted elsewhere in the same organisation, known but not known, there may be fantasies about you and your reputation for being a particular kind of person and particular kind of worker. In many organisations, rumour can run rife, with varying degrees of accuracy or justification. Th. team members now have a chance to test the accuracy of the rumours. The problem comes when they have you fixed in a certain role expectation, and at least for a while try to fit your behaviour to it. Having a reputation for brilliance may be just as difficult to deal with as the opposite. The open team discussion approach suggested for the other two scenarios is again likely to be useful.

The supervisor's own supervisory needs

A major source of worry for new supervisors, particularly in contexts involving work with vulnerable and violent people, is that something awful will happen to a service user – or supervisee – and you will be held accountable. We discuss crisis and trauma specifically in Chapter 7, but the relevance of mentioning these fears at this point is to emphasise that the agency and your own supervisor also carry responsibility and accountability for the work undertaken by yourself and your supervisees. It is to this crucial contextual issue of the supervision of the supervisor that we now turn.

It is unfortunately true that in some organisations there is an assumption that once you become a supervisor, you are – or should be – wholly competent and no longer in need of help or supervision. To need help can be regarded as some sort of weakness – a most curious view that sometimes seems to be associated with certain styles of senior management. We believe the opposite to be true: that it is a sign of strength and a mature professional approach to be able to recognise your own limitations and to judge when you need to seek help from others.

Interestingly, the contemporary imperative to establish and implement quality assurance systems in organisations will require comprehensive staff appraisal arrangements, which in turn will have to be part of supervision for staff at all levels. This is essentially a control mechanism to ensure standards, but in the process it creates a 'supervision of supervisors' framework that is there to be used for other associated purposes. In our view, effective supervision of managers requires a person-centred empowering approach just as much as it does for practitioner supervisees. If quality assurance is to be more than quantity assurance then both the process and relationship issues need to be taken into account, together with the personal experiences and feelings of those involved.

The newly appointed front-line supervisor is in one of the most demanding and crucial posts in the entire organisation, and it is essential that she or he gets good regular supervision. This may or may not be available on appointment, as part of the policy and culture of the agency, or as part of a staff appraisal system. If it is available, it may not be the kind of supervision needed and hoped for. It may, for example, comprise nothing more than the routine checking of administrative and accountability issues, important as these are. There may be no space for discussion of the personal impact of being a supervisor for the first time and all the associated anxieties and feelings about the new role.

Faced with a less than optimum supervision resource for herself or himself, what can the new supervisor do about it? At the time of appointment, it may be possible to negotiate regular supervision as part of the job agreement. Failing that, or if it does not materialise, then it is necessary to be proactive and ask for regular supervision sessions. This is of course much easier if there is a clear agency policy on entitlement to supervision. Much will then depend on whether the supervisor's line manager is not only willing, but also able, to offer what the supervisor, as supervisee, needs and wants.

If getting adequate supervision from the line manager proves to be an insurmountable problem, then we suggest negotiating some sort of agreement whereby supervision with the line manager continues, largely confined to administrative and accountability matters, but coupled with access to other sources of consultancy and support. Examples of possible sources of supplementary help include a mentor, co-counsellor, peer group or consultant. None of these resources is likely to be offered on a plate, and so the supervisor – *qua* supervisee – will need to be proactive in seeking them. Negotiating the agreement of the supervisor to these supplementary resources may be necessary, for example, if the activity is being undertaken in work time or there is a financial cost involved. Insecure line managers may be resistant to the idea that they cannot offer all that a first-line manager supervisee needs from supervision. (Incidentally, this raises an extremely important point for supervisees – at whatever level – to bear in mind. Supervisors have needs too, and the supervisee who gives some attention to meeting their supervisor's needs – without, of course, taking it to the point of role reversal – will usually benefit in improved quality of supervision for themselves.)

Meeting in a group with one's peers is almost always a source of strength and support, and something that often happens naturally – the well-known groupwork phenomenon of being in the same boat. By definition, meeting with others in the same role offers something very different from line supervision, however good that may be.

Training implications

It is normal to be extremely anxious when taking on a new and challenging job like being a supervisor. Major change is never easy. We only hope that the various complexities we are pointing out in these first few chapters are not increasing the reader's anxiety level too much, whilst stimulating awareness of what is involved. We hasten to reassure that later in the book, notably in Chapters 6 and 7, we shall be focusing specifically on the kind of concerns that new and old supervisors have, and suggesting some of the steps that can be taken when difficult situations arise. We are also stressing throughout the book that supervisors should never be left to struggle on their own; good quality training and supervisory support are essential resources for this demanding task.

Training for the post of supervisor is – or at least should be – a major undertaking requiring substantial allocation of agency resources. For this reason we have given a whole chapter (10) to it, and will just mention one aspect here that relates closely to all the previous discussion. This aspect is variously called self-positioning, baselining, self-assessment or self-appraisal. It is not only useful, but necessary, to undertake some form of self-assessment to understand the main elements in one's own personal baseline as a beginning supervisor (it can also be very useful later on in a supervisor's career, though perhaps more specifically focused on supervision competencies). A self-assessment questionnaire for supervisors can be found in Hawkins and Shohet (1989: 77–9). Richards *et al.* (1990) include a range of checklists and exercises including one called 'reflecting on one's supervisory style' (p. 34).

Throughout the chapter we have discussed the significance of past experience for how a new supervisor will start their job. We have looked specifically at the previous experience of supervision, as supervisee, and as student supervisor, and at the internalised model that may be drawn on. We have also looked at the childhood experience of key authority figures and the exercise of power, and how this shapes a perspective that may be mediated or reinforced by the prospective supervisor's later adult experiences. We have indicated the importance of style in the supervision relationship, and emphasised the importance of the supervisor's own supervision.

Perhaps the most common anxiety of the new supervisor is how to handle the authority of the new position and the power that goes with it. Assuming they applied for the job and were not thrust into it, arguably at least some part of their motivation was to seek that power anyway. Power can be sought for very honourable reasons, like wanting to have more influence over policy, wanting to improve services to users, wanting to introduce a more woman-centred approach to practice, wanting to develop an anti-oppressive service to users, wanting to offer staff a much more fruitful and empowering experience of supervision, and so forth. The goal to work towards is to feel comfortable with the power and authority that goes with the position. Supervisees will soon pick this up, and appreciate that you are clear about role and boundaries, thus helping them to be clear also. The issue of power and empowerment, which is integral to the supervisor's self-assessment and all aspects of their functioning, is addressed in the next chapter.

Supervision and power: an anti-oppressive perspective

Issues to do with power, and how it is managed, lie at the heart of supervision and the supervisory relationship. When one person is in a position of formal authority over another a dynamic is created that derives from that inequality of power. Throughout childhood the parent(s) or other adult carers of a child exercise enormous power over the life and feelings of that child. Psychodynamic theory helps us to understand more deeply the repercussions of this formative childhood experience on the attitudes of adults towards those who have authority and power over them, notably in the workplace with their supervisors and managers.

Power is manifest not only interpersonally, but also, and most significantly, structurally in the systems and institutions of the wider society. It is this structural dimension of power that is frequently understated and underestimated in its impact on the supervisory relationship. For example, the perspective of a black supervisee in their initial approach to a white supervisor will inevitably be influenced by their past experience of racism. As a black child growing up in Britain they will have seen that many of the institutions that impinged on their life and that of their parents were controlled by white people, and often discriminated against black families. We are referring to institutions such as schools, employers, housing agencies, commercial companies, and for many disadvantaged black youths, the police.

Another example might be the perspective of, say, a woman care assistant supervisee, with a male supervisor, who as a young girl learned how men can mistreat women. This personal experience will have included the relationship between her parents, and how she herself was treated by her father and, more generally, what she observed at school, among her friends and in the community in which she lived. Institutionally, she will have been influenced by the images of male power and abuse of power on the television. For example, if she happened to turn the television on when Parliament was being televised, she will have had no doubts about which sex controls most of the political power and policy decisions having a profound effect on her future life and opportunities.

These personally, culturally, structurally and institutionally based inequalities of power will all have a profound influence on the supervisory relationship; they will have an effect *in addition to, and interlinked with,* the more obvious power issues associated with the relationship between a supervisor and a supervisee. (When the supervisor is also the line manager, the formal power differential is that much greater.)

In this chapter we shall first outline the two different sources of power inequality, and then attempt to bring them together, with illustrative examples. The latter part of the chapter will examine the responsibility of the supervisor to model and facilitate an anti-oppressive approach by all team members to their work with service users, and to their relationships with one another. We shall also touch on the implications of these power factors for the kind of training and preparation supervisors need to equip themselves to undertake their task from a genuinely anti-oppressive perspective. The illustrations given will refer mainly to race and gender, although many of the points made are directly transferable to other forms of oppression. Specific reference is made to sexual orientation and physical disability, both of which are largely ignored in the supervision and management literature.

The reader may already be puzzling over the apparent contradiction between, on the one hand, the power relations implied in the terms 'supervisor' 'supervision' and 'supervisee', and on the other, the principle and methods of empowerment. 'Supervision' is indeed an unsatisfactory term in some ways. Firstly, it implies that the task of the supervisor is to oversee directly the work of the supervisee, whereas in most social work and community care settings most of the time the supervisor must rely on reported and indirect information about each supervisee's work. Secondly, and more fundamentally, it suggests a one-way relationship in which one person with the knowledge and the authority supervises another who is ignorant and dependent. When referring to professionally trained social workers, there is the further issue of the term's doubtful appropriateness as a description of their professional relationship. Even if social workers are more accurately described as 'bureau professionals', the term 'supervision' seems to address the 'bureau' much more obviously than the 'professional' part of that duality.

Notwithstanding these problematic issues about the term 'supervision', we retain it throughout this book because it is used almost universally in the personal social services – and in many other settings – albeit with some variation in what it actually means. We also use it because it does not fudge the issue of the authority and power vested in the supervisor's role. There are indications (Kadushin 1992: 98) that many supervisors are not comfortable with their authority and power and seek to side-step it in various conscious and unconscious ways. When that dynamic occurs it can only confuse the supervisee, who knows full well that the supervisor is in a position of considerable power over them in respect of their job.

The crucial question to be explored is whether empowerment (defined loosely as development and growth that enhances a person's control over their own life and behaviour) is possible in this unequal relationship? We hope to show that it is, but only when certain conditions are fulfilled. These conditions will become more apparent as the chapter develops, but include:

- recognition of the clearly defined limits of the legitimate power of the supervisor and the legitimacy that derives only from their formal role and position
- understanding that this power is to be exercised constructively in a two-way relationship between people of equal status and worth as human beings.
- recognition of just how much the supervisee has to contribute to the supervisory relationship.

One thing that can get in the way is the need some supervisors seem to have to feel that they have authority *over* someone else. How many of us when we are in the role of supervisor find ourselves talking about 'my staff' as though there was some form of ownership? We know that we have, and we know also that this phraseology is not part of the road to empowerment and reciprocity.

But before getting any deeper into this discussion of the compatibility of empowerment and supervision, we need first to clarify the different kinds of power that are present in the supervisory relationship. These include the potential for empowerment of the supervisee, and indeed, of the supervisor. We shall first summarise the classical accounts of power, drawing particularly on Kadushin's work (1992), then try and clarify the concepts of discrimination/anti-discrimination and oppression/anti-oppression and their relevance to supervision and power issues. We shall finally attempt to bring these different concepts together with some practical illustrations.

Concepts of power in supervision

Drawing on French and Raven's classical formulation (1967) and Kadushin's discussion of it (1992: Chapter 3), we can distinguish those kinds of power that derive from the supervisor's designated authority from their agency, and those that derive from their personal attributes. The former include *position* or *legitimate* power authorised for the role of supervisor and/or manager. They also include *coercive* and *reward* power meaning, respectively, power to require the supervisee to do something and power to offer or withhold rewards, for example, permission to go on an interesting but expensive course. Kadushin and others add *resources* power, which is the control managers have, to varying degrees, over the allocation of resources that supervisees may need to carry out a piece of work, for example, to arrange some transport to enable disabled people to attend meetings of a self-help group.

The *personal* power of a supervisor comes in part from their expertise, in part from what French and Raven call *referent* power, by which they mean a kind of relationship power that comes from the supervisee's wish to identify with their supervisor and perhaps be like them, and, we would also add, in part from the power of *personality*, by which we mean the combination of personal characteristics that make up the presence of the supervisor.

In 1989 Kadushin conducted a follow-up questionnaire with large samples of supervisors and supervisees in the USA, and the replies confirmed his earlier findings.

> Only expertise and positional power were perceived by both groups as salient. Supervisors overwhelmingly saw expertise as the source of effective power. While supervisees generally agree, a high percentage of supervisees saw positional power as the reason for agreeing to do what their supervisors wanted them to do. A negligible percentage of respondents saw referent power, reward, or punishment as significant.
>
> (Kadushin 1992: 92)

We do not know whether a similar survey in Britain would produce similar results, although this seems quite likely.

The emphasis by supervisors in Kadushin's survey on expertise (which is the essence of what a consultant offers) could be interpreted as a possible retreat from fully acknowledging the power of their role and position. The latter, not surprisingly, was seen as crucial by the supervisees. As we shall observe later, there are many situations where the supervisee has more expertise in a given area of practice than their supervisor has, whereas by definition, there are no situations where the supervisee has as much position power as their supervisor. Kadushin, echoing a point we made earlier, comments that

> the supervisor must accept, without defensiveness, or apology, the authority and related power inherent in his [*sic*] position. Use of authority may sometimes be unavoidable. The supervisor can increase its effectiveness if he feels, and can communicate, a conviction in his behaviour.
>
> (Kadushin 1992: 95)

This should be understood in the context of another point Kadushin makes that 'The most effective use of authority is minimal use' (p. 97).

Grimwood and Popplestone (1993), in a chapter on power in their book on *Women, Management and Care* suggest three other kinds of power that influence supervision. These are: *negative* (blocking by the supervisor, for example, making petty restrictions to show who is in charge), *nutrient* (caring for another person as in parenting), and *collaborative* (the power necessary to create innovation and change, which relies and depends on collaborative effort). They set this formulation in the context of an analysis that suggests – and we agree – that in general male managers are more concerned with status and position power than are their female counterparts, whereas most women managers put more emphasis on the personal factors. Thus many women managers are strong on collaborative power, working with team members to innovate and bring about change, even though this is not always supported in large bureaucratic organisations controlled by white male managers.

We return shortly to issues of gender, race and oppressed groups, but first we need to correct an impression that we may have created in this chapter that supervisors are the ones who carry all the different kinds of power in the supervisory relationship. Supervision is of course very much an interactional process. Whatever stance the supervisor takes, whether authoritarian, collaborative or unpredictable, the supervisee can, and often does, also exercise considerable influence and power in the relationship.

In virtually any situation involving authority, that authority depends largely on validation by those subject to it. For example, even in the highly controlled context of a closed prison, prison officers and governors – and prisoners – know only too well that the stability of life in the prison depends crucially on the prisoners acknowledging and accepting the authority of the staff. On the fortunately comparatively rare occasions when they do not, instability and often violence almost inevitably follow. The same principle applies in supervision. The supervisors and the agency – and the supervisees – rely on the system working, which means supervisees accepting and validating the authority of their supervisors. The wise supervisor is aware that this gives considerable power potentially to supervisees and takes this into account in their behaviour as supervisor. Of course we are not talking about a situation akin to a prison riot, but one in which supervisees, particularly if they act collectively, can do a great deal to affect the reputation and future prospects of their supervisor in the organisation.

The paradox in all this, as one of us has observed in relation to groupwork (Brown 1992: 74), is that quite apart from ideological desirability, the power sharing, empowering collaborative approach to supervision is the one most likely to secure the position of the supervisor and their authority. An authoritarian – as distinct from authoritative – approach sets up active or passive conflict that sooner or later may undermine the supervisor's role, and will certainly damage their effectiveness and reputation.

Another example of the power carried by supervisees in supervision is the various games that are sometimes played, consciously or unconsciously, to try and cope with and control the dynamics of the supervisory process. These were identified and characterised in an amusing and vivid, if rather male-orientated and fanciful fashion, by Kadushin (1968). Undoubtedly one way in which supervisees exercise power, and seek to control supervision on their terms, is by the use of various interactional methods and devices. Whilst some supervisees may have recourse to avoidance techniques irrespective of supervisor behaviour, the majority are responsive and much less likely to resort to a negative attitude when the supervisor is empowering, collaborative, and working with them.

Discrimination/anti-discrimination and
oppression/anti-oppression

Julia Philipson's publication on *Practising Equality: Women, Men and Social Work* (1992) is particularly helpful in defining and clarifying some of the terminology. She and others refer to 'discrimination' as both a quasi-legal term used specifically in some legislation, e.g. the Sex Discrimination Act 1975 and the Race Relations Act 1976 and also, in its much more widely used sense, to indicate when a person is being treated unequally because of personal factors such as their race, sex, age, (dis)ability or sexual orientation. She writes:

> Oppression is a complex term which relates to structural differences in
> power as well as to the personal experiences of oppressing and being
> oppressed. It relates to race, gender, sexual orientation, age, and disability
> as separate domains and as overlapping experiences.
>
> (Philipson 1992: 13)

Philipson suggests that whereas anti-discriminatory practice relies on a model
of challenging unfairness, and is essentially 'reformist in orientation', 'anti-
oppressive practice works to a model of empowerment and liberation and
requires a fundamental rethinking of values, institutions and relationships'
(p. 15). Many writers (see, for example, CCETSW 1991a; Thompson 1993; and
Chapter 6 in Brown 1992) have unwittingly blurred this important distinction. However, as a black woman colleague has pointed out to us, getting the
rhetoric right on the terminology and concepts, without addressing the
substance of structural inequalities, means very little.

In the context of the supervisory relationship, examples of discrimination
might be allocating less time to a black worker than to their white counterpart, grooming a male supervisee actively for promotion whilst preparing his
female counterpart only passively, or not ensuring that all relevant team
documents are made accessible to a blind colleague. Oppression is more
subtle and pervasive as, for example, when a young team manager considers
a much older colleague approaching retirement as someone who is not open
to personal development, or when a heterosexual female supervisor subtly,
and quite probably unconsciously, takes a more critical and less openly supportive stance to the child care work of a lesbian colleague than she does to
that of other heterosexual team members.

Conversely, an anti-discriminatory approach to supervision would be one
in which all supervisees are treated scrupulously equally – which does not
necessarily mean the same. An anti-oppressive approach would be one in
which the whole style and perspective of a supervisor communicates a fundamental belief in the potential and ability of each supervisee. This approach recognises and tries to understand the obstacles to growth that
may have developed for that person in the face of their past oppression
and discrimination, and works actively to enable them to increase their
personal confidence and professional competence. To achieve this aim an
empowering interpersonal relationship will often not be enough. The evidence of the supervisor's serious intent needs to be demonstrated in actively
challenging those structural inequalities in the organisation that are oppressive and impeding the supervisee's development. However, anti-oppressive
supervision does not mean colluding with the supervisee if their work is
not satisfactory. Holding to professional standards and meeting agency requirements will sometimes mean confronting difficult issues, whilst valuing
the person being confronted and acknowledging extrinsic discriminatory .
factors.

Thus whilst an anti-discriminatory stance is one that can at least to some
extent be learned and applied intellectually – and legally – an anti-oppressive
approach is one that, to be authentic, has to be wholly congruent with the
understanding, feelings, attitudes and behaviour of the people involved. This

means, especially for white middle-class males like ourselves, listening to what oppressed people are saying about their experience, absorbing feedback about the impact of our own behaviour, and continuously working both to sensitise our own feelings and to develop anti-oppressive strategies on the wider organisational front.

An associated issue is the task of relating the many different kinds of oppression, with their similarities and differences, to each other. For each individual this awareness will start from a different point depending on their own personal position and experience. Here we are entering the difficult territory of the unhelpful but very understandable tendency to prioritise oppressions into some kind of hierarchy. Each of us inevitably has a stronger commitment to some oppressions than to others according to personal experience and interest. For example, the white man with a major physical disability is likely to give priority to disablism, the black woman to racism and sexism, those in the permanently unemployed underclass to issues of social class and poverty, and so on. These biases – which are also strengths – affect all supervisors and supervisees in different ways, depending on who they are. Part of the personal work of the supervisor, and indeed also of the supervisee, is to recognise them and to try to develop a generic anti-oppressive approach with the goal of facilitating empowerment. This then has to be applied sensitively in response to the needs of each individual supervisee. Easier said than done!

When we seek help from the literature we have a bit of a problem. We find that there is now an established general literature on most oppressions. There is a growing though still patchy literature specifically on application in social work students' training and supervision, but very little on the implications for staff supervision. We have found it necessary, therefore, to draw from what is available, combined with our own personal understanding and experience of working with supervisors and supervisees. The most extensive coverage of oppression in the management/supervision literature is given to the position of women. While this is reflected in our writing, there is no suggestion that it is a more important issue for supervision than other oppressions. Although each oppression is unique, much of what is learned in one area can be transferred to others.

There has been a considerable amount of writing and attempts at elucidation of the concepts and processes of discrimination/anti-discrimination and oppression/anti-oppression in recent years. CCETSW (The Central Council for the Education and Training of Social Workers) has given a firm lead, both in their requirements for the Diploma in Social Work (CCETSW 1991a) and in a series of publications. These publications have the training of social work students particularly in mind, but are of wider application throughout social work and community care. Their publications on anti-racist social work education include: *One Small Step Towards Racial Justice* (CCETSW 1991b); *Setting the Context for Change* (CCETSW 1991c); *Improving Practice with Children and Families* (CCETSW 1992a); *Improving Practice with Elders* (CCETSW 1992b); *Improving Mental Health Practice* (CCETSW 1993); *Improving Practice in the Criminal Justice System* (de Gale *et al.* 1993); and *Improving Practice Teaching and Learning* (Humphries *et al.* 1993).

Table 3.1 Black/white/female/male supervision pairings

	Black woman supervisee	White woman supervisee	Black man supervisee	White man supervisee
Black woman supervisor	=	–	–	–/–
White woman supervisor	+	=	+/–	–
Black man supervisor	+	+/–	=	–
White man supervisor	+/+	+	+	=

Key: = race/sex differences do not change the role power differences
+/+ race/sex differences reinforce the role power differences
–/– race/sex differences counteract the role power differences
+/– race/sex differences act in different directions

Power, difference and similarity in the supervisory relationship

To summarise the discussion so far, there are many different kinds of power that influence the supervisory relationship. These fall into two broad categories:

- the formal power that derives from the role and position of the supervisor *vis-à-vis* the supervisee
- the informal power of both supervisor and supervisee that derives from professional and personal attributes, *and from the structurally determined identities and roles based on key characteristics like race, gender, class, age, sexual orientation and (dis)ability.*

It is the latter aspect of informal power in relationships that in our view is given inadequate attention in the literature on staff supervision.

To illustrate the ways in which these different kinds of power can affect the supervisory relationship, we have selected race and gender as variables in the matrix of different combinations of power. Table 3.1 shows that there are 16 different possible combinations (and when we remember that the term 'black' includes people of many different ethnic origins and religions we realise that the reality is much more complex). Four of the 16 combinations are 'like with like', for example, a white woman supervising another white woman. Of the other 12 combinations, some have the supervisory role and social-structural power of the supervisor as mutually reinforcing (either doubly when a white man supervises a black woman, or singly when a white woman supervises a black woman). Some have the gender and race oppressions going in opposing directions, when a black man supervises a white woman, and vice versa. Some have the social-structural power of race and of gender difference both counteracting the role power, when a black woman supervises a white man.

One thing we need to make clear is that the situation is not as symmetrical as the diagram might suggest. In particular, as Brown and Mistry (1994: 12), drawing on Day's (1992) reference to black women writers, have pointed out:

> It would however be a mistake to treat the oppression position of black men and white women as symmetrical in Britain and North America . . . the dominance of black men cannot be equated with the dominance of white men because only the latter is part of the patriarchal-capitalist inheritance . . . black women are not denying that black men are sexist, but some black women identify their position as one where they 'struggle together with black men against racism, while we also struggle with black men, about sexism'.
>
> (Carby 1982: 213, quoted by Day 1992: 19)

To illustrate the relationship dynamics and power issues, we shall now examine some of these combinations in more detail, starting with the situation of a white woman supervising another white woman. As two white women together there may well be a good empowering feeling of mutual identification and solidarity, for example, in their shared experience of the male dominated senior management culture as macho and alienating, and in the kind of understanding the woman supervisor has of the woman supervisee's feelings about working with male perpetrators of sexual abuse with girls. This sameness can be, and often is, a source of great strength and support for the supervisee – and indeed sometimes also for the supervisor.

There are however possible traps to be avoided. One is that a collusive alliance is formed that denies the formal power of the supervisor. For example, if the supervisee is not keeping her records satisfactorily the supervisor may protect her, rather than helping her understand and confront the difficulties she is having, with an expectation of improvement. There could also be a racist collusion – quite possibly at an unconscious level – in which the two white women stereotype, and fail adequately to understand, the needs of black families or individuals.

Furthermore, just because they are both white women does not of course mean that they may not be different and possibly divided by other major factors like age, sexual orientation, ideology or career expectations. For example, one may have a strong feminist perspective on her work, favouring the formalisation of a network of women's staff groups. The other may take the view that the significance of gender in the work is greatly exaggerated, that women's staff groups are a divisive distraction, and what really matters is one's competence and commitment to the job. If the supervisor is the feminist, the supervisee's capacity to hold to her value position may be undermined by her weak position power (she could want her supervisor's positive support in some planned career development), and the supervisor may exploit her own position to try and pressurise the supervisee into a change of view. If the dynamic is in the other direction, and the supervisor is unimpressed by the supervisee's feminism, this could set up an impasse detrimental to both women in the supervisory relationship, particularly affecting the professional development of the supervisee. Another potential source of conflict between two women may arise from the tensions involved in each woman having different priorities concerning having children and seeking rapid career progression.

Let us now consider the dynamic when a white man supervises a black woman, and then vice versa. In the first case we have the maximum power differential possible in our 16 scenarios, which could of course be further reinforced if, say, the supervisee also has a disability and the supervisor is from a 'higher' social class – not an outrageous assumption given the pattern of social structural discrimination in Britain. Various possibilities may develop in this scenario. One of the most likely is that the white man is well-meaning, has had a smattering of anti-racist training, and walks on eggshells because he is so anxious not to appear racist. Unfortunately he has no idea of this – or indeed any other – black woman's experience, and has made no serious attempt to try and find out. As a result he is quite unable to empathise with the current experiences the supervisee is having in her work, which is mostly with white service users, colleagues and other professionals. He may be paternalistic if not patronising in manner, or even sexualise the relationship by being flirtatious. If the supervisee is, say, of Asian origin, he may also use her to brief him about the needs and customs of Asian families, and, just because she is black, ask her to take on responsibility for promoting anti-discriminatory practice within the team.

For her part, the black woman supervisee faces some difficult choices. Should she defer to his power and status (something she has had to do in many other situations in her life in order to survive) and be tolerant of his approach? Should she minimise supervisory contact and seek support elsewhere? Or should she be courageous and confront him with how he is treating her and request a frank reappraisal of their supervisory relationship? If she goes for confrontation she runs the risk that he may counter by defining her as someone with a chip on her shoulder, or insecure, which could disadvantage her in the future. One potential source of strength for her in this situation is active team support.

If the roles are reversed and a black woman is supervising a white man, what then? As in all the previous examples, much will of course depend on the particular individuals concerned, and our illustrations – and they are no more than that – are based on our own experience and that of others shared with us personally or through publications. For the black woman, particularly if recently appointed to her managerial or supervisory position, this may be the first occasion in her life that she has been placed in a position of formal power over a white man. Can she exercise that power and authority without a tendency to defer in the way she has been socialised into throughout her life? Can she on the other hand resist the temptation to exploit this role reversal by taking every opportunity to emphasise her position and power?

The white male supervisee faces the polar opposite predicament. This may well be the first time in his life that he has had a black boss, and moreover nearly all of his previous authority figures could have been male as well as white. These factors may lead him to try and undermine her authority –

quite possibly without realising what he is doing – by indulging in male stereotypical behaviour such as parading his academic knowledge (which could well be inferior to hers), or being patronising or flirtatious in approach.

There are three things to say about these illustrative examples. The first is that we have only selected a few combinations out of the race and gender matrix. We hope, however, that these might stimulate thought about the other combinations in this matrix, and the ways in which other oppressions, such as class, age, disability and sexual orientation interact with the formal position power of the supervisor.

The second is to recognise that the one-to-one interactions take place in a team context that can be very influential. The culture established in the team will affect how both supervisor and supervisee behave with each other. For example, the extent to which the team as a whole validates or undermines the power and authority of the black woman supervisor will affect both her confidence in supervising the white male supervisee, and his attitude to her in supervision. Similarly, if the black woman supervisee has good support from anti-racist colleagues in the team, she will feel much more confident about confronting her white male supervisor if this is necessary. The team ethos will act as a constraint on him, and perhaps motivate him to learn much more about the black experience and anti-racist empowering supervision, and make a real effort to change his behaviour.

The third comment is that the examples given are mostly of the ways in which the effectiveness of supervision may be reduced by 'difference'. Difference can of course also be empowering and fruitful, and below we suggest some of the ways in which supervisors and supervisees can create conditions in their relationship that are more likely to enrich than to diminish the satisfaction and effectiveness of their work together. As a prelude to this, we shall first refer to some of the relevant literature and research.

Information about discrimination and oppression in supervision

As previously indicated, sources on this subject are not easy to find other than on gender, much of which is written by women not men. (Most of the impetus for policy change on gender and race has come from women and black people, respectively, and a similar pattern occurs with other oppressions.)

Gender and supervision

Three publications, taken together, provide a convincing picture – if not scientifically proven evidence – of the experience of women in relation to social work, supervision and management. These are *Women and Social Work* (Hanmer and Statham 1988); *Promoting Women* (Allan *et al.* 1992) and *Women, Management and Care* (Grimwood and Popplestone 1993).

All three texts emphasise the differences in culture, style and priorities that tend to distinguish male and female managers (recognising that these are generalisations and not true in all cases). For example, male managers tend to emphasise status, control and pay, whereas women managers are more likely to stress improvement of services and personal interest in the job (Nicholson and West 1988, referred to in Grimwood and Popplestone 1993: 62). A man is more likely to see a first-line manager post as a stepping-stone to further promotion, whereas many women regard it as their ceiling. It is pointed out (for example, in Allan *et al.* 1992) that most women have greater home commitments, often as the primary carer, and that whereas the career of a man is often positively enhanced by marriage, the reverse is usually true for a woman (Hanmer and Statham 1988). This has various adverse consequences for a woman when the agency work ethos is to put one's job above everything else in one's life; part-time and jobshare management posts are rarely to be found, and good quality child care arrangements are both scarce and expensive.

When women are promoted and in mainstream supervisory positions, the evidence (Hanmer and Statham 1988; Kadushin 1992) indicates that they are accepted by supervisees, both male and female, at least as favourably as their male supervisor peers. There is, however, often a strong pressure to adopt the male ethos and prevailing culture, especially in senior management positions, where a small minority of women often become very isolated. The pervasive male management culture tends to stereotype female managers as either feminine and sexual but not very competent, or the reverse, highly competent but unfeminine.

In a not untypical situation in an SSD, a newly promoted woman child care manager found herself the only woman in a middle management group of ten. At early meetings after her arrival some of the men began to make sexist comments, for example, 'what's it like being a woman amongst all us men?' Before she had the chance to reply, another male team manager made comments implying that in order to have achieved that status, she must of course have the necessary 'male' characteristics. This put the woman manager in a catch-22 situation regarding her response, because if she became angry and aggressive, i.e. showed 'male' attributes, this would prove their point; if she did nothing she would be colluding with their sexism. It was only when she made it very clear in an assertive way that their behaviour was unacceptable, and the men quickly came to realise that she was able to be feminine *and* a competent child care manager, that their behaviour changed to treating her as a respected colleague.

Failure to take account of gender differences is illustrated in the following, not unusual example from the male-dominated world of a university. One woman professor was the only female member of an otherwise all-male senior management committee. At one point the (male) vice-chancellor called a 'toilet break', and when the committee resumed a few minutes later he announced a decision on a previously uncompleted item, quite unaware until it was pointed out to him, that the decision had been reached in the men's toilet in the absence of the only woman!

Two research articles from the USA – to be treated cautiously in terms of generalisation to other contexts – provide further indications of the male-dominated prevailing culture of management influencing supervision style. In a study by York *et al.* (1989), based on a sample of social workers in North Carolina, they found that supervisors were more likely to exhibit what they describe as 'male' leader behaviour than 'female', irrespective of the sex and position of the supervisor.

Nelson and Holloway (1990), researching in the field of counselling, studied the interaction between supervisors and supervisees in the middle phase of supervision sessions. They focused specifically on whether male and female supervisees were treated differently by supervisors, irrespective of the sex of the supervisor. They concluded that

> it appears that individuals in the expert role, regardless of gender, may assume more power in interaction with their female subordinates [*sic*], either by withholding support for the female subordinates' attempts at exerting power or by simply exerting stronger influence with female subordinates. In the supervisory relationship the female trainee may respond to this stance on the part of her supervisor by declining opportunities to assert herself as an expert.
>
> (Nelson and Holloway 1990: 479)

They go on to conclude, not surprisingly, that this can disempower women in supervision and influence their future professional identity.

Race and supervision

The published material specifically on how racial differences may affect the supervisory relationship is mostly from the student supervision context. See, for example, *A Review of the Experiences of Black Students in Social Work Training* (de Souza 1991); *The Black Students' Voice* (Burgess *et al.* 1992) and *Improving Practice Teaching and Learning* (Humphries *et al.* 1993). There is also some information to be found in the general literature on the experience of black staff in social work agencies (for example, Ferns 1987; Ahmad 1990). We refer below to Divine's investigation (1989) into the supervision of first-year probation officers in the West Midlands Probation Service. There the concern arose not only because several black officers were failed by their white senior probation officer supervisors at the point of confirmation, but also because their experience contrasted with that of a much larger number of their white counterparts, all of whom were passed.

Grimwood and Popplestone (1993: 51–2) suggest that more attention has been given to the need to promote black staff to all levels in the organisation than has been given to a similar promotion need for women staff. It may be that the decision of CCETSW in Paper 30 (1991a) in effect to designate racism as the oppression *prima inter pares* in student training has given this impression; although we wonder whether this is really true. Some American research (Jayaratne *et al.* 1992) examined the perceptions of African-American practitioners of their supervisors on the criteria of 'emotional support', 'social undermining' and 'criticism'. Their finding was that in large public organisations being a female African-American supervisor resulted in being most negatively perceived by the black workers, whereas in smaller private agencies it was the white male supervisors who were most unpopular. The researchers suggest that the negative views in both cases may be caused by envy.

Setting the position of black supervisors in the organisational and societal context, as one must, Ahmad (1990, quoted in Humphries *et al.* 1993) argues that 'white professionals, as part of the white collective, have both formal and informal power over their black colleagues even if some of these colleagues are supervisors or managers' (p. 63). Thus, as with gender, the crucial factor is the established culture of the organisation, which is likely to be white-dominated throughout, as well as male-dominated in the upper echelons. As a crucial first step to counteract this, Humphries *et al.* argue that the values of 1960s social work, for example, on being non-judgemental, are outdated. They argue that these values support the power *status quo* that props up racism and other oppressions and discriminations endemic in the organisational structures. What is needed, they say, is a new anti-oppressive value base that identifies with oppressed groups, and recognises that most individual problems have their roots in the socio-political structure.

Experience from social work training (de Souza 1991; Burgess *et al.* 1992) indicates time and again that black students on placement are more likely to encounter difficulties in supervision than are their white peers. The exceptions are when they are attached to multiracial teams or teams that actually practice a well worked-out anti-racist policy. Some of the typical difficulties that arise for black students on placement, usually with a white practice teacher, and which often get replicated in comparable situations after qualification, have been outlined by de Souza (1991). These include (taken from de Souza's headings and quotes from black students in Williams (1987)):

- *Black students as 'race experts'* 'Some practice teachers see the role of the black student as one of helping to challenge a racist organisation or helping them to service black clients'
- *The colour-blind approach* 'At the meeting with my tutor, it was as though I was white. Race or racism was never mentioned. We never talked about racism from clients or colleagues. I didn't know how to deal with this'
- *Organisational culture – the unwritten code* 'As I was about to interview a client on duty, the senior told me that the man may be racist and asked what I would do if he hit me (a woman). I said I would hit him back and left the room. The interview ran smoothly but I was later told by the senior that my remarks were unprofessional and that I could fail my placement. I was offered no support on how to deal with racist clients'
- *Collusion or challenge* The black student has to decide '. . . whether to collude with racist practice and behaviour and pass (their placements) or confront and challenge such practice and behaviour and risk failure'.

Divine's investigation of the first-year experience of 'failed' black probation officers with white seniors (1989) revealed what at best could be described as communication problems. There was a divergence between black staff and white managers in their respective understanding of the purpose of probation work, and little guidance given to black staff on the framework of evaluation. Also, black staff experienced the white supervisors as defensive and punitive in attitude. This was in the context of an oppressive organisational framework, supervision generally of patchy quality, and a frequently racist criminal justice system. The encouraging aspect of this enquiry was that

Divine's recommendations to remedy the problem were taken seriously by the agency, and he later reported positive improvements in the supervision of first-year probation officers and confirmation procedures in the West Midlands (Divine (1991) in CCETSW 1991b: Chapter 13).

While both race and gender are at least getting some attention in relation to management, supervision and promotion issues, the position of some other oppressed groups, notably disabled, lesbian and gay staff, seems to have been virtually ignored. This omission is reflected in the absence of a supervision literature on the issues in relation to these groups. Much of the above discussion and the examples given can be translated conceptually into the context of other oppressions, but that does not begin to do adequate justice to the experiences of the people – supervisors and supervisees – facing the consequences of their particular oppression(s).

Disability and supervision

The general literature on disability and social work (see Oliver 1983; Oliver 1991; and Stevens 1991) indicates the widespread discrimination against disabled people throughout society, including disabled social workers and service users. An example taken from the social work training context illustrates some of the prevalent attitudes to disabled staff in social work and community care. The example concerns a student with severely impaired sight who required an SSD placement. Team after team said they were unable to take him. It was never stated openly, but all the indications were that in most instances the reason was his sight impairment. It was only after his tutor pointed out to a senior manager in no uncertain terms that this response was wholly at odds with the agency's alleged equal opportunities policy that suddenly a placement was found. In the event, the student had an excellent non-discriminatory practice teacher, and did exceptionally well in all areas of assessment. This excellence was particularly marked in administration where the nature of his disability necessitated him being much better organised than most fully sighted students are. One can only speculate on what this tells us about how disabled staff are treated generally, both in and out of supervision, and on the reasons why there are so few disabled managers and supervisors.

Lesbian and gay staff and supervision

As with disability and supervision, the literature is mostly silent on lesbian and gay staff and supervision. The general principles, processes and issues discussed in this chapter are relevant, but again there are particular issues facing lesbian and gay supervisors and supervisees that need to be addressed. The very fact that lesbian and gay social workers and managers face agonising decisions about whether to 'come out' is indicative of the widespread discrimination they face from many colleagues and service users, as well as in their private lives. We are most grateful to a lesbian colleague for assistance with the following illustrations of some of the ways in which this occurs:

- *In the supervisor–supervisee relationship* The 'coming out' dilemma causes all kinds of tensions and difficulties that get in the way of an effective, facilitating supervision relationship. Examples of this are: relations between a 'closet' supervisor and a supervisee who has 'come out'; mutual hesitancy and uncertainty regarding the other person's sexual orientation; dormant fears of homosexuality being restimulated; the confrontation of a supervisee of the same sex by a gay supervisor being diminished and reinterpreted as 'thwarted lust'.
- *Heterosexist attitudes and assumptions about lesbian and gay workers* This shows in various ways, including: negative stereotypes, for example, assumptions that lesbian child care workers are 'perverted' and will harm children; presumptions that lesbian supervisors who criticise male workers' competence are 'anti-men'; gay people experiencing their home life as being treated as invisible; difficulties about touch, and assumptions that gay people are promiscuous and attracted to all members of the same sex.
- *Equal opportunities* Agency equal opportunity policies often treat heterosexism as the most marginalised oppression, added in as an afterthought as if to appease rather than include.

Implications for anti-oppressive/empowering supervision

In this final section of the chapter on anti-oppressive supervisory practice we discuss the various positive steps the supervisor – and the supervisee – can take to develop an empowering climate for both supervision and practice. Differences, which hitherto have been viewed as problematic, are now seen to be potentially positive opportunities to enhance the quality of supervision for all concerned. For these opportunities to be realised, there are a number of preconditions:

- provision of adequate training for the supervisor
- negotiation and implementation of an anti-oppressive/non-discriminatory supervisory relationship
- supervision that enhances anti-oppressive practice with service users.

Anti-oppressive training of supervisors

The starting point must be a combination of a progressive agency policy on anti-oppression, and a supervisor with the necessary commitment to a well worked-out personal position. The latter requires self-preparation, the baseline for which will vary greatly among first-time supervisors – and indeed all supervisors – depending upon a whole range of factors including their:

- personal experience of different oppressions
- previous training content
- previous experience as a supervisee (see Chapter 2)
- personal ideology.

Formal training of supervisors needs to be permeated throughout with an anti-oppressive perspective of empowerment, and to include an early opportunity for each supervisor to make a self-assessment of their personal position and to identify personal development goals. For white, middle-class, heterosexual men, the agenda will obviously be very different from that for those supervisors who may have had to spend their entire lives learning strategies for coping with discrimination and oppression. Our view is that this kind of training needs to be both experiential and cerebral, integrating experience and knowledge, and should be viewed as a continuous process. (See Chapter 10 for a fuller account of the training of supervisors.)

An anti-oppressive supervisory relationship

The first prerequisite is the development of an open honest relationship in which anti-oppressive issues are constantly on the agenda. The supervisor needs to acknowledge right from the beginning the differences in power, both of formal position and of identity. He or she needs to encourage exchange of the feelings each participant has about how these power differences are likely to affect the supervision relationship. For example, if the supervisor is heterosexual and the supervisee is homosexual, or vice versa, this could be an open item on the supervision agenda right from the initial contract discussions onwards.

As part of this kind of discussion the supervisor may need to acknowledge that the supervisee did not choose her or him, and that, at least initially it is an imposed, coerced relationship. (There are some contexts, notably in residential work, where there may be scope for a choice of supervisor, but generally 'you get who you are given'.) For example, a woman supervisee with a male supervisor might have greatly preferred to have had a woman supervisor, or a black supervisee to have had a black supervisor of similar ethnicity. The first thing is for the supervisor to understand these preferences and to recognise that she or he cannot meet some important needs of the supervisee. They should actively support – rather than feel threatened by – any wish on the part of the supervisee to have access to other sources of support such as a consultant, peer support group, or mentor of similar personal background. This should not be seen by either party as an alternative or a threat to supervision, but rather as an important complementary resource based on a clear understanding of the respective functions of supervision and consultative relationship(s). Other measures include incorporating into supervision regular feedback, review and evaluation meetings, preferably linked to an agency system of staff appraisal and development. This whole area needs to be a core part of supervisor training.

Much will depend on the level of trust established in the relationship, and this has to be earned. It can help if the supervisor makes it explicit from the outset that critical feedback about their own behaviour when this is experienced as oppressive will be positively welcomed and acted upon, and not be used to the supervisee's disadvantage in any way. Another test is how the supervisor reacts when a supervisee reports discriminatory behaviour against her or him from a service user. To redefine the problem as belonging to an oversensitive supervisee with a chip on their shoulder can be devastatingly disempowering and disillusioning. What is needed is for the supervisor to listen carefully to the supervisee's account of their experience, to take what is said and felt very seriously, to offer maximum support, and to take whatever action may be necessary.

An anti-oppressive approach to supervision content

This chapter has concentrated on process and the power issues in the supervisory relationship. However, the primary aim of supervision is to provide the best possible service for the service user, and to carry out agency policy (not always the same thing). A central task of the supervisor is to ensure that each supervisee, and the team as a whole, work with service users in an anti-discriminatory empowering manner.

All the principles and values outlined in this chapter relating to supervision, apply equally to practice. There is a parallel process of inequality of position power in the worker–user relationship, meshed in with identity and personal power factors that may reinforce or counteract the worker's position power. Thus the supervision contract agreement on being open about the use of power in the supervisory relationship needs replicating in the worker–service user relationship. Both supervisor and supervisee have a responsibility to ensure that the approach they take when discussing the supervisee's work with service users is anti-oppressive. For this to work there needs to be a preparedness on the part of both participants to check each other as necessary.

Our use here of 'each other' highlights the reciprocity that is possible in a supervision relationship when both people are secure in their shared understanding and acceptance of the power differences and dynamics. Clarity about roles and boundaries creates the conditions for maximum freedom to be two people in a professional/personal relationship. While one has the formal power position, each has potentially much to learn from the other. However, as we stress throughout the book, the one-to-one relationship has to be set in the team and agency context. The pervasive influence of institutional discrimination and oppression is a more intractable challenge than the personal relationship.

Getting started:
contracts and boundaries

So far we have built up a picture of the background and contextual factors that influence the practice of supervision. In this chapter we discuss the first steps in entering into a supervision relationship, and the importance of negotiating a clear agreement, or contract, between supervisor and supervisee. This may help both to clarify the parameters of supervision, and set the tone and style of the future working relationship.

Among the many issues to be considered are those to do with boundaries: what is and what is not appropriate activity for supervision. As we shall see in this and subsequent chapters, getting the contract right does not of itself in any way guarantee successful supervision, but it does provide a firm foundation for effective work. Without a meaningful contract endorsed by both supervisor and supervisee, supervision is likely to be beset with difficulties and misunderstandings.

The major part of the chapter will identify and discuss the main elements that need to be in a supervision contract, and some of the associated issues. The latter part will illustrate some of the difficulties that can occur when the boundaries of supervision get confused, for whatever reason.

Key elements in the contract

Readers may already have drawn up their own list of what they think needs to be included in contracting sessions, reflecting upon the particular context within which they work. We have made our own selection of key elements to facilitate this process. We think all of these elements, suitably adapted to each situation, are likely to be relevant for supervisors and supervisees in a wide range of social work and social welfare contexts. The elements are:

- forming the relationship, including sharing each other's past experiences, values and expectations of supervision

- type of supervision
- accountability
- focus
- issues of timing, frequency of meetings, and other practical arrangements
- confidentiality
- preparation, agenda setting, record-keeping and methods
- values and anti-oppressive perspectives
- provision for evaluation and review.

Each of these elements will now be considered in more detail.

Forming the relationship: sharing experiences, values and expectations

Contracting is not only about planning the nuts and bolts of working to-gether – important as these are – but also about beginning to forge a rela-tionship based on mutual trust and respect. In many instances a new relationship is being formed, but in others it is a question of working out a different role relationship from that experienced previously. Particularly if you have been promoted to manager within your team, the power relation-ship between you and your former colleagues and peers suddenly becomes fundamentally changed.

One way of both exchanging important information and developing the relationship, is the sharing of past experiences of supervising and being supervised. It is important that this is a two-way process, with the supervisor demonstrating at this early stage her or his preparedness to self-disclose in a mutual way, and not just draw out information from the supervisee. These first messages – especially in new relationships – can have a profound effect on future work together. It is important that these shared experiences are explored to the point that the lessons learned can be incorporated into the supervision contract.

Another important aspect of contract negotiation is sharing mutual expec-tations of purpose and what is likely to be involved in supervision. Serious misunderstandings can occur when the respective expectations of supervisor and supervisee are not shared at the outset. In providing training and con-sultancy to social work supervisors, we are constantly surprised at how often an unstated difference in assumptions about what kind of supervision is being provided underlies what can seem to be intractable difficulties. This is a problem that affects not only new supervisors, but even the most experi-enced – as Illustration 4.1 demonstrates.

Illustration 4.1

Two colleagues worked together as trainers on a short introductory course on supervision. Throughout their planning, there were no obvious indications that they might run into difficulties. It was only once the course had begun that each felt at odds with the other, despite a strong commitment to a cooperative and supportive working relationship.

*As the workshop progressed, it became apparent that once they scratched
the surface each had a quite different internalised model of supervision. One,
for example, placed a strong emphasis on structuring the supervisory
relationship, and the supervisor's managerial responsibility; while the other
placed an emphasis on the process of the supervisory relationship, and the
supervisor's professional responsibility. Only after the course were they able to
acknowledge the influence of their formative experiences (see Chapter 2).
Before becoming trainers each came from a very different social work context,
and hence had very different experiences of supervision. One had worked for
many years as a psychiatric social worker in a local authority, the other as a
drama therapist in a voluntary organisation. As a result, they not only
placed a different emphasis on the managerial and professional functions, but
also on how accountability influenced the relationship between supervisor and
supervisee. Had they shared these past experiences and different assumptions
in advance of their work together, at least some of the difficulties could have
been avoided.*

Types of supervision

'Supervision' is an umbrella term for many different but related activities,
and this sometimes causes confusion and misunderstandings about purpose.
Hawkins and Shohet (1989: 44) have identified four main types of supervision:

- *Tutorial supervision*   The supervisor assumes the role of tutor and offers
  educational input
- *Training supervision*   Another educational role used when the supervisee is
  a student or trainee, and the supervisor holds some responsibility for their
  practice
- *Managerial supervision*   The supervisor is the line manager of the supervisee,
  and the relationship can be characterised as manager – subordinate
- *Consultancy supervision*   The supervisor has no direct responsibility for the
  supervisee or their work, and is in a purely consultative capacity.

In social work and community care agencies most supervision falls within
the category of managerial supervision. However, particular work contexts
and developmental influences of the kind discussed in the next chapter may
lead supervision closer to the other three categories.

While these categories represent important cornerstones, the variety and
diversity of social work supervision is not adequately conveyed by this classification. We therefore propose the use of a map, Figure 4.1, to locate both the
current position of supervision at the outset and the direction and boundaries
of change over time. It can be an interesting exercise for both supervisee and
supervisor to locate individually where on the map they see their current
supervisory relationship and then to compare and discuss the similarities
and differences.

The formal nature of the supervisory relationship can be thought of in
terms of two main continua, as shown in Figure 4.1. Both supervisee and
supervisor need to be clear about their agreed starting point in a new supervision relationship. This brings us to the next contract element: accountability.

Figure 4.1 Types of supervision

Accountability

The first (vertical) continuum in the figure represents the degree of accountability the supervisee has, to the supervisor at one end, and to themselves at the other. The issues that will influence the position of supervision on this continuum at the start of a new contract are:

- the line management relationship between the supervisor and supervisee (e.g. much greater if the supervisor is also the line manager than in cases where the supervisory responsibility has been delegated to a senior colleague)
- the social and political demands on the organisation for accountability (e.g. much greater accountability to the supervisor is required in statutory child protection work than in a voluntary advisory service)
- the degree to which the supervisee is experienced and acknowledged as competent and responsible (i.e. a new worker will need to be very closely accountable to the supervisor for all aspects of their work initially, but later may be expected to carry greater accountability for their work themselves).

Across this axis in the figure we have tutorial and consultancy supervision, which emphasise the accountability that supervisees have to themselves (towards consultancy), while managerial and training supervision emphasise the supervisee's accountability to the supervisor (towards management).

Contracting is also the time to clarify lines of accountability in more complicated circumstances; as, for example, when more than one supervisor is involved with the same supervisee, in interdisciplinary supervision, and in group and peer supervision models. When third parties are to be involved in the supervision arrangements they should also participate in at least some of the contract negotiations.

Focus

There are several aspects of focus in supervision, and one of these is indicated by the horizontal continuum in the figure. This continuum concerns the extent to which supervision deals primarily with current specific practice issues, or aims to develop a wider, more general, learning and understanding of the approach to future work. This also is likely to be affected by a number of different factors:

- the place of the supervisee in their own professional training and development (e.g. social work students on placement, and new workers, are more likely to have global needs to be addressed, while experienced workers will have addressed many of these needs already, and are more likely to be struggling with the exceptions rather than the rules that emerge from their current practice)
- the nature of service delivery (e.g. forms of service delivery that call on the worker to draw upon and examine themselves are more likely to require a general developmental emphasis than more instrumental forms of service delivery)
- the pressure on service delivery (e.g. in social work departments where there are very heavy workloads, there will be more time spent on specific issues than in less pressurised settings)
- the degree of latitude in service delivery (e.g. if there are legal requirements relating to service delivery, as in court work, the specific issues are likely to be emphasised more than if some latitude is permitted, e.g. running a group for offenders).

As will be noted from the various issues raised so far, some of the influences on the formal role of the supervisory relationship are fixed, while others may vary over time. Difficulties can arise later in supervision unless both supervisor and supervisee have clarified together in the contract the extent to which the supervisory relationship is expected to develop and change. Assuming a healthy and effective supervision relationship, over time it can be expected that the nature of that relationship will become increasingly consultative. We have shown this in Figure 4.1 by representing Consultancy supervision as a developmental magnet towards which all other types of supervision are drawn as the relationship develops. The developmental process within supervision is discussed in greater detail in Chapter 5.

There is another aspect of focus that sometimes leads to misunderstandings and frustration among supervisees. This is the focus of the content of supervision sessions, and in particular the extent to which the supervisee, as opposed to the work, comes under scrutiny. A frequent complaint from supervisees is that they went into a supervision session expecting to talk about the needs of their client only to find the spotlight on themselves personally. Sometimes the complaint is the opposite: that the supervisor becomes too task-orientated, giving insufficient space or encouragement for the supervisee's personal concerns or professional development. The common factor and essential point is that misunderstandings come when the parameters and focus of the discussion have not been clarified. Both parties need to have a very clear idea about how supervision agendas are established (another contract topic covered later) and how the focus of discussion is determined.

Timing, frequency of meetings, and other practical arrangements

Arrangements about the duration, frequency, and flexibility of supervision sessions may seem rather simple practical issues that could easily be skated over. Our experience, however, suggests that these time factors often have a critical influence over the development and quality of the supervisory relationship, and we shall therefore discuss them in some detail.

Illustration 4.2

As a new manager, one of us took great pains to assure staff that they could have as much supervision as they needed. 'If you need to talk about something, however small, just let me know, and I'll arrange a supervision session.' Well, you might think this was a foolish offer, and you would be right, not because it opened the floodgates, but rather the opposite. Two months passed, and not one of the eight team members had asked for supervision. Further enquiry revealed that the requirement on supervisees to ask for supervision meant that they felt they had to have a problem worthy of this special arrangement. Not only that, but in asking for supervision, workers felt that they were in a sense making an open declaration both to their manager and the team that they were not coping. However well intentioned, ad hoc arrangements restrict supervision to crisis management, and are often no more than a euphemism for no supervision.

The regularity of sessions can be critical to the way in which supervision is used. All too often supervision gets repeatedly rescheduled in the wake of new pressures and crises, sometimes with serious consequences. It is well understood in developmental psychology that the more secure the child is in the knowledge that, whatever happens, their parent will always be there, the freer they are to leave their parent and explore the world. Conversely, if the child learns that the parent is unreliable, then the more they cling and refuse to venture out. Likewise, the supervisee needs to feel secure enough to venture out into the work with confidence, and to use the supervisory relationship as a source of strength, without becoming over-dependent or clinging. For that to happen, supervision must be reliable and regular. The supervisee must know that it will always be there, and that it will not be buffeted about by competing demands and pressures, however tempting that may be. In some ways, supervision needs to be a safe haven, a constant in a sea of change; a time and place when the supervisee can stand back, take stock, reflect, and then prepare for return, revitalised. The regularity also helps both supervisor and supervisee think of the sessions not as separate meetings to discuss current difficulties, but as being developmentally linked, providing a sense of direction and purpose.

If supervision is used simply as a forum for checking off tasks, then there is no reason why the session should not end when that checking has been completed. However, supervision is more often not about the work *per se*, but about the supervisee who does the work. In the previous paragraph, we described supervision as a safe haven and illustrated the importance of constancy within that relationship. We believe, therefore, that whatever time boundaries are agreed for the duration of the session, these should be firmly maintained. In effect the boundaries of the supervision session provide a container inside which the supervisory process occurs. The less we know about that container, the less it can be trusted; and the less trusted it is, the less valuable the material that will go into it.

On training courses we often find that supervisors react against this apparent inflexibility, so it is worth exploring a little further. The first objection usually comes in the form 'but what if we simply run out of things to talk about after half an hour? Do we just sit in silence staring out of the window, or what?' This is a very real concern, and we have experienced many times the panic and unease that such situations can create for the supervisor/tutor and the supervisee/student. But is it really possible that after even just one day's work there is nothing that merits discussion? We think this is unlikely, and are much more convinced that after a week, two weeks or a month (the usual intervals between sessions), if the supervisee still feels there is nothing to talk about, something is seriously wrong.

It is perhaps more likely that there is so much to talk about that it is difficult to know what is appropriate or where to start. The supervisee may feel that only certain types of problem are appropriate for supervision, or that supervision is only about difficulties and never opportunities. Maybe they still have to learn how to make the best use of supervision, or perhaps it is the supervisor who is operating within a too restrictive model. Alternatively, there may be some interpersonal dynamic operating between supervisor and supervisee that is blocking communication and undermining trust.

In summary, when a supervisee says they have nothing to talk about, they may mean that they do not know what to talk about, or how to talk about it. They are sometimes too anxious to raise the difficult or personal issues that are troubling them. That is where the supervisor's skill comes in. Often the beginning of the session will focus on surface issues, and when these are exhausted, the supervisee may struggle for a while on the brink of moving into deeper, more difficult but relevant explorations. If the supervisor interprets this as closure, then they will devalue the sessions implicitly and substantially restrict opportunities for development and creativity.

A related problem sometimes occurs when, just as the time for the session is almost up, the supervisee raises a difficult and stressful issue. This is sometimes referred to as 'the doorknob syndrome'. The natural inclination might be to extend the session, although we feel that the disadvantages heavily outweigh the advantages. Why has the supervisee waited for so long before introducing this item? If the disclosures come late because the supervisee is not yet ready to go any further, shifting the boundaries may make it feel even less safe. Furthermore, the supervisor might already be winding down, out of supervisor mode, and not be psychologically prepared to address the new issue. There is also the practical problem of other work commitments that may have to be rearranged. Even if this is not an immediate issue, the supervisor needs to consider whether a pattern is being set for the future, and what kind of modelling they are providing.

Our preference would be to maintain the time boundaries of the session whilst empathising with the supervisee's feelings and anxieties. If the issue can wait, it can be put on the agenda for the next session as a priority item. If it is too urgent for that, then the chances are that the supervisee is wanting the supervisor to wear a different hat (most likely that of manager, but possibly counsellor). In such cases a separate meeting could be scheduled in the very near future to respond to the crisis, the separation being important to clarify changing roles and functions.

Finally, both participants need to know in what kind of circumstances either of them may cancel or interrupt a session, and whether as a general principle lost supervision time will be made up. Discussion of this issue at the contracting stage may help to strengthen one of our central tenets, that supervision is taken very seriously and given high priority. It also sometimes happens that either supervisor or supervisee fails to turn up at an arranged session, without any prior agreement or notification. What happens then? The important thing is to establish from the beginning that such unaccounted-for absence is taken just as seriously when the supervisor is at fault, as when it is the supervisee.

Confidentiality

One of the difficulties about confidentiality in social work supervision is that it cannot be absolute in the same way that it sometimes can be in a doctor–patient or therapist–client relationship. We believe that the supervisor must address this from the outset. She or he may, for example, have to write reports or appraisals on the supervisee; if the supervisee reveals malpractice, then the supervisor must act; and certainly, they will need to make explicit their own need to talk about the relationship in their own supervision.

To find a way through this, it is perhaps as important to establish principles as it is to make rules. For example, if the supervisor feels that they need to discuss anything that arises in supervision elsewhere, then they will normally talk to the supervisee about it first. It is worth noting that the supervisee also has some responsibility for confidentiality. It can be galling for the supervisor to discover that while they have drawn clear boundaries of confidentiality around supervision, the supervisee has been gossiping to all and sundry. The important issue about confidentiality is that the supervisee feels confident that their disclosures will be treated with respect and integrity, and that they are not misled into believing that confidentiality is absolute when it is not.

In a research study (not yet published) by Iain into group supervision, it was noted that in one group almost four hours were devoted to discussing confidentiality, and that despite this the issue continued to resurface in later sessions. The agreement worked out was of virtually legislative proportions, with a ruling on almost every eventuality. The problem is, whatever is decided, it still depends on whether you trust that decision. This is not to deny the importance of trying to be explicit about confidentiality issues, simply that they are meaningless without trust.

Preparation, agenda setting, methods and skills to be used, and record-keeping

Contract discussions need to clarify how decisions will be made about what will be worked on in supervision. The right of both participants to contribute agenda items needs to be established, and a clear system for doing this to be agreed – including how agenda priorities are set. It is useful to plan for some items to be known ahead of the meeting, so suitable preparation can be undertaken by both participants, but also leaving space for unexpected items that may arise between meetings. It is important that the supervisee's most pressing concerns get high priority and are not marginalised by a supervisor–driven agenda. The supervisee in turn has a responsibility to be proactive about making requests to discuss their items.

Like most things, supervision sessions are usually more effective when the participants have prepared themselves properly. This includes psychological preparation, which means, for example, the supervisor making every effort to start supervision with an uncluttered mind, temporarily freed of other concerns and worries. The supervisee is entitled to undivided attention throughout the session. This is much more easily said than done, as we both know from the shortcomings in our own practice. However we know from our own experience that when we allow a little time before a session to reorientate and prepare mentally, and when we are able to hold that concentration in the session, the supervisee/tutee almost invariably benefits. There is also of course the more tangible kinds of preparation to be done, in the form of reading any background papers, thinking about agenda items and so on.

It is good practice to agree to keep an open supervision record of topics covered and any decisions made. Apart from any direct benefit to the supervisee, it is particularly important for a relatively new supervisor to monitor their supervision as a basis for improving their own practice (for example, they may on occasion seek the supervisee's agreement to audio- or videotaping supervision sessions for this purpose).

What about the skills needed in the session itself? A brief and accurate answer is to say that virtually all the interviewing, group and communication skills developed as a practitioner are needed as a supervisor. They do, however, need some adaptation because the supervisee is a colleague and the task is different. Supervisees frequently complain about being 'social worked' in supervision, forgetting sometimes that they too have sophisticated interpersonal skills that they can use. There is a fundamental difference between using constructively whatever skills you have to achieve the best possible use of the session, and using those skills to play games, oppress the other person, or avoid difficult issues. Some recognition of these issues at the contract stage can be useful.

Turning to methods and techniques of supervision, the supervisee will be interested to know whether other techniques besides talking – which itself has many ramifications and subtleties – are envisaged by the supervisor. We are thinking, for example, of the use of role-play and other dramatic techniques to replay or rehearse tricky situations; the use of pictorial and diagrammatic representation; viewing a video together for a defined purpose; completing and analysing self-assessment questionnaires; use of games and exercises; sculpting in group supervision and so on. All these possibilities should be discussed at the contract stage, with both parties sharing their particular skills and their feelings about using different methods. An imposed technique is unlikely to be productive, and can reinforce supervisee defences against openness and self-disclosure.

The anti-oppressive dimension in contract negotiation

So far we have mostly referred to 'the supervisor' and 'the supervisee' rather as though they were objects in roles, not people with bodies and feelings. We thought this was necessary to establish a general framework applicable to all supervision contexts, but now we need to recognise that the supervisory relationship is not only a professional and managerial one, but also a personal one. Moreover it is a personal relationship in which – as we discussed in detail in Chapter 3 – authority and power are distributed unequally. This needs to be acknowledged explicitly as a matter of great significance right from the beginning.

It is vital that professionally relevant personal matters are, if possible, shared and discussed during the early stages of a new supervisory relationship. This is not about being unacceptably intrusive, but recognising that for all of us, and particularly for those who experience oppression, there can be no clear separation of the personal, the professional, and the political. Moreover, it is important that the assumptions that each makes about the other are not in any way restrictive or stereotypical. Whether or not the supervisor and supervisee share similar experiences of oppression, there is a need from the beginning to talk about how these will be handled within the supervisory relationship.

Some very significant experiences of oppression (e.g. that of lesbian women, gay men, and of survivors of sexual abuse) may not be obvious or known at the outset. A colleague of one of us commented that every time she had to disclose that she was a lesbian in a new supervision relationship, it was like leaping from a cliff because of the enormous risk involved. If the supervisor can, from the outset, genuinely demonstrate their own awareness of different oppressions and discrimination, and how this can affect confidence in supervision, then such supervisee disclosure could feel more like a step than a leap. Appropriate sharing by the supervisor of their own characteristics, experience and perspectives, can demonstrate that it is not one-way traffic, and encourage the supervisee to feel safer about doing likewise. The complexity is that the intangible nonverbal attitudinal communications are likely to have more impact than verbal statements, important as the latter are.

We know that for many people it is not easy to articulate values and attitudes in a vacuum, especially if you do not have an explicit recognisable ideological position; be it feminism, Marxism, Catholicism, gay rights, anti-racism, humanism, socialism or something else. Even when a clear position is held there may be an understandable reluctance to proclaim it at the beginning for fear of getting stuck with a label for the duration. Labels are of course often attributed irrespective of any disclosures, and supervisors need to guard against this.

One approach we have found useful at the beginning of student supervision is for practice teacher and student to explore each other's value bases, and their compatibility, indirectly through discussion of potentially contentious topical issues. These might be, for example: abortion on demand; transracial fostering and adoption; decriminalisation of cannabis; gay foster carers; domestic violence; ritual abuse of children; euthanasia; electronic tagging; assisting disabled people sexually; sending young offenders abroad as part of their training; and so on. If these discussions are linked to current instances, whether local or national, they may be particularly effective catalysts for mutual exploration of values.

This initial sharing of attitudes, needs and values as part of contracting might also include discussion of potential situations that might arise in the supervisory relationship, and how these might be helpfully addressed. For example, an early discussion about the option for a black female worker of having access to a black female consultant legitimises any future requests. In the absence of any initial discussion, the uncertain black worker may hesitate to ask when the need is there, and the insecure white supervisor may experience such a request as personal failure on their part.

Not every supervisee is going to bare their soul at the beginning of a new relationship, and we would be worried if they did. As we saw in Chapter 3, the person who has suffered continuous and hurtful discrimination and oppression for much of their life has no reason to trust someone in power over them until or unless that person – particularly if they are from an oppressor group – has demonstrated that they are not personally oppressive and can be trusted. This means that early exchanges of the kind referred to in this section may have a long-term impact on the supervision relationship. The responsibility of the supervisor at the contracting stage is to begin to create a supervision culture that the supervisee gradually experiences as safe, supportive and empowering.

Provision for evaluation and review

Whilst drawing up an initial contract is in our view an essential prerequisite for effective empowering supervision, it is only the beginning – a necessary but not sufficient condition. For example, initial discussion of the deeper, more intangible aspects of contract sometimes has a slightly unreal theoretical air to it until tested in practice. It is rather like equal opportunity policies, which are vitally necessary in any organisation, but only take on true meaning when discrimination actually happens and the policy is tested for real. It is important, therefore, to build in periodic reviews of supervision, in which both supervisee and supervisor try to be as candid as possible in sharing their own experience of their work together, and suggesting how it might be improved. This can if necessary lead to renegotiation of elements of the contract.

Boundary issues

What is and what is not appropriate business for supervision? One of the most likely causes of problems occurring at the contracting and subsequent supervision stages, is supervisor and supervisee confusion about where the boundaries of supervision lie. Supervisees, almost inevitably, will sometimes experience not just confusion but contradictions and competing demands in their job. Consequently, the supervisor has a responsibility to assist them in their search for clarity. To embark upon this task the supervisors must, themselves, be able to search for clarity within the supervision relationship. At the most basic level, they must at least have an understanding of what belongs within the supervision session and what goes elsewhere.

Earlier we commented on the danger of supervision becoming synonymous with management. Since the supervisor has, at some level, managerial responsibility for the supervisee, the tendency for supervision sessions to slip into individual management meetings can be insidious and pervasive. Richards *et al.*'s (1990) description of supervision as straddling management and practice provides a useful reminder of an appropriate balance. It can also be helpful to remember that very often the supervisor does not see the work of the supervisee first hand. To be accurate, therefore, it is often not the work that is being supervised but the worker. Putting these ideas together, we have the three elements of management, practice, and the worker, to which, as we shall see in the next chapter, the team can be added.

This division of supervision into functions, while valid and potentially useful, also contains dangers. Most obvious is the trap of assuming that supervision is a convenient hybrid of three different kinds of meetings, all held simultaneously. On training courses we often encounter supervisors who organise their sessions by devoting (say) a third to business matters, a third to practice, and a third for personal support. No doubt this is a simple and fair way of dividing time; unfortunately it takes little account of the interrelatedness of the subject matter or the real needs of the supervisee, and runs the risk of reducing supervision to a rote practice capable of maintaining only minimum standards.

Hawkins (1982) made a useful contribution to the understanding of supervision as a dynamic process by paying attention to the tension operating between management, client, and worker systems. In Chapter 5, with a slightly different emphasis, we have called these the Agency, Practice, and Worker Systems, and added the Team System. Normally, these primary systems have their own arenas (separate from supervision) for discussion, exploration, and decision-making. These may include staff business meetings, task reviews, and staff sensitivity meetings. To replicate the work of these meetings within supervision makes little sense. Therefore, the importance of these issues to supervision is limited to the induction phase (see Chapter 5) for new workers, where there is a need to ensure that the supervisee is well-grounded in all aspects of their work responsibilities.

After the induction phase, effective supervision is less concerned with these systems in isolation than the supervisee's efforts to understand the ways they impinge upon each other:

- how does the worker balance their own needs against the demands of the client?
- how do they reconcile individual workloads with membership of a team?
- what is their loyalty to the team when tested against loyalty to the agency?
- what happens when their personal beliefs are in conflict with the agency, the team, or those of service users?

The list can go on, but these examples illustrate how the supervisee will have to struggle to make connections between the different systems.

Before returning to the problem – faced by both supervisor and supervisee – of what is relevant to the supervision session and what should be dealt with elsewhere, we need to say some more about our concept of supervision, and the underlying values.

A vision of effective supervision

We believe that the supervision process can be:

creative
engaging
enabling
ensuring.

It offers an opportunity to reflect upon practice in its entirety: the good, the not so good, and the problematic.

It is a time out, a safe haven, and an opportunity to take stock.

It is a time for:

exploration
reflection
learning
problem-solving.

Carried out in a responsible way, this process will benefit:

the **worker** *personally*
their **practice** *with service users*
their *collaboration within the* **team**
their *ability to work within the* **agency** *remit, and toward* **agency** *goals.*

Credibility is given to the notion that good workers explore the questions provoked by their work, while insecure workers tend to present a studied image of coping. Thus the expression of doubts or confusion become signs of strength not weakness.

Finally, but most importantly, it is fair, and it is empowering.

A skilled supervisor understands what, in a given context, belongs within a supervision session and what does not (and through discussion helps supervisees to reach a shared understanding). As we shall see, failure to apply this distinction can lead the supervisor – and the supervisee – into considerable difficulty. How one decides what belongs within supervision will inevitably vary according to the presence or absence of other staff structures. For example, the presence of a team business meeting reduces the relevance of pure managerial issues in supervision. What is not reduced, however, is the relevance of the interplay between managerial and personal or professional issues.

The supervision session is a forum for reflecting on, and facilitating the work. It is not the place to do that work; a point that becomes all the more obvious when we consider that an experienced social worker may spend less than one per cent of their work time in supervision.

It may be helpful at this point to illustrate, with some examples, the distinctions we are making about what belongs in, and what belongs out, of supervision.

Illustration 4.3

Rosa is a hostel manager providing supervision to each member of the team individually. With the team working in a highly interdependent way, it is inevitable that as staff examined their work in supervision, they would touch upon the work of their colleagues. When tensions developed within the team, several team members used supervision to express their dissatisfaction with the others. Although Rosa wanted this to be discussed in a team meeting, those concerned felt that they needed to use supervision to explore their dissatisfaction first; and that to call a meeting on the basis of what had been discussed would breach the confidentiality of their sessions.

Rosa has a real dilemma on her hands. If she listens to their complaints in supervision she risks being drawn into a web of collusion. If she pulls down the shutters, and refuses to hear any of their complaints, she runs the risk of neglecting both their needs and those of the team. If she confronts the whole issue in a team meeting, how safe will staff feel to bring issues that trouble them to supervision in the future? These are major issues which need to be anticipated, and fully worked out when contracting the supervision relationship. We believe that this should include a clear understanding of the principle of responsibility; that when difficulties arise between colleagues, it is their responsibility to resolve them directly. Rosa would need to be careful not to get too involved in the detail of those problems, but rather encourage more direct ways of resolving them. The focus should be on the process of problem resolution, rather than the problem itself. It may be worth noting that one advantage of group supervision is that it does provide more direct opportunities to work on such team issues.

Illustration 4.4

A manager of a locality fieldwork team becomes aware during a supervision session that the supervisee is not maintaining up-to-date records of their work. It is a matter of some urgency, and indeed the worker has been warned about this before. The matter clearly must be resolved, yet there are obviously concerns about the supervision session becoming a disciplinary meeting and how future sessions will be used. Our view is that while the supervisor must raise the issue with the worker in supervision, the focus should be on exploring the supervisee's difficulties in record-keeping. That is not to dodge the uncomfortable reality that disciplinary action may be necessary, simply that a disciplinary meeting separate from supervision is the appropriate forum. Undertaking disciplinary action, whatever the forum, will inevitably affect the future supervisory relationship. It need not, however, cloud the purpose of supervision, provided the supervisor and the supervisee can establish clear boundaries to the relationship.

Illustration 4.5

A senior training officer in a training department supervises another training officer. They work in the same office. Furthermore, most of their work is shared, and they spend much of their time planning and delivering courses together. The problem comes when trying to decide how to use supervision. The temptation is to plan and review more courses, but that is what they do outside supervision. In such cases we believe that supervision should focus more on the developmental needs of the supervisee, featuring a stronger emphasis on work themes, and viewing the work within a broader context. If there are any relationship problems between them as colleagues, these are likely to be particularly difficult to address. Obviously an attempt should be made within supervision to resolve such problems, although it needs to be accepted that in some cases a third party may need to be consulted.

To underline the importance of this message about supervision boundaries and focus, we share the following experience.

Illustration 4.6

In the early 1980s Iain managed a residential therapeutic community. Once a month a line manager from head office would spend a day at the project, during which an hour and a half was devoted to individual supervision. This was conceived as an opportunity to explore role difficulties and personal needs, and it offered an opportunity for support. Purely managerial issues could be addressed elsewhere. None the less, Iain found himself using an entirely self-defeating strategy to avoid his own supervisory needs. The fact that the supervisor was under a lot of pressure to achieve all her management tasks in one short visit provided the basis for the avoidance. The supervisor would begin each session by checking and clarifying the purpose of the session. Then she would say something like 'Let's start by talking about how things have been going for you generally, and perhaps later we could draw up an agenda for the rest of the session.' Iain would agree, but then might pull out a wad of memos, letters, reports, checklists, policy documents, and invoices, and suggest '...It would help me to get a few practical matters sorted first...' With practice, it became possible to maintain discussion on these diversionary matters for the full hour and a half. At the end of each session the supervisor would say 'I had hoped we could spend more time on you... maybe next time.' This strategy, with some twists, was maintained 'successfully' for almost two years.

Earlier we observed that the 'drift towards supervision sessions becoming individual management meetings can be insidious and pervasive'. The above experience was not so much a drift as an avalanche! Of course, the strategy was totally self-defeating, and any potential for these meetings to help with anything other than surface issues was soon lost. We suspect that men may be somewhat more prone to such obstructive tactics than women!

Supervisor insecurity

Another reason why contracts are not always frank and comprehensive concerns the supervisor's own insecurity. Being elevated to the position of supervisor indicates a certain level of confidence by others in his or her ability. At first flattering, it can quickly become quite daunting and anxiety-provoking. particularly when faced by a skilled and experienced supervisee, the supervisor may feel very exposed by having to show their own skill and wisdom directly. Lacking confidence, they may then unconsciously collude with unclear expectations and boundaries, because these confuse the supervisory relationship, and make their own role more obscure. Supervision of the supervisor can rarely be more important than in these kinds of circumstances. It is worth noting that this applies equally to experienced supervisors, who may feel that they are being caught up and overtaken by their supervisees.

Failure to enter into frank discussion and negotiation of the supervision contract, including all the surrounding assumptions, can only lead to difficulties and a potential for power abuse. The supervisor has a responsibility to demystify and spell out what they have to offer, their expectations of the supervisee, and the nature of the supervisory relationship. They do not have to be the fountain of wisdom, nor an expert in all aspects of social work practice. In fact, it can be very reassuring to have a supervisor who is secure enough to share their vulnerabilities as well as their strengths.

Supervisee insecurity

As this book is written primarily for supervisors, most of the chapter has concentrated on their roles, responsibilities and issues at the contracting stage. However, they must constantly remind themselves that whilst they are often (justifiably) anxious about approaching a new supervisory relationship, supervisees are likely to be even more so. Supervisee anxiety is often high initially for fairly obvious reasons, including their own 'one-down' position in a relationship in which the supervisor can – and sometimes does – wield considerable power over their professional lives. One way for the supervisor to keep in touch with supervisee feelings is to examine their own feelings about their own supervision and supervisors, past and present.

Supervisee anxiety can impede effective contract negotiation if it results in them taking a fairly passive and cautious role in the whole process. The skilled supervisor will detect this and attempt to forestall it by a reassuring open facilitative approach. If the dynamic has already developed, the supervisor may refer to the difficulty explicitly, encouraging the supervisee to try to express their feelings and anxieties.

Conclusion

The supervision contract places boundaries around the supervision process. If those boundaries are safe, secure and known, then it is more likely that the supervisory relationship will be trusted to hold important and perhaps sensitive material. It is not possible to overstate the importance of this, and subsequent difficulties can often be traced back to inadequate or superficial contracting.

We need to recognise, however, that whilst an initial supervision contract is essential, it is only a beginning. Social work is a highly stressful occupation, and no amount of structure, planning and goodwill can prevent supervision situations arising in which tempers fray, anxiety is high and mistrust occurs. Pressure may be on either party at any time arising from their work, their relationship with each other and/or issues in their personal lives. This makes it all the more important that the supervisor conveys – in actions as well as words – a belief that the ability to explore both strengths and weaknesses in work is usually a positive sign of a good worker. Indeed it is our experience that the supervisees who say everything is fine, or that they have nothing to talk about, are almost always the ones that cause the greatest concern.

Ways of understanding and approaching the normal difficulties that can arise in the supervision relationship are the subject of Chapter 6, while issues of stress and trauma, as they affect supervision, are addressed in Chapter 7.

A model for practice

In the last chapter we identified management, practice and the worker as the principal concerns of supervision. We also noted that some authors, usually following Kadushin (1992) have preferred thinking of the supervisory process in terms of its constituent functions: administrative, educational, and supportive. The picture is further complicated by the addition of functions such as consultative (Brown 1984) and mediation (Richards *et al.* 1990). Since ours may not be the only text that the reader consults in relation to supervision, we shall now share our own way of bringing some order to the confusion, by attempting to provide not so much a prescription, but a map of the terrain, identifying some of its landmarks and contours.

A model based on four primary systems

The four systems that form the basis of our model are:

- the practice system
- the worker system
- the team system
- the agency system.

The notion of practice in this respect is complicated by the diversity of social work service provision. Hawkins and Shohet (1989) have used the term 'client' to describe the corresponding system in the counselling and psychotherapy field. The assumption, however, that the recipients of a social work service are either willing participants, or even that they benefit from it is not always tenable. The truth of social work may often have more to do with carrying out unpalatable tasks on behalf of a largely unappreciative society – removing children into care, working with unwilling residents, supervising probation orders, having people detained under the Mental Health Act, explaining to people that they are not eligible for certain benefits, and so on. To call the recipients of these alleged services 'clients' only adds insult to injury. No, if we were to use the term 'client' in such cases, it would not refer to the person receiving the service, but those that demand it: the courts and the public.

The notion of a single client, as opposed to a group, or community can be equally misleading. While knowledge of legislation, policies and procedures was once the domain of lawyers, managers and administrators, now they are as much a part of social work practice as welfare and other person-centred work. When we refer to the practice system in this context, we refer to the focus of the social worker's efforts in all the work undertaken. This is just as likely to be participating in a case conference, meeting with leaders of a local community group, or negotiating a care package with a provider of services, as it is working with a family or counselling an individual.

The team system has been included because the way in which the supervisee both works and relates to colleagues has a very significant impact on the quality of their work, whether or not that work is shared. This dimension is largely missing in previous formulations of supervision, perhaps because it is assumed to be part of a management focus or administrative function. Given the influence of political and contextual factors in social work, this conceptual merging can confuse very significant and different influences.

The Worker System acknowledges that in order to carry out many social work tasks, the worker will have to draw as much upon their personal resources as upon their professional expertise. The extent to which a supervisee can effectively carry out their duties will be heavily influenced by their own psychological health. In Chapter 7 we explore in further detail the critical role that supervision can play in preparing for, and protecting the worker from the worst effect of work-related stress and trauma. In addition the Worker System incorporates the worker's needs for professional development, and the examination of the appropriate and inappropriate use of self.

The Agency System involves all those aspects of the work that are specified by the agency, either as a matter of organisational culture and choice, or by legislative requirements. This may include Codes of Practice, Policies, Procedures and Guidelines which set the parameters within which the supervisee must operate.

Based on these four systems, we have developed a model (Figure 5.1) operating at three levels of increasing complexity, each representing a developmental phase.

The first, shown in the inner circle, proposes that explorations in supervision can be mapped out into the four distinct primary systems in a relatively discrete way during the early or *induction phase*.

The second level, the *connection phase*, shown in the middle ring, proposes a more sophisticated level of exploration represented by the connectedness between each pair of systems, as follows:

- professional (practice–worker interface)
- collaborative (worker–team interface)
- managerial (team–agency interface)
- organisational (agency–practice interface).

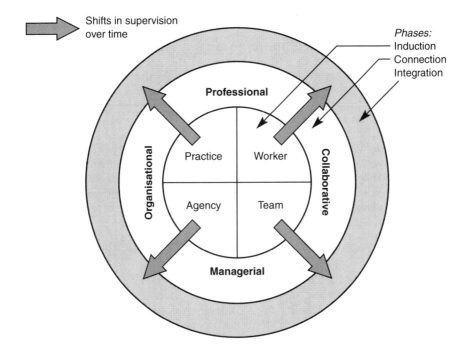

Figure 5.1 A model of supervision

The third level, the *integration phase*, represented by the outer ring, is a synthesis of all four systems.

The model provides us with a way to describe what goes on in supervision. The developmental element is the gradual change of focus of supervision over time, as experience and competence increases, from the first, through the second, to the third level (or phase).

At the first level, the focus is on each of the four primary systems for supervision, separately. This requires that the supervisee has a sound operational knowledge of each as a prerequisite for effective work. Supervision will normally only focus on these areas in their pure form during the induction phase when the worker needs to be firmly grounded, and the supervisor needs to ensure that the essential parts of the work are well understood. Beyond this induction phase, these nuts-and-bolts matters would normally be addressed more appropriately through specified arenas outside supervision, for example, in case conferences, team meetings, business meetings, personal counselling etc.

Once the induction issues have been addressed, supervision may begin to tackle some of the more complex and connected issues that are likely to require constant review, and may be the source of difficulty for the more established supervisee. These are the (second level) link areas of connection between the four primary interfaces for supervision.

Professional: the practice–worker interface (connection phase)

During the induction phase, the supervisor may assist the worker in becoming sensitised to the needs and experience of the client or to the contours of their task, with a view to identifying appropriate strategies for providing an effective service. In the connection phase, however, the supervisor begins to address the more complex interconnectedness between the worker and their practice. This may involve an exploration of the way that the worker's own identity, situation and needs impinge on the work, and how the relationship issues can be addressed in order that they assist rather than impede service delivery. Recognition of transference and countertransference from previous relationships may also provide part of the discussion. It may be the area in which the worker explores how they are similar or different to those they are working with, and how this can lead to collusion, blockages, overemphasis or denial within the relationship. Issues of power, its use and misuse within the relationship, and anti-oppressive practice represent further cornerstones. It is the focus which acknowledges that the use of 'self' is the primary tool and vehicle for much of social work practice. As a consequence, attention must be paid to the toll that the work may take from the worker (see Chapter 7), with the supervisor having a direct responsibility to assist the supervisee in maintaining their own psychological well-being.

Often we encounter workers whose own personal time – time to attend to their own needs and the needs of those who share their non-work lives – becomes eroded by the needs of increasingly demanding service users. Indeed, should we expect otherwise? Any of us, confronted with immediate tragedy or overwhelming need might feel impelled to give of ourselves unconditionally. Yet questions need to be asked, and the answers challenged in supervision. Whose needs are really being met, and conversely, whose are being denied? Does a preoccupation with one piece of work lead to a neglect of others? The worker, undoubtedly, will be responding to some need within themselves: perhaps following a life script, a spiritual journey, a passionately held ideology, or maybe they are compensating for something in their own lives.

Just as the worker may be addressing personal needs through their work, so the service user will also be using the experience. Sometimes the transaction will be straightforward: there is a request for help, worker assesses the need as appropriate, and the required service is provided. Often, however, the transaction is complicated. Someone wants a service, but not believing that they will get it, sabotages their own efforts. Or maybe the worker, having been tricked and deceived in their own life, begins to see practice encounters fraught with treachery and deception. The practice–worker dimension examines in fine detail: why we do the work, what we get out of it, what the costs are, how we protect ourselves from the pain, how we find an appropriate balance between our own needs and those that draw upon us, how we hone our own skills to maximum effect, how we maintain or generate enthusiasm.

Most social workers carry heavy workloads. Demand upon their services can be inexhaustible. Cases may churn up long-forgotten experiences and reactions. Or maybe the worker finds parallels between their own lives and those whom they help. Indeed, perhaps if the worker is not stirred up by these encounters, then that says as much about what the worker has screened out as it does about the service user. However such reactions are interpreted, what is undeniable is that the relationship between the worker and their practice is highly complex and deserves close attention in supervision.

Collaborative: the worker–team interface (connection phase)

Here the concern is about how the worker relates to other colleagues and the team as a whole. Are they making full use of the resources and expertise within the team, or are they keeping others at arm's length? Equally, are they making their own resources and expertise available to others? In many contexts, particularly residential and day care, other colleagues directly share the same work. In these instances, issues regarding the balance of responsibilities, good communication and working relationships will be paramount. It is important, however, that one-to-one supervision does not attempt to find solutions to any interpersonal difficulties that exist (other than those in the supervisory relationship itself) as these necessarily involve other parties. Rather, supervision can help the supervisee gain the clarity and confidence to feel sufficiently empowered to address and work through such difficulties directly.

Frequently the supervisor may hear the supervisee complaining about or expressing difficulties with another team member. Our view is that it may be an error then to analyse the faults of the third party, or indeed to provide justification for their behaviour. Rather, we would prefer an approach that encourages the supervisee to achieve a more considered view of themselves in relation to the team. This may include a valuable opportunity to apply their understanding of group process and systems thinking to their own immediate experience. Such opportunities to take a 'meta', or 'outside-in' perspective should not be underestimated.

Managerial: the team–agency interface (connection phase)

There is often a very alive dynamic deriving from the supervisee's dual membership of both an immediate team and a more distant organisation. Splitting can lead the supervisee to project all negativity out on to a faceless organisation when its origins may lie within the team itself. Ultimately this can only block the chances of resolution. Equally, the agency culture may have an oppressive systemic influence upon the supervisee's relationships within the team, sometimes with little awareness of this by the supervisee themselves. It is essential that the supervisor/manager maintains an openness in supervision in relation to the agency, and is prepared to be active – and be seen to be active – in trying to influence policies or practices that are manifestly oppressive to supervisees.

Organisations, like people, have individual characteristics. Each may value some things while downgrading others. Even within an organisation these characteristics can change according to fashion, permeating systemically down through the prevailing political climate. These organisational characteristics can have a profound effect on the operation of an individual team. An organisational creed, for example, that sees better management as an answer to all problems may serve to disempower non-managerial team members while placing unrealistic expectations on the team manager. In a similar way, an overemphasis on value for money based on quantifiable output may lead to divisive competition and friction between team members.

Supervision needs to address the team–agency dynamic with a view to assisting the supervisee gain a balanced assessment of the various influences affecting them, and in so doing, find positive ways of responding to those influences. In some cases the team–agency focus may help the supervisee not only to see their difficulties with other colleagues as more than a matter of personal conflict, but also to acknowledge that some conflict may be inevitable given their respective roles. The converse can equally apply – leading to workers denying interpersonal difficulties within the team and projecting responsibility for these out on to an unresponsive or malign organisation. While it may be seductive to believe that the organisation is always wrong, the supervisor needs to confront this myth. Equally the supervisor needs to be clear that they are not operating as company spokesperson. The supervisor must act in a personally honest and balanced way; to act otherwise would not only demean all involved but throw away any credibility that supervision may have as a vehicle for effective change.

Organisational: the agency–practice interface (connection phase)

In representing the four systems as having a circular rather than linear relationship we are able to draw attention to the importance of the relationship between the Agency and Practice. We believe that this makes good sense, and is consonant with modern management thinking, current notions of quality assurance and general good practice. What it means in terms of the supervision of a worker may seem more difficult to grasp. This is, however, just as important an area for supervision as the others. As suggested earlier, there is often a tension in social work between the person who is the recipient of a service and those who benefit from that service. This may be particularly evident in some areas of statutory social work as, for example, in the supervision of offenders in the community. The supervisee may encounter difficulties in knowing how far to foster a positive relationship, when the nature of that relationship may be far from unconditional and could involve having to work against the individual's wishes.

Another important aspect of this dimension is the need for the worker constantly to check the quality of the service offered against the agency's mission. This will include ensuring that practice is carried out within an anti-oppressive framework. Additionally, as the example below demonstrates, it is important to note that in an organisational sense 'quality' is not an absolute concept, but conditional upon certain stated core policies and values.

There is now a clear policy for all probation departments, spelt out in national standards (Home Office 1992), about the terms under which a probation officer works with those offenders whom they are supervising. These terms, *inter alia*, require the worker to concentrate on offending behaviour rather than welfare work. A situation could then develop in which a probation officer supervisee embarks on some intensive housing and social security negotiations on behalf of a probationer, whilst virtually never discussing their offending behaviour with them. The outcome may be successful not only on the welfare front, but also in stopping further offending. The approach taken will necessarily be a matter of concern for discussion in supervision because, notwithstanding that it was effective, it breached agency policy.

This example also illustrates how opportunities may need to be made available for the supervisee to explore differences between how they feel the agency should be providing its services to its clientele and the way it actually does. Sometimes this can be a starting point for effective change; at other times it may be more a question of looking at how the worker can remain effective given an imperfect situation. Unless these issues are tackled openly and explicitly they are likely to go underground, only to resurface later when least needed or expected.

Integration: focus on the work as a whole (integration phase)

As mentioned earlier, this is the area most likely to become the focus of supervision with supervisees who are experienced workers. For new workers, time spent in this area is more likely to be part of a review process brought on by a need for staff appraisal, rather than as a natural consequence of the developmental process. It represents an opportunity for the supervisee to stand back and take a look at their work as a whole: its shape, balance, character, and direction. It may also provide an opportunity for longer-term considerations, including career planning. With a more developmental focus, it acknowledges that more experienced workers operate out of a more intuitive and internalised set of rules, each of which becomes more elastic as general principles converge with specific demands. Supervision acts to help the supervisee challenge and refine their generalisations and accumulated wisdom, and in so doing to keep these as responsive and adaptive mechanisms. More experienced workers, however, can either be excellent supervisees – who know their own needs, and how to have these met through supervision – or among the most intransigent. The latter may have achieved a certain eminence, and act to hide their current practice behind reputation and prior experience, or an illusory notion of experienced professional judgement.

One of the major concerns in supervising experienced workers is to prevent stagnation and ossification on the one hand, while fostering their creativity and providing a sense of challenge on the other. In doing so, the supervisor may have to acknowledge that they can no longer provide answers, and that in many ways the supervisee may be more expert in their particular field. This shift moves the relationship further in the direction of that between consultant and consultee, with the learning style moving further along the pedagogic–androgogic axis. Peer consultancy may become a more appropriate vehicle for learning and development at this stage.

Developmental themes: the supervisor–supervisee interaction

In the previous section we mapped out, in broad strokes, the three developmental phases for the supervisee, calling them the induction, connection and integration phases. Here we would like to elaborate further upon these ideas not only from the supervisee's and supervisor's perspective but also from the perspective of the interaction between the two.

There is nothing new in the idea of developmental models of supervision. Indeed, Holloway (1987: 209) calls these models 'the zeitgeist of supervision thinking and research'. She also notes that Worthington (1984) cites no less than 18 different models of supervision referring to developmental principles in the 'psychiatric, psychological, and social work divisions'. Most often these conceptualisations have come from within the counselling, clinical psychology and psychotherapy fields (Stoltenberg 1981; Loganbill *et al.* 1982; Blocher 1983 being among the most influential), while Gardiner (1989) has provided another, drawing upon his research with social work students. Our formulation draws on the work of these writers, together with that of Ronnestad and Skovholt (1993), who have provided an illuminating survey of the research literature (including their own). Our own contribution is twofold. The first, already shown diagramatically in Figure 5.1, is to integrate the developmental themes into the map of supervision functions. Second, we hope that we will be able to include in the approach some of the greater complexity and diversity encountered in social work tasks.

Referring back to Figure 5.1, it is important to note that this is a map to help the supervisor respond appropriately over time to changing supervisory needs, and that these needs are predicated upon the supervisee's – rather than the supervisor's – development. The supervisor's development, however, is also a key factor, and we will attempt to draw this into the discussion in the next section.

Let us start by considering the concept of 'experience' in relation to supervision. This term is used for the sake of simplicity, and in its most general sense; clearly it is possible to be new to a job and to a supervisory relationship, and yet be a very experienced practitioner. There are, in fact, many shifting layers of experience within the developmental process, and we have mapped some of these in Table 5.1.

Each supervisee, and indeed each supervisor, will have a different portfolio of experience. It is important to include in these portfolios life experience, which may be just as significant for supervision as professional experience. Typical examples include being a parent; a member of a minority ethnic group; a survivor of childhood abuse; a recovered alcoholic; someone who has known prolonged unemployment. The concept of experience is particularly important if we consider it in dynamic rather than absolute terms (i.e. an acknowledgement that experience in one arena interacts with inexperience in another). The developmental model of supervision that we propose is based upon the assumption that the supervisor will not operate *carte blanche*, but make judgements as to the supervisee's level of experience in each arena.

Table 5.1 Types of experience relevant to supervision

Low experience <<<<<		>>>>> High experience
<<<<<<<<	of being supervised or of supervising	>>>>>>>>
<<<<<<<<	of the current supervision relationship	>>>>>>>>
<<<<<<<<	as a member of the current team or project	>>>>>>>>
<<<<<<<<	of delivering the current form of service	>>>>>>>>
<<<<<<<<	of working with the current client group	>>>>>>>>
<<<<<<<<	of social work in general	>>>>>>>>
<<<<<<<<	of life beyond social work	>>>>>>>>

Consideration of experience is both a matter of degree and type. When we examine any specific supervision relationship, it quickly becomes apparent that the supervisor will not necessarily be more experienced than the supervisee in all the areas outlined above. For example, a supervisee may have induction phase needs through membership of a new team and entering into a new supervisory relationship, while also having integration phase needs in relation to their experience of social work, the client group, and of life. Effective supervision requires the acknowledgement of such variations.

For the sake of clarity, however, and to map out some of the developmental issues in broad strokes, we shall start with an assumption that the supervisee is a professional novice, and then note the changes as he or she gains experience. At this point the worker would be in the induction phase, where the supervisor needs to ensure that the worker is well grounded, and the supervisee needs to know what is expected of them and what the rules are. Gardiner (1989) notes that the focus during this stage in social work training is on the content, rather than the process of learning. Ronnestad and Skovholt (1993) report that supervisees at this stage value specific skills and supervisors who emphasise these, while supervisors who do not have this skill focus are generally criticised, and disappoint supervisees.

During the early stages inexperienced supervisees tend to prefer a relationship with their supervisor that is more directive than reflective (Fisher 1989). Similarly, Heppner and Roehlike (1984) report that supervisors who taught, offered support and encouragement and gave feedback were most liked by inexperienced supervisees. These supervisees are generally more anxious, dependent, and technique-orientated than more experienced supervisees (Reisling and Daniels 1983), and supervisors tend to engage in more emotional supportive behaviour and less confrontational behaviour (Cross and Brown 1983).

Much of the research cited above (apart from Gardiner) was undertaken in the American context and with graduate student counsellors and psychotherapists. Our own experience confirms that for the truly novice social worker in Britain, the findings apply equally here: new workers, and experienced workers in new positions and settings do tend to have concrete needs, and value hands-on advice and guidance. However, we now need to introduce two qualifications to this consensus. The first is that many newly qualified social workers are mature students with a wealth of relevant life experience that they bring to their work and to supervision. This suggests that in fact there may be relatively few true novices in social work.

The second qualification is about styles of learning. In Chapter 2 we proposed a model of adult learning that emphasises the supervisee's capacity for self-learning. It is important to note, however, that this is a state that often has to be worked towards, rather than be assumed. For those supervisees trained in traditional learning styles, initially supervision may have to be more content-focused, directive, didactic, and skills-based, offering ample feedback within a supportive rather than confronting relationship. For others trained to be self-directed learners (see Burgess 1992), the supervisor's task will be complicated, because on some counts (e.g. content) the supervisee will be a novice, yet their self-directed learning style and the associated high level of confidence will not sit comfortably with an initially dependent supervisory relationship of the kind we have described.

Notwithstanding these two caveats, the general principle of a shift in the emphasis of supervision over time, which is very clearly established in the literature, applies to all supervisees. It is just that some will have more advanced starting points and initially richer experience portfolios than others.

Krause and Allen (1988) found that supervisors reported collegial and consultative relationships with increasing frequency as supervisees became more experienced. Kadushin (1974) and Fisher (1989) report similar findings. Kolb and Fry (1975) suggest two modes of learning that have relevance to supervision: the 'preferential mode', where the worker is helped to develop their own style and build on their strengths; and the 'compensatory mode', which pushes the worker to confront areas of weakness. They argue that learning for the inexperienced worker should start with the preferential mode, and move into the compensatory mode as they develop confidence and competence in their work.

Various authors have proposed different levels or stages within supervision. Hawkins and Shohet (1989) in the counselling/psychotherapy supervision field, and Gardiner (1989) in the social work student field, provide two such examples, which are outlined in Table 5.2.

Each formulation shows a development from a relatively narrow and short-term focus toward a wider and longer-term focus, the Hawkins and Shohet model emphasising the focus of professional concern while the Gardiner model emphasises the type of learning that the supervisee engages in. The complexity and diversity of experience commonly found in supervision, however, can make it difficult for the supervisor to apply simple stage models to specific relationships. More useful, in our view, is to note the kinds of changes that might be expected over time, allowing for the likelihood that

Table 5.2   A comparison by stage of two developmental models

Hawkins and Shohet (1989)	Gardiner (1989)
Level 1 is characterised by dependence on the supervisor, is essentially self-centred, and addresses the supervisee's anxiety as to whether they can make it in this work.	*Stage 1* a surface-reproductive conception of learning, characterised by a predominant focus on the content of what is to be taught and learnt (i.e. facts or procedures).
Level 2 is characterised by fluctuations between dependence and autonomy, and between over-confidence and being overwhelmed. The supervisee's concerns tend to become less generalised, and more focused on their anxieties about helping particular clients.	*Stage 2* is characterised by a focus on the process of learning (i.e. an active-constructive search for meaning from experience).
Level 3 is characterised by greater professional self-confidence, less dependency on the supervisor, and a more collegial relationship. The focus shifts to the processes involved in their work, and addresses anxieties about the relationship aspects of working with clients.	*Stage 3* is characterised by a focus on meta-learning, and learning to learn (i.e. being able to use and evaluate qualitatively different approaches to different learning tasks).
Level 4 is characterised by an integration of all aspects of the work, and a shift towards deepening wisdom. By this stage supervisees will often have become supervisors themselves.	

each of these may change at quite different rates. As we saw in Chapter 4, one of the tasks facing the supervisor at the contracting stage is discussing with the supervisee what supervision will focus on, and what expectations they and the supervisee have, both of themselves and of one another.

Table 5.3 highlights a number of bipolar possibilities, along each of which, at any stage in the supervision relationship, the supervisee and supervisor may find themselves. As such it may provide a useful means of charting the nature of the supervisory relationship, not only at the outset, but also as it changes over time.

In looking at the difference between inexperienced and experienced supervisees, apart from finding a substantial number of variables (e.g. those shown in table 5.3), certain factors appear to remain equally important throughout all stages and levels. These include clarification and facilitated reflection, of which Ronnestad *et al.* (1984) suggest that 'these methods may constitute the creative, explorative, and integrative processes of supervision'. They are, in effect, the preconditions for any effective helping relationship. Additionally, the importance of offering feedback remains constant throughout all stages of the supervision process (Worthington and Roehlike 1979), although

Table 5.3 Developmental shifts in the supervisory process

Low experience	>>>>>>>>>>>>>>	High experience
Induction phase	Connection phase	Integration phase
The supervisor is:		
Directive	>>>>>>>>>>>>>>	Non-directive
Non-challenging	>>>>>>>>>>>>>>	Challenging
Didactic	>>>>>>>>>>>>>>	Reflective
The supervisee's needs are:		
Immediate/short-term	>>>>>>>>>>>>>>	Long term
Concrete	>>>>>>>>>>>>>>	Abstract
Context-free	>>>>>>>>>>>>>>	Context-specific
The focus is on:		
Content	>>>>>>>>>>>>>>	Process
Information and Advice	>>>>>>>>>>>>>>	Self-direction
Skills	>>>>>>>>>>>>>>	Relationship
Supervisee anxiety and fear of failure	>>>>>>>>>>>>>>	Supervisee creativity and sense of achievement

following Kolb and Fry (1975), the nature of this feedback might vary with time from preferential to compensatory mode.

Development as a supervisor: implications for the relationship

At this point we would like to introduce into the picture the supervisor's own stage of development (in their role as supervisor). Following the same schema as we have for the supervisee, we need to outline the induction, connection and integration phases in terms of the supervisor's own development.

During the induction phase, the supervisor is finding their feet, trying to establish a model of supervision for themselves, and trying to make sense of the transition in role from experienced practitioner to supervisor. It is a time of both excitement and anxiety, of questioning and confusion. The new supervisor will often be more than usually concerned about what their supervisee thinks of them (Ronnestad and Skovholt 1993), have a strong desire to feel competent, and like the supervisee, focus on the 'concrete' as a coping strategy (Hess 1987).

During the connection phase, the supervisor begins to feel more confident in taking a more analytical or exploratory stance in relation to some of the thornier and less tangible problems. They may take more risks, and begin to regain some of their own practitioner skills and reapply these to the supervisor role. The supervisor also begins to gain a more realistic assessment of their own limitations, and feels more comfortable in sharing their own ignorance and discomfort in supervision, both when supervising and being supervised.

Table 5.4 Scenarios arising from different supervisee–supervisor development phases

		Supervisor		
		Induction	Connection	Integration
Supervisee	Induction	Scenario 1	Scenario 2	Scenario 3
	Connection	Scenario 4	Scenario 5	Scenario 6
	Integration	Scenario 7	Scenario 8	Scenario 9

During the integration phase, the supervisor works increasingly with hunches and their own intuition, joining with the supervisee on a journey of professional discovery. It is, however, absolutely essential that the supervisor, as their confidence grows, undertakes some form of self-evaluation lest their own supervisory practice becomes grandiose and unboundaried.

Taking this a little further, it can be seen that if we assume that both supervisor and supervisee can be located in one of three developmental phases, then nine typical scenarios exist. These are shown in Table 5.4.

While it is beyond the scope of this book to examine all of these scenarios, a few examples may help the reader use this kind of analysis to fill any relevant gaps.

Scenario 1 (where both supervisee and supervisor are in their own induction phase) raises certain considerations. Hess (1987) has noted that in focusing too much on what is concrete, there is a danger that the supervisor may unknowingly close off too much complexity, and thus enter a stagnant rather than a developmental route. There is also the increased danger, with both parties negotiating their way in the supervisory maze for the first time, of becoming irretrievably lost. At least in scenario 7, where the supervisee has significant experience of being supervised, they may be able to let the novice supervisor know when they are going off course. On the other hand, in scenario 1, the supervisor's anxiety about their new role, if not too great, may help them identify and empathise with the supervisee's situation more easily.

Scenario 3 (supervisor is in the integration phase but the supervisee is in the induction phase) can also pose significant difficulties. As Ronnestad and Skovholt (1993: 399) note, 'given the high need of the beginner for specifics, the vague abstract quality of some expert's advice will be frustrating for the new student'. Given also that the new supervisee tends to work in a context-free way, while the experienced supervisor may work in a context-specific way, this problem may be exacerbated. One example would be of the new supervisee who is very anxious to make sure that they know how to do their work, yet feels that they already have too much to take in to think about the supervisor's continued insistence on an anti-oppressive approach. If this happens, the first task for the supervisor will be to help the supervisee to understand that anti-oppressive practice is not only about context but is absolutely central to the work itself. (Note that the opposite scenario may also apply, with the newly qualified worker well trained in anti-oppressive practice, and the experienced supervisor much less developed in this area.) These issues require great sensitivity, and perhaps the best advice that we can offer to supervisors is to make sure that they have their own needs for supervision properly met.

Scenario 7 (experienced worker, inexperienced – in the supervisor role – supervisor) frequently occurs when a new manager is appointed into a team containing very experienced practitioners. Here there is a danger of carrying too much of their managerial role into supervision, either as a compensation for the lack of confidence in supervising the professional side of their work, or to reinforce their new role. As we have seen, however, the supervisee who is at the integration stage is unlikely to find their needs met in such a concrete focused style of supervision, and one might expect considerable difficulties to ensue.

Scenario 9 (both supervisor and supervisee in their own integration phases) can be immensely rewarding, although it often fails to live up to its promise. There is a danger that each become too comfortable with the other, laziness sets in, and challenges are avoided. There is also a danger that discussions become overly esoteric and distant from practice. At this stage, the supervisee themselves, rather than internalising rules, may be making up their own. Under these circumstances the supervisor needs to become increasingly challenging, rather than collusive. The supervisor's process skills may be more important than their expertise in this scenario.

Conclusion

In this chapter we have introduced a model of supervision that highlights both the importance of a systems approach and an understanding of developmental themes. The relevance of different types of formative experiences (see also Chapter 2) has been discussed, and some illustrations offered to show how this can influence the starting point for the supervisory relationship and its subsequent development.

Before we move on, it is important to recognise that there remains much more to be said about the developmental themes and issues within supervision. In Chapter 6 we concentrate in more depth on the supervision relationship itself, using practical examples to illustrate the kind of difficulties that can arise, and to suggest possible resolutions. In Chapter 7 we shall provide a model of a worker's emotional adaptation to work stress and trauma, and indicate the role and responsibilities of the supervisor in that situation.

6 The supervision relationship

Introduction

In this chapter we shall consider some case studies that illustrate many of the difficulties and tangles that can occur in the supervision relationship. We are only too well aware from our own experience that there are no easy answers, but we hope that our three-stage framework of scenario, analysis, and possible supervisor responses will provide a useful basis for thinking about the issues involved in the struggle to understand and, as necessary, act.

The case illustrations can be used in various ways. Supervisors can choose between reading right through each illustration, including our comments; or you may prefer only to read the scenario first, and develop your own thoughts before proceeding. If you are a trainer, the scenarios may provide useful material for your courses; either as specific case studies, or as triggers to open up discussion around particular issues.

Before introducing the illustrative material, we need to point out that the extent to which the supervision relationship needs to be on the supervision agenda will depend on various factors including:

- the nature of the task of the supervisee, and in particular how central the idea of relationship is, or is not, in that task. For example, there is a significant difference in amount and type of relationship content between counselling work with a sexually abused child, and purchasing respite care
- whether there are relationship difficulties between supervisor and supervisee that are impeding the effectiveness of supervision and/or the effectiveness of the supervisee's work with service users
- whether focus on the relationship is potentially empowering for the supervisee and/or enhances their professional development
- the unique chemistry of a given supervision relationship. The arbitrary nature of supervisor–supervisee selection means that there is great variation in the degree of similarity and difference between any two participants in supervision.

Although we are focusing on the one-to-one relationship, much of what occurs can only be understood in the wider context. As we have seen elsewhere in the book, the separate personal and professional histories of the participants have a profound effect. So too do service users, the nature of the task, the team, the setting and agency policy. The supervision relationship is also a microcosm of the wider society, with all the inequalities that derive from differences in sex, race, age, sexuality, class and physical ability (see Chapter 3). At the end of the chapter we mention briefly some of the theories that influence our own attempts to understand and respond to issues arising out of the supervision relationship, including those that extend beyond the one-to-one pair.

What distinguishes supervision from most other personal relationships is the formal authority and power vested in the supervisor by their role in the agency. It is a compulsory unequal relationship that has not been chosen by either person (cf. parent–child relationship). It can also have a significant influence on the supervisee's future career. This power factor lies behind many of the distortions that can occur in the supervisory relationship, and which get in the way of effective productive work.

The discussions that follow are based on at least two assumptions. One is that some form of contract negotiation and agreement has occurred – in the way outlined in Chapter 4 – but that situations will arise and highlight areas that, for whatever reason, were not adequately covered at the initial stage. Another is that although the issues are posed from a supervisor perspective, there is no assumption that they are necessarily of the supervisee's making. Sometimes the issue will be mainly or entirely the responsibility of one or other party, but mostly we shall seek to understand and look for possible responses by focusing on the interaction and communication between the two people involved.

We also recognise that each illustration is open to a wide range of interpretations, and we are very much aware that readers' views are likely to be just as valid as our own. We have both gained from discussing together our ideas for this chapter – and indeed for the whole book – and hope that readers may benefit similarly from shared discussion of the struggle to understand.

Illustrations of common relationship issues

We have chosen to illustrate ten kinds of relationship issues, which are some of the most common encountered in supervision:

1 the new supervisor in the established team
2 personal/professional complications
3 gender and race issues
4 ideological conflicts
5 transference
6 the 'parallel process'
7 personal information

8 sexual orientation
9 'no problem' supervision
10 unacceptable behaviour.

Each of the above topics will now be considered in turn, using the same three-part framework:

- an outline scenario
- an analysis of the issues
- some suggestions for possible responses by the supervisor

As suggested earlier, you might want to approach the illustrations in a number of different ways. We would suggest that you approach at least two of them as follows:

- read only the scenario at first
- make notes of any potentially important issues or themes within the scenario
- read the analysis, comparing the issues or themes that you have identified with those that we have chosen to highlight
- make further notes on any appropriate responses that might be available to the supervisor
- read the responses that we have suggested, and compare with your own.

We hope the illustrations stimulate much debate!

Illustration 6.1 The new supervisor in the established team

Setting: day centre
Agency: local authority social services department
Service users: adults with learning disabilities
Supervisor: Jenny. Black, African-Caribbean female, Centre manager, aged 36. New to the Centre, promoted from deputy manager in another day centre. Qualified.
Supervisee: Paul. White, male, assistant manager, aged 29. Quite recently completed CSS, and is only other qualified member of staff. Has been at the Centre for five years.

Scenario

During his last two years in post, the previous manager had been largely absent through ill health. During that period, the Centre lost direction and attracted widespread criticism from within the department. There was some difficulty filling the vacancy, and Paul acted up as manager for three months. He did not apply for the post himself. While the Centre continued to lack direction, Paul managed to hold the team together and maintain morale.

When Jenny arrived, she quickly identified the absence of regular supervision as a problem, and introduced a system whereby she would supervise Paul and the other assistant manager, while they would each supervise half of the rest of the team. There was little, if any, voiced resistance to this system. Three months later, the supervision system is now established, but

Jenny is finding the wider process of change much slower than she would have hoped. Her supervision sessions with Paul feel difficult, and he seems to be keeping her at arm's length. He will discuss other staff and agency issues, but will not allow himself to become the focus of supervision. Jenny also suspects that when he supervises other staff, he is supportive to the point of being collusive, and any exploration of their practice is at best minimal. She wonders if this might partly explain the slow rate of change.

Jenny often feels tense, angry, and frustrated both during and after sessions with Paul. She has begun to doubt her own judgement, and wonders whether she is really up to the job. She feels that Paul is somehow holding a threat over her and that he doesn't respect her. While she would like to challenge him, she has little to go on, and fears making matters much worse. Paul feels ambivalent and confused. Although he has not been criticised, he feels as if he has. He doesn't want to be obstructive, but finds it difficult to be relaxed with Jenny.

Analysis

This is a complicated, but not uncommon scenario. We have provided information from both parties, although in practice, it is much more difficult to get an objective synopsis of the other person's feelings.

Changes in leadership are often beset with problems, and there is always a danger that expectations, from all sides, may be unrealistic. In this case Paul's position is particularly ambivalent. Either he didn't want the manager's job, or he felt he wasn't ready for it. None the less, for a period, he was catapulted into that role. When Jenny arrives, she is not so much replacing the manager that has gone, but Paul who is still around. Whether or not he really wants the job for himself, he may feel that this is a step backwards. Given that his was a holding role of uncertain duration, compared with the longer-term developmental role available to Jenny, he may feel that he will be judged poorly against her. He may have nothing against Jenny herself, and while agreeing with the changes that she is implementing, he may feel that these constitute a criticism of him.

Jenny's position is difficult because she is the newest member of the team, yet she is assumed to hold the greatest power to influence it. The way she came into the post can't help. The fact that the post had been vacant for a long period could lead her to feel that she was chosen only because no one else wanted it. Having been promoted from a similar but more successful Centre may raise questions in Paul's mind about her loyalty to the project. While there is no obvious reason for suggesting that the race and gender differences have been particularly crucial in creating the tension between them (although see Illustration 6.3), they may be an obstacle in reaching a resolution. Paul may feel that he doesn't want to express directly his feelings about the situation because he fears being labelled 'racist' or 'sexist'. Jenny wants to be seen as a good manager in her own right, not as a good black female manager. In any case, the relationship feels far from safe enough to explore these issues properly.

In addition to the above possibilities, the role of the other assistant manager may be crucial. The real rivalry may not be between Jenny and Paul, but between him and the other assistant manager. If so, the supervisory structure set up by Jenny may have unintentionally reinforced these tensions, and the possibility of deep divisions developing within the team cannot be ignored.

Response

While strong interpersonal dynamics (see Illustration 6.5) may be operating, it is only really possible to deal with these once other structural and systemic influences have been addressed. The fact that Jenny has now been in post for three months offers an ideal opportunity to conduct a wide-ranging review of the changes (including supervision) that she has initiated. Provided this review actively seeks feedback from all involved, the likelihood of Paul feeling that he is being identified as the problem may be reduced. A further exploratory step might be to set up tandem supervision sessions with both Paul and the other assistant manager, specifically to look at the supervision of the rest of the team.

Within the supervision relationship itself, Jenny may wish to seek direct feedback from Paul as to what he finds is helpful, unhelpful, and what he would like to see change about their sessions. It is important that this process is seen as a mutual one, and Jenny should also give her own feedback. If it has not already happened, Jenny may need to put a number of other issues on the agenda: Paul's own career plans, and how he would like to see his own role within the Centre develop; how they each experience the race and gender differences in their relationship; how the changes have affected each of them personally and professionally.

Jenny will also need to use her own supervision both to review to what extent she may be undermining her own confidence unnecessarily and as a source of support.

Illustration 6.2   Personal/professional complications

Setting:	locality team
Agency:	probation service
Service users:	offenders
Supervisor:	Mary. White, female, recently appointed senior probation officer/team manager, aged 40.
Supervisee:	Joan. White, female, aged 42. Experienced probation officer.

Scenario

Mary and Joan have been close colleagues and personal friends for several years. When the previous senior probation officer left, they were two of the applicants interviewed for the post. Mary was successful, and Joan was not. They both found the process of competing for the same post very painful. Before the interview they went to great pains not to let the situation affect their relationship, agreeing that whoever was appointed, their friendship would not be affected in any way.

In the first two supervision sessions, Mary made it clear that she still saw them essentially as equals, and she regarded supervision with Joan as consultation on a mutual basis. They both acknowledged that Mary's role as team manager did mean that things were different in a formal sense, and so they discontinued their previous pattern of having lunch together at least twice a week. However, they continued going out together regularly in the evenings and sometimes at weekends. Joan was the one who tended to initiate these frequent social occasions, and although Mary felt a little uneasy, she always agreed. 'After all,' she reasoned to herself, 'why the hell shouldn't I continue a friendship I enjoy in my own time away from work?'

Nothing was said openly to Mary about this issue by other team members, but both she and Joan were aware of some tensions in the team, and Joan was becoming increasingly isolated. It got to the point where Mary began to dread team meetings and individual supervision because of the increasing tension. She also noticed that the two male members of the team were being particularly difficult.

Analysis

Internal promotion is quite a common event, and often causes pain and ill-feeling, particularly when other team members have applied for the same job. Major adjustments are needed in role relationships, which often are fudged to avoid some of the tensions evoked when a former peer becomes the boss. In this scenario, Mary and Joan are trying to preserve the close friendship they had before. If only the two of them were implicated they might have sustained their avoidance of confronting their changed role relationship. However, they are both members of the same work group, and the repercussions are affecting the whole team and their work together.

Joan's increasing isolation is partly due to envy, and partly because she is not trusted with information that her colleagues do not want communicated to management. The two men resent the perceived exclusivity of their woman colleague and line manager. When Mary and Joan were both probation officer colleagues that was one thing, but now the roles have changed and Mary is their manager, they resent it.

Response

Looking at this with the benefit of hindsight, Mary could have called a team meeting soon after her appointment to discuss as openly as possible with her former peers the feelings aroused, and the need to work out a new way of working together. Additionally, in her first individual supervision sessions with Joan, it would have been helpful to have a very open exchange about the new situation, and the steps they would both need to take to manage it.

However, given that – very understandably – she did not deal with the issues adequately at the outset, what can Mary now do to try to retrieve the situation? There are at least three arenas in which action can be taken: in her own supervision by seeking help from her own supervisor; in confronting the issue directly with Joan in their supervision sessions; and by open discussion in a team meeting. None of these steps is easy, and an alternative might be to take the indirect approach and change her own behaviour by demonstrating much more clearly that all team members are being treated equally in the professional context. However, whatever strategy she adopts with the team, she will still have to have some kind of dialogue with Joan. If difficulties persist, one option is to bring in a team consultant, and another is for either Mary or Joan to join another team. Understandably, they may resent even considering the latter option on the basis that they are entitled to their friendship, and they may feel 'why should we be punished for the feelings of others?'.

Illustration 6.3   Gender and race

Setting:	*locality office*
Agency:	*large voluntary*
Service users:	*children and families (child protection)*
Supervisor:	*Chander. Black (Asian), male, team manager, aged 52. Five years as team manager, many years as practitioner.*
Supervisee:	*Christine. White, female, aged 27. Qualified three years, joined this team a few months ago.*

Scenario

Both Chander and Christine are finding their relationship very difficult and sticky. Chander experiences Christine as quite distant, keeping supervision to the minimum amount of contact required. She does her work satisfactorily, if not brilliantly, and they have fairly low-key conversations in supervision, mostly about some of the families with whom Christine works. Chander hopes things will improve, and just wonders whether it is anything to do with him being black and/or their age difference.

Chander has been wanting to raise the issue of their rather tense and distant relationship for some time, but has felt apprehensive about opening up difficult personal areas, sensing that powerful feelings are involved. Then one day he hears on the team grapevine that Christine has let it be known that she would like to change her supervisor.

Analysis

This is a not unusual example of differences in age, sex and race affecting a supervision relationship, whether or not one or more of these variables is the actual root cause of the difficulty. One can speculate about a range of possible explanations of both Christine's and Chander's behaviour. What is clear is that they have not been able to create a supervision environment in which either feels confident and trusting enough to pursue quite difficult interpersonal issues.

It may be, for example, that although race is perhaps the most obvious factor, and the one that preoccupies Chander, Christine is quite clear (but has not told Chander) that she wants to have a woman supervisor. This could be due to having had a bad previous experience with an older male supervisor who treated her in a patronising sexist manner that she experienced as deskilling and disempowering. It could also be because she finds it much easier to talk with women than men about her work with sexually abused girls and their families.

Christine may be reluctant to share her wish for a change of supervisor for fear of being thought racist, and Chander may be holding back from getting involved in what he sees as dangerous territory. We can surmise that at the contracting stage there was some acknowledgement that they were of different age, sex and race, but no serious attempt was made to explore how this might affect their supervision relationship.

Response

When there is the kind of personal apprehension being felt by Chander, it is often helpful to discuss the difficulty with someone else. Chander's own supervisor would be the obvious person, but he may not feel confident enough in that relationship to disclose his concerns. If this is so, there are other options, including peer team managers and/or a black managers' group to which he might belong.

The fact that Christine has apparently been talking about it to at least some team colleagues means that Chander needs to grasp the nettle as soon as possible. This will probably mean arranging an additional supervision session in the near future, unless the regular one is imminent. It may be helpful to start by acknowledging that the supervision relationship is not what it should be, and that it seems important to try to understand what the difficulties are. It can be reassuring to convey the expectation that neither of them is to blame, but that it is something that they need to try to sort out together.

At this stage it may not be appropriate to speculate together on possible reasons, although this may become necessary if Christine does not respond. In the latter eventuality, Chander might suggest a mutual brainstorming of all the possible explanations, which may make it easier to get at the issues. Alternatively, if he has a strong hunch, he may take the risk and say (in his own words) something like 'I am aware that I am being affected by the basic differences between us, and that being a black man, and older, may be an issue.'

One anticipatory step that Chander could take prior to the meeting is to think about possible other resources that could be helpful to Christine, to supplement what he is able to offer directly as her supervisor. For example, if she is able to say that she finds it much easier to speak with a woman about some aspects of her sexual abuse work, he could accept her feelings on this issue, and explore with her alternative (female) consultancy resources for this part of her work. It could also be useful to renegotiate the supervision contract to cover the problematic areas, including an agreement to review their working relationship at least every three months.

Illustration 6.4   Ideological conflicts

Setting: *locality team*
Agency: *probation service*
Service users: *offenders*
Supervisor: *Kirsten. White, female, aged 45. Senior probation officer for the last seven years.*
Supervisee: *Alison. White, female, aged 29. Qualified six months ago.*

Scenario

Kirsten has a reputation as a task-orientated professional who is very committed to good quality practice, and who encourages her staff to develop effective ways of getting offenders to confront their own offending behaviour.

Alison is a self-styled radical, with political views reflected in her activities in left-wing organisations. She has a well worked-out structural analysis of crime and the criminal justice system, viewing much criminal behaviour as being the consequence of poverty and oppression (an approach that won her considerable praise on her social work qualifying course). She argues that whilst probation officers have necessarily to do some of their work at the micro level, the only meaningful way of confronting offending behaviour is to confront the causes of crime in offenders' lives. By this she means tackling the oppressions of class, race and gender as manifest in poverty, poor housing and unemployment; and confronting the racism and sexism that permeate the criminal justice system. She sees forming alliances with community groups as an important part of her job.

Kirsten experiences Alison as a personable committed probation officer, but her idealism and radical approach is beginning to irritate, not least as it is starting to have repercussions in mutterings by the judiciary, the police and senior managers, including her own supervisor. The latter expects her to confront Alison about the approach she is taking, by indicating that she needs to spend less time on contextual factors and more on confronting offenders with their own responsibility for their offending behaviour.

Analysis

This is a situation in which there is an ideological clash between supervisee and supervisor. As with many supervision relationship issues, this one is often fudged. Both parties have a vested interest in minimising differences in order to settle for a relatively quiet life. Alison may have deliberately played down her ideological value base at interview as a conscious tactic to increase her chances of getting the job. At the initial contract-making stage of supervision, exchanges about respective values and ideologies might not have occurred, partly because they can be difficult to articulate (see Chapter 4 for a suggestion on this during contracting), and partly to avoid possible conflict at an early stage of the relationship. If the supervisee is not doing her job properly, ideology may soon become a supervision agenda item, but when as in this case Alison is doing her job very well – but differently – then the approach needs thinking through carefully.

One possibility is that Alison's ideology is one that Kirsten held herself – perhaps even more strongly – when she was a student many years previously. Her approach has changed in the intervening years under the influence of the agency task, criminal justice policy and her middle-management role; but a residue still remains. This may result in her either colluding with Alison as the vicarious expression of a radical zeal she once possessed, or taking a fairly punitive approach to try to insist that Alison makes the adaptation she has had to make herself.

Response

This is another issue that might have been picked up at the contract stage, but was not. The priority is for the supervisor and supervisee to try to communicate with each other about it. If the supervisor gets a semi-complaint, for example, a judge raising their eyebrows at the politicisation of an otherwise very good pre-sentence report, this gives the supervisor an entrée if she feels she needs one. It should be possible to avoid a confrontational encounter and to seek to have a reflective discussion about the issues, whilst validating Alison's many strengths. This might lead to Alison modifying her approach, whilst not betraying her fundamental beliefs.

If there is a resonance from Kirsten's own political past, she needs to consider how to manage her own feelings so they do not bias her supervisory response to Alison. One option is to be quite open and frank with her, sharing the development and change over time in her own approach, and the reasons. This could be a way of showing she understands, and also acknowledging her own dilemmas in how to help Alison work at the issues she faces as a recently qualified probation officer with high ideals. Alison may see Kirsten as having compromised and 'sold out', but there is now the possibility of a creative discussion on how Alison's talents might best be expressed within the boundaries of the agency requirements.

Illustration 6.5 Transference

Setting: *children's resource centre*
Agency: *local authority social services department*
Service users: *children and families*
Supervisor: *Marcus. White, male, deputy manager, aged 38. Experienced social worker.*
Supervisee: *Jane. White, female, resource centre worker. Recently qualified and newly appointed.*

Scenario

As part of her induction, Jane has been working together with a more experienced white male resource centre worker, Patrick, with a number of families. Mostly this has worked out very well, but over the past two weeks there has been one family in particular that has been causing her some concern.

Initially she brought this to supervision and spoke of 'experiencing a real sense of unease' when working with this family. Nothing had been said, but each time she spoke within a family session, the father would frown, look confused, or in some other way express disapproval. On several occasions, while her colleague was attending the mother, or one of the children, the father would catch her eye and give her a 'withering and hateful stare'. In contrast, he would respond very positively to Patrick's interventions. The effect has now got through to her so much that she feels intimidated, undermined and deskilled to the point that she can hardly open her mouth in sessions. Patrick is supportive, but has not experienced this side of the father, and feels he hasn't got anything on which to challenge him. He also feels that to say anything to the father on Jane's behalf would further undermine her, and reinforce his own position with the family.

In supervision, Jane expresses both her rage at the father and a sense of hopelessness and desperation. She would much prefer never to see him again, but also refuses to give in to 'this man.' Furthermore, she feels that if she doesn't get this sorted out, her confidence will be permanently undermined. She acknowledges that he has stirred something in her that she thought she had dealt with in her past.

When asked about this by Marcus, she says it is not something that she could talk to a man about. Marcus has also asked if she would like him to talk to Patrick to see if there was a way in which he could intervene without undermining her. At this point she turns and screams at Marcus, 'You just don't understand, you always think that there's an easy answer!' and storms out. Marcus is left feeling very concerned, upset and confused.

Analysis

Jane's out-of-character reactions, both to the father and to Marcus, suggest, as she acknowledges herself, that something from her own past has been triggered. This is not, however, to deny that the father's behaviour is quite offensive in its own right. We might surmise that the father, or his behaviour, remind her of someone in the past who aroused painful feelings in her. It is not the business of supervision to help Jane work through that past relationship, or the feelings aroused by it. It is, however, important that supervision helps her disentangle her reactions to the father from those originating in her own past relationships.

The situation is made more complicated by the fact that the material stirred up in her appears to be extending beyond the family itself, and affecting her relationship with both Patrick and Marcus. Just as Jane may be finding it difficult to separate the father from the 'significant other' from her past, so she may be finding it difficult to separate Marcus and Patrick from her reactions to others who may have been involved at that time. The fact that they are all male is likely to be highly significant, and may undermine their capacity to directly assist her in disentangling some of the interpersonal dynamics.

The transference (an unconscious replaying of past dynamics within a current relationship) is made more likely by the fact that there is an inequality in the power relationship between Jane and Marcus, and to a lesser extent

Patrick. However, it would be inappropriate to make this assumption solely on the evidence given. Jane's reaction to Marcus may have been momentary, based on a sense of panic that he was about to delve into her private and personal life.

The dilemma for Marcus is that, while he may feel disempowered himself, he still has a responsibility both to Jane, and to the family.

Response

Marcus needs to arrange to see Jane soon, to help her work out the various options that are open to her, and assist her in putting whichever seems most appropriate into action. He has to clarify with her that he has a responsibility to ensure that the situation with the family gets resolved, but that how this is approached is negotiable. He will reassure her that he has no intention of forcing her into anything against her wishes. He needs to accept that his responsibility to oversee the process does not mean he has to be involved in all aspects of it. Jane may, for example, prefer to explore with a female consultant those personal aspects of the case that may be linked to her own gender and sexuality. Marcus does not need to know the detail of these sessions, but will expect Jane to keep him up to date with her current work with the family.

If Jane is having a genuine transference reaction to Marcus, then in the first instance they need to see if they can sort this out between them. Readers who question the psychodynamic notion of transference (and countertransference), may find Mearns's (1991) person-centred concept of supervisor–supervisee congruence more accessible. He suggests that to avoid supervision relationships becoming restrictive, regular time outs are incorporated where both supervisee and supervisor explore the following areas:

- unclarified differences of opinion about the aims and practice of both work and supervision
- the worker's unvoiced reactions to the supervisor
- the supervisor's unvoiced reactions to the supervisee
- the worker's unexpressed assumptions about the supervisor
- the supervisor's unexpressed assumptions about the worker
- the worker's unexamined assumptions about how the supervisor experiences their behaviour
- the supervisor's unexamined assumptions about how the worker experiences their behaviour.

While this is intended as a proactive strategy to maintain a healthy and uncluttered supervisory relationship, it can also provide a structure for examining a relationship within which hidden or perhaps unconscious forces are suspected to be at work.

If this proves too difficult, Marcus may need to negotiate a third-party consultant to help them work through their difficulties. In all of this it is easy to forget Patrick, and we would suggest that he is involved, perhaps in a tandem session as early as possible.

Illustration 6.6 *Parallel process*

Setting: *family resource centre*
Agency: *large voluntary organisation*
Service users: *children, and their families*
Supervisor: *Mary. Black, African-Caribbean, female, centre manager, aged*
                        42. Five years in post. Previously worked in child guidance.
Supervisee: *Beverly. Black, African-Caribbean, female, resource centre*
                        worker, aged 27. Three months in post. Previously in statutory
                        child protection.

Scenario

Beverly is highly committed to her current post, which she feels allows her the opportunity to provide the kind of service for which she originally came into social work. Typically she comes across as a bright, skilled, focused and committed worker. Mary has been very impressed with Beverly's preparation for and use of supervision. Both she and Beverly have looked forward to their sessions and found them rewarding.

Recently, however, Beverly has taken on a number of new cases that seem to be having an effect on her. Mary has become quite alarmed by Beverly's muddled thinking and distractibility in supervision. Mary has found her lack of focus quite irritating, and it has become difficult to get a clear picture of how individual cases are going.

The only case about which Beverly has expressed any concern involves Lucy, a young single mother with three children. Although Beverly likes Lucy, she finds it very difficult to pin her down to any one thing. She seems to have so many needs that to sort and prioritise these in any way seems impossible. This is not helped by the fact that Lucy talks incessantly, and generally goes off at a tangent. Exasperated, Beverly has found herself trying to shout Lucy down. She has begun to wonder how Lucy's children cope with her.

Mary has noticed herself becoming uncharacteristically authoritarian toward Beverly, and this makes her feel guilty. She is concerned that Beverly has become overstressed, and is worried about the quality of service she is offering clients. There is, however, no other indication that anything is amiss with Beverly's work.

Analysis

While Mary is right to be alert to the dangers of stress (see Chapter 7), in this case there is another possible explanation for Beverly's behaviour. It appears that something is happening in the relationship between Lucy and Beverly, which Beverly is at present unable to recognise or name. It is, therefore, difficult to bring this to supervision directly. At an unconscious level, however, she continues to struggle with it. In supervision, her role is not dissimilar to the role her clients take on with her, and this provides the conditions for her to act out unconsciously in supervision the behaviour that she finds puzzling in Lucy. In turn Mary behaves, untypically for her, in the way that Beverly has been responding to Lucy. The parallels may seem obvious when written out here, but when caught up in it they can be easily overlooked.

This phenomenon has been called mirroring, the reflection process and the parallel process by different authors. Mattinson (1975) describes it as follows: 'The processes at work currently in the relationship between client and worker are often reflected in the relationship between worker and supervisor' (p. 11). The importance of this phenomenon is considerable for at least two major reasons. If Mary does not recognise it, she may well make an inaccurate assessment of Beverly as 'unfocused, muddled and distractible' and become increasingly authoritarian herself. Secondly, as Doehrmann (1976) points out, behaviours not only duplicate themselves in supervision, but also in reverse, back into the practice relationship. Thus, how Mary responds to Beverly holds not only implications for their own supervisory relationship but also for Beverly's relationship with Lucy.

It may be helpful to note that parallel processes can also be understood in terms of systems theory.

Response

Parallel processes can provide rich material for casework supervision because they offer a very direct way of exploring what might be happening in the practice relationship, drawing upon the immediate experience within the supervisory relationship. The skill lies in the supervisor noticing, and trusting their own reactions as a source of evidence during the supervision session. Three important questions that Mary must ask of herself are 'do I generally find myself becoming more authoritarian, or is it just with Beverly?' 'If it's just with Beverly, is it restricted to our supervision sessions?' 'Is there any evidence that Beverly is "confused, muddled and distractible" outside of supervision?' 'If this occurs only within supervision, then is it only when talking about certain cases?' The answers to these questions will help distinguish parallel processes from more general developments.

Recognition of such processes can come as an enormous relief to supervisees, and is relevant however much or little process work is involved in their method of service delivery. Without such recognition the supervisory process can be seriously impeded and distorted. The degree to which parallel processes are explored and used will depend upon both the nature of the supervisory contract (has the use of 'here and now' processes in supervision been negotiated?), and the amount of process work involved in the supervisee's practice.

One way of opening this up might be for the supervisor to think aloud 'I've been very impressed with the quality of your work, but just lately I've been feeling irritated by your loss of focus, and I fear I've been overcritical and bossy towards you. I'm not sure what this is about, but I wonder if there might be a clue in the relationship you have with any service users?' Alternatively, Mary might pose the three questions suggested earlier out loud, and invite Beverly to join with her in a problem-solving process. If the parallel process can be acknowledged, they can then both use their own experiences in the current supervision relationship to throw light upon what may be happening in the practice relationship.

Illustration 6.7 Personal information

Setting: family centre
Agency: large voluntary organisation
Service users: children and families
Supervisor: Fiona. White, female, aged 38. Project director of the family centre.
Supervisee: Jim. White, male, aged 39. Has recently joined the staff after previously working for a locality child care team in a social services department.

Scenario

Jim is quite an experienced worker who has recently joined the staff of the family centre. He came with good references, and has settled into the team where he is already appreciated as a hard-working, committed worker with a nice sense of humour. He is showing himself to be a thoughtful, sensitive practitioner, particularly in his work with children and as co-facilitator of a parents' group. However, it has been observed that he sometimes seems preoccupied and rather tense and depressed.

In an early supervision session, Fiona notices that in discussion about one family that Jim has been allocated, he seems to get quite tense when the physical abuse of two of the children is discussed. Initially this reaction was not regarded by the supervisor as particularly unusual or anything to worry about unduly, and she decided not to raise it in supervision – not least because she had been favourably impressed by his work since he came to the Centre. However, when in a subsequent discussion of this family, Jim expressed considerable anger towards the children's abusing father (with whom they were no longer living), Fiona became increasingly concerned. She was in a dilemma about whether to wait for any further indications (the 'quiet life' syndrome), or to back her hunch that something important was underlying Jim's responses with this family, which might need exploring in supervision.

Analysis

The response of the supervisor is understandable, and typifies an approach that is based on a reluctance to refer to personal reactions in a supervisee unless there is some evidence that their work is not satisfactory. The personal information in this case is that shortly before transferring from a local authority child care team to the family centre, Jim had a traumatic experience whilst attending a child protection course. A particularly graphic portrayal of physical abuse of a young child touched on his own buried childhood experiences when he was severely beaten by his own father. Furthermore, it reminded him of an incident before he became a social worker, when he was under temporary suspicion of physically injuring his own son. Medical investigations eventually confirmed that the injury was accidental and ex-onerated him from any blame; it was that incident that finally led to his decision to become a social worker with children.

Jim never disclosed these personal experiences during training, and chose to keep them to himself subsequently. The main reason he had not disclosed his own experience of having been abused, and particularly of having been, temporarily, a suspected abuser, was his fear that although he had been completely cleared and knew himself that he was not an abuser, it might put him under suspicion with his peers and managers. This was a realistic fear because if he discloses, Fiona might find herself having to cope with feelings that there may just be a possibility that he could be a potential risk to children at the Centre.

This kind of situation is not something that could have been anticipated whilst drawing up the supervision contract. The most relevant aspect of the contracting stage is likely to be the extent to which Fiona modelled being open and personal in the approach she took, and the level of trust she has been able to develop in the supervision relationship.

Response

One skill in a supervisor that cannot be directly taught is reliance on per-sonal feeling responses as a source of evidence that may be just as valid as more concrete indications, such as the content of what a supervisee says. In this case, when Jim was tense and angry about the abuse and the abuser, Fiona could have taken a risk and commented on his behaviour. For exam-ple, she might have said, 'Is this setting something off for you Jim?' If he has a strong emotional reaction and shares his personal experiences, it will obviously be important that Fiona responds in a supportive way. This may include offering Jim the choice of sharing more with her, and/or seeking counselling support elsewhere, perhaps in a survivors' group. At an appropri-ate point she will need to discuss with him any implications for his work at the Centre.

An alternative response from Jim might be a defensive one, either denying his strength of feeling or justifying it as appropriate to the gravity of the abuse – but not making any connections with his personal life. The super-visor is then faced with a dilemma about what to do next. She might say, 'Fair enough, it just seemed to me that there might be something that this case triggered off for you personally', hoping that he might go away and think about it, and then await developments. Another option might be to disclose some relevant experience of her own when abuse of a child triggered off personal things and affected her feelings and responses to the situation. Whatever she does, affirmation of the good quality of his work is likely to be important.

A general point here is that all kinds of personal background issues are constantly affecting a social worker's practice. This does not of itself, how-ever, entitle the worker's supervisor to that information. On the other hand, the disclosure, if made, is likely to enable the supervisor – and indeed the supervisee – to be more effective. What the supervisor can do, therefore, are the sorts of things suggested above to make it more likely that the supervisee will feel able to disclose relevant information. If he still does not, and his work is perfectly satisfactory from a supervisory point of view, then the supervisor will have to settle for not knowing.

Illustration 6.8 Sexual orientation

Setting:	*residential centre*
Agency:	*voluntary agency*
Service users:	*young adult men, aged 16–25*
Supervisor:	*Pat. White, male, project leader, aged 58. Has been working in various social work settings for 30 years.*
Supervisee:	*Ben. White, male, social worker, aged 27. Recently qualified, new to the project, and on a one-year contract.*

Scenario

Ben is a bright, skilled and caring worker. During his training he made a positive decision to 'come out' as a gay social worker despite the fact that there was a not inconsiderable risk that this might endanger his chances of finding work with adolescents, his specialist interest. In order to stay in his home area he took this temporary one-year post. Politically and personally he feels strongly that all lesbians and gay men should come out, and be proud of their sexuality. After his interview, Pat approached him, and said that he was impressed by his courage and conviction.

In the contracting stage of their supervisory relationship, Pat assured Ben that his disclosure was not an issue so far as he was concerned, and that he wanted him to feel free to discuss any work issues arising through his sexuality. Ben felt that this was genuine, and trusted Pat.

Last week, however, Ben saw Pat in a gay bar, although they did not speak at the time. One of Ben's friends knows Pat well, and confirmed he is gay. Ben now feels torn. He appreciates that Pat has been supportive to him, but feels that he is getting caught up in a collusion against his own principles. Ben thinks that if he in effect endorses this secrecy, he will be betraying his principles.

Ben confronted Pat in their next supervision session. Pat acknowledged that he is gay, but when he entered social work, to come out would have meant dismissal, and the end of a career that he felt passionate about. To come out now would involve more personal pain than he could bear.

Ben finds it very hard to respect a supervisor who covers up in this way, and urges him to come out. Pat, however, refuses; he has found his own way of living with his sexual orientation, and feels that it is too difficult to change now. He respects Ben for his stand, but also thinks he is entitled to his own privacy. In any case it feels like too great a step: he would have to renegotiate all his relationships; to have others review his past performance as a 'closet gay'; and perhaps lose the confidence of some of the young homeless men he works so hard to help.

The situation is compounded by the fact that in coming out, Ben has put issues of sexuality and sexual orientation on to the agenda not only within the project, but for the organisation as well. Previously, Pat could get by simply by not having to engage in discussions around sexuality; that is no longer possible.

Analysis

Ben may not be demanding that Pat 'come out' but unless he can respect Pat, the relationship will be seriously undermined. It seems ironic that this should happen within a relationship that otherwise holds so much potential. The consequences are likely to extend well beyond the supervision relationship itself. For Pat he may risk being ostracised and losing face among colleagues if his 'secret' becomes known. His self-esteem may already have been undermined by his failure to live up to Ben's (and perhaps, his own) expectations.

Ben may only be able to see the foreground (Pat's refusal to come out), while Pat is trapped as part of the background (his history, and other's expectations of him). There is the risk of a very promising supervisory relationship being damaged. The problem here is not Pat or Ben or their relationship, it is the heterosexist oppression in British society, and the discrimination against lesbians and gay men in many social work teams and agencies, not to mention among service users.

The issue of personal information is discussed further in Illustration 6.7, while ideological conflicts are the focus of Illustration 6.4.

Response

This is a potentially painful situation for both Pat and Ben, due not least to the prevalence of homophobia and heterosexism. In other circumstances, we would recommend that Pat discusses his dilemma with his own supervisor. Here, however, this course of action would require both that he was already willing to come out – which he is not – and that his supervisor was aware of the issues involved – which may not be the case. Being head of a unit in a small agency, the only supervision Pat gets is monthly meetings with a line manager from head office. His supervisor uses these sessions to discuss the management and funding of the unit, and is the last person Pat would choose with whom to discuss personal matters.

Another course open to him could be to seek some independent advice; as a first step, a phone call to a confidential gay helpline may provide an entrée. One pressing reason for doing this is that the chances of his sexual orientation becoming known in the unit are increasing all the time, in a situation over which he has little or no control. Pat will need a source of support and advice should this happen.

It is important that Pat doesn't see Ben as the problem. The fact that they are both experiencing the consequences of oppression is a point on which they can unite, and which is a shared basis for their continuing debate on a basis of mutual respect. This may be experienced as liberating for both Pat and Ben, although both may feel a sense of frustration that these discussions have to remain within the confidentiality of supervision. However Pat decides to resolve the situation, what he needs from Ben is time, and this needs to be negotiated. If he does decide to come out, this should not be a panic measure, but a positive choice. On the other hand, Pat has as much right to privacy as anyone else, and should not be afraid to assert that right if demands are placed upon him to disclose his sexual orientation. One thing for Pat to watch is that this issue could take over most of Ben's supervision sessions, the primary purpose of which is to assist Ben in doing his work as effectively as possible. It may, however, become a direct supervision issue if Pat is able to help Ben respond to the quite possibly homophobic responses he is likely to encounter from residents, and perhaps from some colleagues in the team.

Illustration 6.9   'No problem' supervision

Setting:	*residential therapeutic community*
Agency:	*large voluntary organisation*
Service users:	*young adults with mental health problems*
Supervisor:	*Mary. White, female project leader, aged 38. In post for four years. Qualified.*
Supervisee:	*David. White, male project worker, aged 28. In post for six months. Unqualified, previous experience limited to voluntary work with people with learning disabilities.*

Scenario

David is a likeable and committed worker who enjoys his work, and has developed a natural and easy rapport with the residents. He is seen, and sees himself as the practical member of the team, and comes into his own when gardening, or decorating with individual residents. Mary feels that her major strength is her groupwork and process skills.

While David seems to take everything in his stride, Mary senses that there are some parts of the work with which he is not engaging fully. During resident meetings, for example, he often looks bored, and is largely silent. When he does contribute, it is usually to suggest short-cut solutions to very deep problems, and in so doing, brings discussions to a premature closure. Mary has raised this both in the post-group discussion and in supervision, but with little response, other than an acknowledgement from David.

The difficulty between Mary and David is most obvious in their supervision sessions. Mary feels that these are sterile and very hard work, while David doesn't feel that he has any problems to bring, and consequently finds them a waste of time. A typical session will begin with Mary asking how things have been going, and how would he like to use the time. Generally, he will say that things have been fine, and that he hasn't anything pressing to talk about. If Mary persists, he will randomly select a topic, but both are left with the overriding feeling that they are just going through the motions and filling in time. She feels that he is either resistant to her, or to the idea of supervision.

Analysis

While it is quite possible that David is being resistant, there are many other explanations that need to be considered first. David may feel that he has to prove that he is a competent worker, and fear that any expression of need would reflect badly on him. It is also possible that Mary has unwittingly conveyed an impression that supervision exists to talk about problems, weaknesses, and generally things that are not going well. Should such an expectation have been set up, the need for supervision may take on a wholly remedial nature predicated upon crises, and be dependent upon David not coping. Thus, for David, the need for supervision may have become equated with failure.

Alternatively, David may feel that his practical strengths are being under-valued by Mary, or maybe he feels threatened by her process skills. He is quite new to this post, and may still be relying upon skills drawn from his previous voluntary work, without yet having identified and developed the particular skills needed in his new work setting. If this is the case, he may not yet be able to articulate his needs in the way that Mary expects, because the contours of his work are not yet clear to him. Equally, if his process skills in working with residents are relatively undeveloped, then it is unrealistic for Mary to expect him able to make use of them in supervision. In this respect, Mary may not have taken their different developmental needs and level of experience (see Chapter 5) sufficiently into account.

Furthermore, age and gender dynamics cannot be ruled out, nor can trans-ference and countertransference reactions.

Response

Mary may need help to recognise that her interpretation of David's behav-iour as resistant is premature, and perhaps more an expression of her own frustration. To share such an interpretation with David could lead to him closing off to defend himself, and then he really might become resistant.

Recognition that the problem may exist between them, and not belong to one of them provides an important first step. Account, therefore, needs to be taken of the inequality in the relationship. Mary has more formal power, is more experienced, has more developed process skills, and is more familiar with the concept of supervision. Consequently, while resolution of problems through open-ended discussion may be a desirable longer-term goal, at this stage it may simply perpetuate the existing dynamics and place David at a disadvantage in the problem-solving process.

The onus is on Mary to attempt to provide a safe and structured frame-work within which to conduct the problem-solving process, and to ensure that the structure, methods, and stages are well understood by David (Dixon and Glover 1984 propose a simple and useful five-stage model involving (1) problem definition (2) goal selection (3) strategy selection (4) implementa-tion of strategy (5) evaluation). This may not only reap benefits in identifying, understanding, and resolving the problem between them, but also help David to have access to a model of problem-solving for his work with residents (a process which, as noted earlier, he tends to short-circuit). An agreement to suspend judgement, be open to all solutions, and avoid temptations to take short cuts to anticipated solutions would provide some of the ground rules.

Without going into all the possible outcomes of such a process, possible solutions may include: renegotiating the supervision contract; providing more structure and direction in the early phases; spending more time on developmental work – agreeing short- and longer-term goals, identifying and building on strengths, assessing training needs; conducting a tandem supervision session with another supervisee who can provide David with a model of how to make good use of supervision.

Illustration 6.10 Unacceptable behaviour

Setting: child care locality team
Agency: social services department
Service users: families
Supervisor: Mary. White, female, aged 43.
Supervisee: Charlie. White, male, aged 36.

Scenario

Charlie has been in the team two years. During this period Mary has been his supervisor, and she has had a number of concerns about Charlie's work, She has, however, been unable – and sometimes disinclined – to substantiate them. Service users have on occasion commented on his unreliability; there have been incidents of unaccounted absences during the working day; his records tend to be behind; he is frequently away from work with various physical complaints; and he is unpopular with some other team members. A few attempts to confront him with his shortcomings have been responded to very defensively. The knowledge that he lost his son tragically in a road accident a year ago, and that his wife is in poor health, has made it even more difficult for Mary to confront him.

Then one day Mary receives a letter containing a catalogue of complaints about Charlie from a service user, a woman (Mrs Smith) whose two children are on the child protection register, though not currently a cause of great concern to the department. Mrs Smith is complaining that several times Charlie has not turned up for scheduled home visits; that when he does come he is sometimes very abrupt and talks sharply to the children; and also that he did nothing to get the younger child into a day nursery as he had promised he would. Mary visits Mrs Smith and gains the impression that most of these complaints are almost certainly justified. Charlie has been informed about the complaint, and has reacted characteristically with a flat denial. Mary has arranged a special supervision session with Charlie to discuss the situation.

Analysis

There are times when supervisors have to confront supervisees about unacceptable professional behaviour, and the process is usually experienced as very fraught and extremely painful. These situations bring into sharp relief the 'ensure' part of the role of the supervisor, who for much of the time offers the much more congenial 'enable' function. Sometimes a specific complaint of this nature is partially welcomed by the supervisor as a peg on which to hang a discussion about the generally poor standard of work. Alternatively, the supervisor dreads knowing that what may well develop into a confrontation cannot be postponed any longer.

It is surprising how often there are difficulties, if not tragedies, in the personal lives of staff in this position, which makes confrontation even more difficult and stressful. Yet the supervisor is entrusted with upholding good professional standards on behalf of the agency, and must keep her eye on the task and the needs of the children as the paramount consideration. A further dimension is likely to be the reaction of the other team members. It is not unusual in a situation like this for team members who have quite openly criticised a colleague's work and reliability to support him against management, however irrational this may be.

Charlie's denial is difficult to interpret in isolation. Possibly the traumas in his own life have left him very brittle and depleted, with his lowered tolerance showing itself both in the face of demands by the children and family, and from Mary. It is likely that, despite his apparently cavalier attitude, he is very anxious about the forthcoming meeting.

Mary is in an invidious position. She has talked it through with her own supervisor, but still lies awake in bed at night rehearsing what to say. On the one hand she is angry with Charlie for the way he has behaved and put her in this position. On the other she feels guilty that her action is likely to exacerbate the pain of a man who is worried about his wife's ill health, and is still grieving the death of his son.

Response

Mary cannot avoid taking some action. The question is how to do it. There are a number of things – not necessarily in this order – that might help in the early stages of the supervision session. The first is to explain to Charlie everything that has happened so far, including her meeting with the woman who made the complaint. The second is to inform him of his rights in the situation if, as seems likely, some kind of disciplinary action is under consideration. Thirdly, she needs to make sure Charlie has plenty of space to give his own account and explanation of events alleged in the letter of complaint. Fourthly, Mary needs to try and create a non-hostile atmosphere, and to bear in mind all the time that she has to try to manage the meeting in a way that will not be too damaging for their future supervisory relationship.

Charlie may behave in one of two extremes. He may either become very contrite and express feelings of uselessness and inadequacy, or more likely he may become very angry and accuse Mary of taking the client's word against his own. He may also throw in for good measure that he knows Mary has always had it in for him and she is now grabbing the opportunity to 'get' him.

However Charlie reacts, and however much Mary may at times feel sorry for him, she needs to hold on to the fact that her first responsibility is to ensure that service users get a good professional service from the agency. The welfare of staff is important, but the welfare of the children is paramount. This could well be a situation where it is not possible for Mary simultaneously to offer Charlie support as well as control. If this is so, Mary might need to think through where, and for how long, he might gain that support.

A framework for reviewing supervisory relationships

As may be apparent from the preceding illustrations, supervision relationships can be extraordinarily complex. The reader may welcome, therefore, a framework for reviewing such relationships. We would strongly suggest that any such review include both the supervisor's and the supervisee's perspectives. It can be very helpful if the template (Table 6.1) is used within the supervision session itself, with both supervisor and supervisee simultaneously filling in their side of the table, and then sharing and comparing their own perspectives.

Table 6.1 An illustrated framework for reviewing supervisory relationships

	Supervisor	*Supervisee*
Prior facts		
Current supervision		
Feelings		
Thoughts		
Actions		

Useful theories to aid understanding

We have selected four theories that we have found helpful in making sense of the supervision relationship, and which have influenced the case analyses and suggestions in this chapter. We do not see each theory as competing with the other for an ultimate truth, rather that each helps us look at the same situation from a different perspective, and so increases our range of options.

There is not space here to do more than note these theories, and give a few examples of which illustrations were influenced by which theories. The references indicate further reading for those who wish to pursue them further.

- Psychodynamic theory (Hollis and Woods 1981) helps us to understand the effect of unconscious processes on the supervision relationship. The two illustrations where this was most central were 6.5 and 6.6. 'Transference' is a core psychodynamic concept, and while the 'parallel process' can be explained in systems terms, we presented it as something that occurred at an unconscious level. Unconscious defence mechanisms are a possible explanation of David's resistance in Illustration 6.9.
- Humanistic theory (Rogers 1961; England 1986) emphasises the importance of authenticity, openness, warmth, empathy and self-disclosure as the basis for working together effectively. It is established, as well as being self-evident from personal experience, that the supervisor – or social worker – who is open and honest about their own experience and feelings is more likely to elicit that openness in those they are working with. We had an example of this in Illustration 6.7, with the suggestion that if the supervisor disclosed some of her own personal responses to child abuse, this might enable the supervisee to disclose the personal experiences that were affecting his responses to an abusing father.
- Systems theory (von Bertalanffy 1971; Goldstein 1973; Specht and Vickery 1977) is based on the notion that there is often a dynamic connection between different arenas of activity, when these apparently discrete activities have permeable boundaries. Thus to understand the dynamics of what is happening in a one-to-one supervision relationship, it may be necessary to understand what is happening in other connected systems like the team and agency. This framework is relevant to all the illustrations, and is central in 6.2, where a personal friendship between a supervisor and one of the supervisees is causing ripples throughout the team.
- Structural theory (Corrigan and Leonard 1978; Dominelli 1988; Langan and Day 1992) sets the supervisory relationship in the institutional and societal context of inequality and the oppression of less powerful groups by those with more structural power. This framework was used in Chapter 3 when examining how different kinds of power affect the supervision relationship. Illustration 6.3 demonstrated how the interpersonal supervisory relationship was being affected by the interaction of age, gender, and race differences. Similarly, the tensions in the supervisory relationship between two gay men in Illustration 6.8 were a product of the structural context of oppression and discrimination.

Skills for resolving relationship difficulties

Finally, we list some of the core skills suggested in the various case illustrations in this chapter:

- genuineness, empathy and warmth
- use of self and personal feelings
- ability to reach for underlying feelings
- ability to discuss the process of the relationship
- ability to use authority and power positively, including the skill of challenging another person constructively
- capacity to work with and manage anxiety and stress
- effective use of own supervision and/or consultancy
- skills in working anti-oppressively
- problem-solving skills
- group skills
- mediating skills.

It is likely that each supervisor will find that they feel rather more comfortable with some skills than with others. We would recommend that the reader reviews their own strengths and weaknesses in relation to each set of skills, and formulates a plan for their own skill development. It may be particularly helpful to elicit direct feedback from their own supervisees in relation to each set of skills.

7

Stress and trauma: the supervisor's response

. . . social services and health systems are often the least effective at dealing with traumas in a manner that protects staff from their impact. In fact because of the stress on the larger system, intervention by administration often adds to the problem rather than helps staff cope with it. In contrast, support for staff during traumatic times can pay off in the long run with positive staff morale and more effective services to clients.

(Shulman 1993)

You might like to try this exercise. First of all think of a colleague that you respect. Imagine that they are your supervisee, and you are together in a supervision session. Now imagine them looking up at you. Their eyes are bloodshot, and full of tears. In a faltering voice they say 'I feel so ashamed . . . useless . . . I'm letting everyone down, including myself . . . I've had enough . . . look at me . . . I just can't go on . . . what should I do?'

What are you feeling, thinking, doing? Situations similar to this can be among the most demanding and distressing that the supervisor will have to confront. Much of our work demands that we draw extensively upon our own personal resources, and these are likely to be worn down through constant use. This applies as much to the supervisor as it does to the supervisee. Sometimes the accumulation of stress may be gradual and insidious, and sometimes it arrives suddenly and overwhelmingly. The systems that are expected to provide support are not immune from the effects of stress themselves, and may end up compounding rather than alleviating the problems faced.

There is no immunity from stress and trauma. The supervisee's psychological well-being both prior to and after crisis strikes are, however, central concerns for the supervisor. A proactive approach will place this unequivocally on the supervision agenda from the very beginning. Failure to do so may result in social workers feeling like this: 'How do you get senior colleagues to notice you are suffering from acute burnout? Do you send a memo, or collapse in tears? . . . I want to be bright and helpful but instead I am prickly and defensive. I feel dispensable, disposable, and despondent' (letter in *Community Care*, June 1984).

The difficulty of the supervisor's task is often compounded by the fact that as the supervisee's stress increases, they may find it increasingly difficult to make good use of supervision. Typically, they may become more defensive and prickly, as suggested in the above quote, and this may make it difficult to acknowledge their own needs and seek help. The supervisee may also become crisis-bound, reactive, and unable to stand back to look at situations objectively. The supervisor's often critical influence over the supervisee's career opportunities undoubtedly makes it more difficult to express needs directly, especially if this is associated with fear of being negatively assessed. Equally, the supervisor, while wishing to help and support, may be blamed and rejected for being part of the organisation that is seen to be responsible for the stress. If that is not enough, the supervisor may have feelings of guilt themselves, or may be operating under such personal stress that they cannot respond to the supervisee's needs.

In this chapter we will begin by identifying the various stressors the supervisor may have to address. In the second section, further consideration will be given to accumulation of stress, and appropriate preventive and remedial supervisory strategies. The final section will focus on the supervisor's responses to supervisees who experience trauma or potentially traumatising incidents through their work.

Sources of stress

Stresses may originate from many different sources in the supervisee's life. As a starting point it may be helpful to identify these, and relate them to the primary systems used throughout this book: the worker, practice, team, and agency systems. This can provide the supervisor with a framework for carrying out regular checks (see next section), in supervision, of the stressors affecting the personal well-being and work-effectiveness of their supervisees. In Table 7.1 we have summarised some of the more common stressors, while in Figure 7.1 we show the relationship between these.

Although we have shown the stressors as being discrete, in reality they are often inextricably linked. The following illustration may help.

Illustration 7.1

Joe has been working on a particularly stressful child abuse case, which not only has churned up feelings from his own childhood (2b), but has also resulted in him receiving threats (2a) from the father. This case has occupied so much of his emotional energy that he has not been able to keep up with his workload. This has led to some resentment from other team members (3), who see themselves as 'carrying' him. At the same time his relationship difficulties with his partner (1) have been steadily getting worse, partly because he was so preoccupied with work, and partly because of financial difficulties. He had hoped that the latter might be relieved by going for promotion. His managers, however, are aware that he is struggling, and his

Table 7.1 Stressors acting on the supervisee at each level within the
system

System Stressors	Stressors
1 Worker (personal)	Stressors emanating from the supervisee's personal life, for example: • relationship difficulties, including separation, divorce, problems with children • illness, or illness of someone close • loss and bereavement • financial difficulties • oppressive abuse
2(a) Practice	Stressors emanating from the supervisee's practice, where they become the victim, for example: • being the victim of physical assault (e.g. by a client or their relative) • being on the receiving end of racism, sexism, disablism, homophobia and other forms of oppressive abuse • being subject to threats of violence, assault, or indeed having one's family threatened
2(b) Practice	Stressors emanating from the supervisee's practice, where the experiences of others stir up strong feelings for the supervisee, for example: • disclosure of abuse • bereavement and loss • terminal illness • clients whose life mirrors that of the worker • large workloads, with a high proportion of difficult and protracted cases
3 Team	Stressors emanating from the supervisee's membership of a team, for example: • personal conflicts with other team members, harassment and bullying • scapegoating or other dysfunctional group processes • feeling isolated or undervalued within the team • involvement with other colleagues' work stress
4 Agency	Stressors emanating from the supervisee's contract with their employer: • reorganisations • competition for promotion • closure of units • threats of redundancies

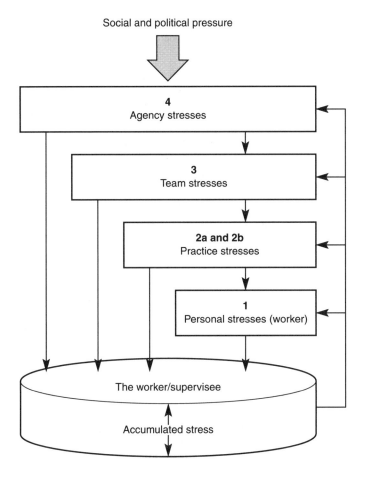

Figure 7.1 The flow of stress through the social work system

immediate prospects are slim (4). The fact that he does not feel he can cope with his own problems is affecting his ability to work with the child abuse case, which in turn increases pressure on other parts of his work load, which in turn . . . and so on to the point of collapse.

Sitting with Joe in a supervision session as he catalogues his crumbling world, it is easy to feel deskilled. The first and most important thing to do will be to listen, and actively engage with him at a feeling level. Only once he has felt that he has told his story fully, and that it has been properly listened to, is it likely that he will be responsive to further help from the supervisor. At this point it may be helpful to begin an unpacking process by encouraging Joe to map out the relationship between each stressor on paper

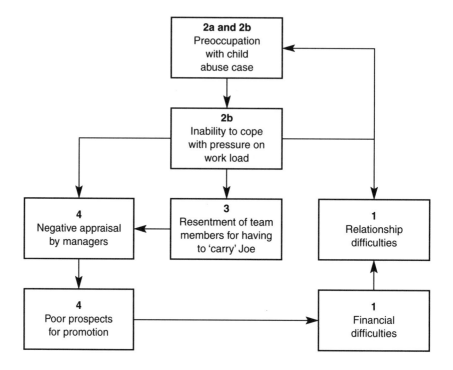

Figure 7.2   Stressors in Joe's life

(see Figure 7.2). We will talk more about this mapping process later. At this stage, however, we simply want to illustrate how stress emanating from one part of the system interrelates with stress from other parts.

Accumulated stress and burnout

In addition to the specific stresses indicated above, there may be many other more insidious stresses, which can accumulate over long periods of time to such an extent that they become debilitating. These can emanate from public attitudes towards social workers, lack of professional consensus as to the social worker role, role ambiguity and conflict, passive leadership and lack of recognition.

The container at the bottom of Figure 7.1 shows how stress can be accumulated from all parts of the system. It is worth noting that stress can move around a system in both directions. The worker can accumulate stress from each of the areas outlined in the previous section, while also acting as a stressor to other parts of the system. In Joe's case, for example, his stress was also a stressor to his supervisor, the team, his partner and for those involved in the child abuse case.

The ripple effects of stress within teams

The consequences for other team members, when a colleague is in crisis, can be far-reaching and profound. Some of the ripple effects for the team are identified below. When one member of a team becomes significantly overstressed, other team members may:

- recognise the stress suffered by their colleague, but not know how to respond without making matters worse; in effect they ignore it, but may still feel the guilt
- choose not to notice the stress for fear of having to acknowledge it in themselves
- need to reassure themselves that they are different from their stressed colleague; in distancing themselves, they may become critical and blaming
- become overcautious, particularly if the stress was created through a work-related trauma
- become angry with the agency and the supervisor for failing to protect their colleague against the stress
- turn the guilt in on themselves and their fellow team members, leading to a loss of trust and confidence in the team
- deny their own need and entitlement for support, which may seem insignificant in comparison to that of their colleague
- lose a sense of being in a team, and feel increasingly isolated.

This list is far from exhaustive, but, as can be seen, might easily exhaust any team where the individual stress felt by the worker is not actively managed. Supervision is not the only place where this needs to happen, but if the supervisor neglects the opportunity, it may prove very difficult to pick up elsewhere.

Equally, the cost to the agency can be immense. Staff may leave, or require extended periods away from work; staff morale may drop, and anger toward management increase; organisational failings may be exposed and attract adverse publicity. The service users may also suffer: services may be withdrawn or reduced; established relationships may be undermined, or replaced; and just as the worker's colleagues may feel guilt, anger, or sadness, so might they. All these factors, and many more, can have the effect of the stress being passed both up and down the system. Without a proactive approach, the pressure on the agency may become overburdening, and result in a bureaucratic, minimalist style of management that elects to deny that pressure.

We hope that an awareness and sensitivity to these factors alone would encourage employers to take the welfare of their staff seriously. As we write, however, a court case in Northumberland will help ensure that worker stress is no longer pushed under the carpet:

> A social worker made history yesterday when a High Court judge held his employers liable for a nervous breakdown which ended his career. John Walker, aged 57, who was retired on medical grounds after two breakdowns, is the first employee in Britain to sue an employer for stress from overwork. Lawyers said the case could open the flood gates for damages claims.
>
> (*Guardian*, 17 November 1994)

Undoubtedly, the role of supervision in managing worker stress will become an increasingly central one. For much of the remainder of this chapter we will consider how the supervisor may discharge that responsibility from within the supervision relationship itself. While the emphasis in this book is on the role of the supervisor, it should be remembered that ultimately the responsibility for managing and minimising stress levels is an organisational one.

A proactive supervisory response to worker stress

There is an extensive literature on work-related stress and professional burnout, which the reader may wish to pursue for themselves (e.g. Edelwich and Brodsky 1980; Freudenberger 1980 etc.). In this section, we will keep our focus on the issues as they arise through the supervision relationship. Rather than attempt to provide comprehensive coverage of the subject, we will consider some of the common stress reactions, note how they might develop over time, and provide indications of the work that needs to be undertaken within supervision.

We believe that good supervision addresses work-related stress before it occurs. None the less, many readers will have turned to this chapter because they have more immediate concerns. It may be, for example, that the reader is about to take over the supervision of a worker who is already underfunctioning, where the opportunity for preventive work is not available. This remedial work will be considered as we move through this section, alongside the recommendations for preventive work. Below we summarise some of the most common signs of work-related stress.

Physical signs of stress

- fatigue and exhaustion, without apparent expenditure of energy
- loss of weight and loss of appetite
- insomnia, or disturbed sleep patterns
- increased complaints of migraine headaches
- body tension such as aches and pains without apparent cause, perspiration, and gastrointestinal problems
- substance misuse: alcohol, tranquillisers, drugs. The supervisor may recognise a deterioration in the supervisee's facial skin tone, and the eyes may look tired.

Behavioural signs of stress

- progressive self-imposed isolation
- taking work home so that it takes over more and more of their life
- becoming increasingly indecisive
- overly self-critical
- mechanical approach to work, combined with loss of enthusiasm
- tasks become overwhelming and inertia sets in

- becomes blaming and cynical
- resists innovation and change
- becomes impatient and irritable
- others, clients, colleagues, managers become stereotyped and dismissed
- breakdown in social and personal relationships.

Many of the signs develop slowly and insidiously, so that over short time periods, changes are not obvious or apparent to those who are in regular contact. As a result, we believe it is important that the supervision relationship incorporates regular stress checks. Ideally these should be introduced early on in the supervision relationship, as experience suggests that to introduce them later is likely to arouse suspicion and resistance in the supervisee. A stress check involves the supervisor and supervisee using a framework similar to that suggested earlier to map out together the potential and actual stressors originating from each of the four primary systems (practice, worker, team and agency). Each stressor might then be reviewed in terms of how they are affecting the supervisee, and how they are being managed. It may also be helpful to map out the relationship between stressors, as in Joe's case, illustrated earlier. A problem-solving approach may assist in identifying appropriate stress management plans. If this process is planned on a regular basis (e.g. every six to eight weeks) it might become possible to compare the stress checks over time, and pick up trends that may not otherwise be apparent.

Stage one: initial enthusiasm

Interestingly, many authors identify initial enthusiasm as the first stage of professional burnout. This is most apparent with new and inexperienced workers, and particularly with workers who may have recently made a midlife change of career. It is also common, however, even with very experienced workers who have moved job, particularly if the job is a promotion or within a different organisation. They come into the work not only uncluttered by relationships, previous history, past disappointments and full workloads, but also filled with hopes, aspirations, and a desire to make their mark or prove themselves. The new job is, in a sense, a fresh chance and a new hope. Because of this they may have more energy and enthusiasm for the work than many of their colleagues. This in itself may lead to difficulties including:

- indiscriminate volunteering, which may result in heavy, unbalanced workloads later on. It may also result in the supervisee finding themselves quickly out of their depth, or that the work they have taken on has diverted them from their original work aspirations
- resentment from other staff, who may feel exposed by the new worker's energy. This may make it more difficult to become a member of a supportive and collaborative team
- other team members may become overreliant on the supervisee's energy, and in so doing, set them up as some kind of saviour.

In the latter case particularly, the supervisor must be particularly careful not to collude with this almost messianic wish. The new worker may internalise this expectation, and feel a sense of failure and frustration when it is not realised. Others may also experience difficulty in adjusting their expectations.

We are not suggesting that enthusiasm is to be avoided or discouraged, rather that the process of harnessing it effectively requires an active supervisory process; and that unless that happens the supervisee may experience unnecessary stress. In the very early sessions, in addition to the work suggested for the induction phase (see Chapter 4), there are a number of important discussions that could usefully be included on the supervision agenda:

- a review of the supervisee's previous work history to help ascertain what can be learned from it, and how past ambitions and aspirations have been achieved or thwarted
- a realistic mutual assessment of the supervisee's strengths, weaknesses, and needs. This should also include not just discrete skills, knowledge, attitudes and personal qualities, but also more complex patterns and processes
- a stress check, as mentioned earlier, to identify and plan for actual and potential stressors. We should point out here that the goal is not removal of stress, but establishing a level of optimal stress whereby the supervisee is challenged sufficiently to allow them to work at their best, without that stress becoming debilitating
- setting of realistic and achievable short-term and longer-term goals that foster a sense of accomplishment.

Harnessing enthusiasm in this way serves not to dampen it, but to give it focus and direction, while protecting against premature disillusionment. By addressing stress fully, early on in the relationship, the supervisor conveys that stress management is a central aspect of supervision, and not an irritation to it.

Stage two: premature routinisation

Let us now assume, for a moment, that the initial enthusiasm has not been harnessed appropriately. Typically there are two likely outcomes. The first is that the worker throws themselves headlong into the work in a relatively unprotected way, which may leave them unprepared for the rejection, sense of failure, or hurt that they may experience from service users. When this happens, the most common response is some form of withdrawal, which will be described more fully in the next section on trauma. The second, which we will focus upon here, leads to the premature routinisation of the work. The worker's initial high hopes have become tarnished, distant, increasingly unobtainable. As the supervisee becomes more established, the work may come to feel less exciting and exotic. The initial enthusiasm may have subsided somewhat, and the daily challenges seem less significant. Successes no longer attract a buzz, and service users may cease to be talked about as people, only as tasks. It is as if the worker has accepted a minimal return from the work, perhaps just to get through it. Boredom may feature strongly.

Appropriate work undertaken during the initial enthusiasm stage may protect against the most severe routinisation, and make it more manageable; it cannot, however, preclude it altogether. The supervisor must be prepared to tackle this openly and fairly. If the work identified for stage one has not been carried out, there may still be a chance of carrying it out now, before the situation gets any worse. If it has, this is the first point for revisiting and re-evaluating that work. In addition, new issues coming on to the agenda may form part either of the general developmental work undertaken with the supervisee or of a remedial stress management strategy:

- exploration of how the worker uses, and protects him- or herself emotionally in the work with clients; case discussions focusing on interpersonal processes can provide one opportunity for this work
- exploration of how they keep their personal, non-work lives healthy and separate from their professional lives. Early signs that problems may be developing in this area include: staying at work longer than is expected or required; taking work home; repeatedly volunteering for overtime (e.g. in residential settings); giving up routine social and recreational activities; socialisation restricted to colleagues; lack of physical activities
- reinforcement of small achievements the supervisee glosses over
- challenging supervisee comments that suggest a dismissive, stereotypical or mechanical response to the work
- examination of small pieces of work in detail; this may be particularly helpful when the supervisee has begun to foreclose prematurely on explorations, and where the complexity of the work is being avoided or denied.

This work should not be undertaken in one emergency session, but rather woven explicitly and openly into the continuing supervision process.

Stage three: self-doubt

If the process continues without positive intervention, the routine of the previous phase may become internalised in such a way that the supervisee ceases to search out positive experiences. Ultimately, this can lead to a form of self-doubt. Depending upon the supervisee's personality, the duration of this stage can vary between days and years. Initially the problem may be their own perception of low effectiveness rather than its reality. Later, the supervisee may begin to sabotage their best efforts, and cease to engage meaningfully with colleagues and service users. As a result they may no longer be gaining any rewards from the work, and may begin to question seriously their own value as a worker, and perhaps as a person. The supervisee's thoughts are likely to be very centred around themselves, and consequently, their perceptions of others can become distorted.

During this stage the supervisee may expend considerable energy in attempting to keep their distress hidden. If they have not yet had any experience of exploring the effect the work is having on them within the current supervisory relationship, attempts by the supervisor to broach the matter at this stage are likely to be rebuffed. This may be the latest stage at which interventions within supervision can be initiated with a realistic expectation of success, for example:

- all the work outlined from the previous stages will need to be completed
- the supervisor might help the supervisee map out their emotional history from when they started the job, in order to help them put their current experience in context
- the supervisor should share their own observations of the supervisee directly. It is important that the feedback given by the supervisor is personally owned, clear, specific, relevant, and balanced. If work-related stress has been on the agenda from the outset, and the supervisor's attitude to it has already been articulated, the supervisee is far more likely to accept the feedback
- current stressors need to be clearly identified and their influence mapped out
- the supervisor should also clarify other sources of assistance that may be available and help the supervisee to think through how those resources (support groups, counselling, stress-management courses) might be used
- it is important that the supervisor accepts the limitation of their role, and avoids becoming the supervisee's therapist
- all current work needs to be sensitively reviewed, particularly where there are people at risk or others who may pose a risk. The supervisor cannot avoid their responsibility to service users, and to ensure that the service they are receiving is at least acceptable and safe
- the supervisor should also ensure that they are receiving appropriate supervision for themselves.

At all stages, but at this one in particular, the supervisor may need to be taking an active managerial role beyond the confines of the supervision session. This may involve intervening within the wider system to reduce the influence of stressors, and to mobilise resources, for example:

- reallocation of cases
- change of work priorities
- direct mediation between parties in conflict
- changes in work setting or work pattern
- provision of appropriate training opportunities.

Stage four: stagnation, collapse or recovery

Once the supervisee's stress has proceeded beyond stage three, the progression is largely dependent upon:

- the work that has already been undertaken earlier
- other supports available to the supervisee
- a range of complex factors relating to their own previous history and their personality
- the extent to which the agency has been able to recognise and fulfil its responsibilities to the worker's well-being.

It is quite possible that the result is simply stagnation, i.e. that they lock themselves into a kind of depressive state in which they avoid all changes and challenges. In this state they can be totally exasperating for others to work with, and this may lead them to feel little understood, and often scapegoated. As a result, they may become resentful, cynical and blaming. Physical illness becomes increasingly likely, as does substance misuse, most often through heavy drinking. Overeating and undereating are also common.

While this state of stagnation and low effectiveness may continue for years, it will usually arrive at a point of crisis. This often arises through some other event, for example the breakdown of a relationship, allegations of malpractice, an accident, financial demands or a bereavement. The crisis places the supervisee in a position where it is no longer possible to deny the gravity of their situation. This may lead them finally to accepting help and beginning on a road to recovery. Alternatively, it might signal imminent collapse. They might, for example, suddenly hand in their resignation, and refuse any further involvement with the agency. Little is known about what happens subsequently in these situations, but undoubtedly some will suffer longer-term mental health problems, and many will never return to social work.

Working with the supervisee throughout this stage can be extremely demanding and stressful in itself. As the supervisee's stress becomes increasingly obvious to others, the supervisor may feel under pressure to be seen to be doing something. They may also question their own part in their supervisee's distress. Have they done everything that they reasonably could, or have they colluded with the agency against the individual? Support from within the line management structure needs to be sought. It may, however, be difficult to resolve these questions internally, and in such cases, an independent consultant may be able to offer some objectivity.

In this phase, the supervisor's role is more likely to become that of a mediator whose purpose is to:

- identify sources of professional help, discover what they have to offer, negotiate financial assistance from the agency and facilitate the take-up of services by the supervisee
- ensure that the supervisee's rights are respected and that they are treated well by the organisation
- keep colleagues informed in such a way that reduces gossiping and increases sensitivity and respect.

The need for regular supervision, however, still remains, particularly in order to:

- monitor how they are responding to their changing situation
- show an interest in their well-being
- help the supervisee face the choices that they have before them, and, if necessary, help them to feel able to leave their job with dignity.

Most social workers experience a degree of work-related stress or professional burnout. Over the length of their career most supervisors will encounter colleagues who are suffering from debilitating levels of stress. That is a long way from suggesting that the decline from enthusiasm to collapse is inevitable, or conversely that good supervision will necessarily prevent it. All we can suggest is that good supervision helps, and even when collapse cannot be averted, it may help maintain the respect and dignity of all concerned.

Work-related trauma

The current wave of interest in post-traumatic stress might easily lead us to believe that it is a rather more glamorous and exotic process than the eroding effects of 'ordinary' stress – although we have yet to hear anyone suffering from post-traumatic stress describe it as such! It is a much more common condition than might be expected, and most social workers will already have worked with traumatised clients: people who have been raped, physically and sexually abused, assaulted; parents who have lost their children through sudden death, or through removal under a court order; people involved in accidents, and life-threatening experiences. When it happens to a colleague for whom you have supervisory responsibility, however, it can feel quite different. With stress, you can often see it building up, and may have the time to prepare yourself to deal with it. With trauma, it happens suddenly, often unexpectedly, makes immediate demands, and may implicate the supervisor him/herself.

Often supervisors and managers respond to trauma in the same way as they do to stress; they assume that if you can decrease the demands on the worker or increase their resources, then she or he will be able to regain equilibrium. While this may be true for stress created through working under high pressure and constant demand, when considering trauma it may significantly underestimate the complexity of needs.

One of the major reasons for this difference is that unlike accumulated stress, traumatic stress is primarily maintained by internal rather than external stressors. These internal stressors originate from re-experiencing some of the effects of the traumatic incident that happened at an earlier time. Trauma describes a sudden, massive and overwhelming threat to an individual's safety, integrity or identity. The consequences of this may lead to what is typically described as traumatic stress, where the demands placed upon the individual may be significantly increased internally by re-experiencing the trauma (e.g. through nightmares and flashbacks), while the resources are depleted through disturbed arousal (e.g. insomnia, hyper-alertness, startle responses). A person who becomes traumatised often experiences it as a major rupture with the past, after which they will often describe themselves as 'a changed person' or that they will never be able to look at life again in the same way.

The distinguishing feature determining whether a person becomes traumatised by an incident is not the size of the incident, but whether it challenges a person's core beliefs about both themselves, and the way they see the world. It is important to note that it is the worker's subjective experience that is all-important, not the specific nature of the incident triggering their reaction. Thus in some circumstances being spat at may be experienced as more traumatic than being threatened with a knife. To understand this we need to know more about the individual's core beliefs about themselves, and their beliefs about the world.

We all have deep-seated beliefs about ourselves and our world. Sometimes these are articulated through religion or philosophy, but many are not recognised until they are challenged. These beliefs can often be logically refuted, and yet we still hold them because they allow us to go about our daily business without having to take every possibility into account. For example, we would imagine that most readers of this book will hold a core belief about a full life expectancy. We might all know that we could die within the next twenty-four hours (be run over, involved in a crash or an explosion) but if we really believed that our life might not last beyond tomorrow, we would probably urgently seek more fulfilling activities than reading a book!

One of the earliest indications that a supervisee might have been traumatised is often found in what they say a day or so after the incident. Typical examples are:

- '...why me?'
- '...I can't understand it, I thought we had such a good relationship'
- '...what kind of God can let this happen?'
- '...I never believed that people could be like that'
- '...I don't know who I am any longer'
- '...I can't believe it has happened'
- '...it feels like a rug has been pulled from under me'
- '...I've completely lost it, nothing seems straightforward any more'
- '...I always believed that people could depend upon me'.

Each of these statements indicates some kind of challenged belief the supervisee is desperately trying to come to terms with. It might help to think of trauma as similar to any other loss, perhaps a bereavement. The difference is that the grief process relates not to the loss of someone else, but the loss of oneself and the world one knew.

In anticipation of a trauma

Although trauma can occur at any time, it is important that some preventive and anticipatory work is undertaken within supervision:

- the supervisor should convey a positive attitude to the needs of workers who might be shaken up through experiences at work
- at an early stage it is worth checking with the supervisee whether they have gone through a traumatic experience before. This may help place it on the agenda, and also provide the supervisee with an experience of talking about trauma before it happens
- some supervisees, particularly those that have not been traumatised, talk as if they are surrounded by a protective bubble – others may be assaulted, and while it is possible that they could too, they do not really believe it. This needs to be explored, and a fruitful line of enquiry might be to ask the supervisee to imagine what it might take to burst the bubble, and to consider the consequences
- in reviewing the supervisee's work, the supervisor should ensure that an appropriate assessment of risk is made, and that the supervisee is taking appropriate precautions for their own safety

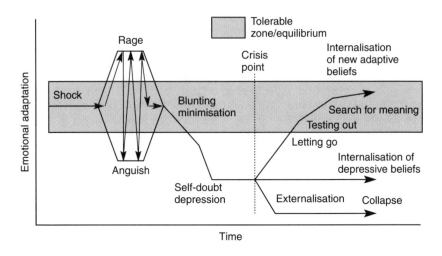

Figure 7.3 The process of adaptation to challenged core beliefs

- since the supervisor will often not be immediately available following an incident, it is important that they ensure that the supervisee knows what to do, and what their rights are (these are normally laid down in departmental policies on violence)
- additionally, they should ensure that all other staff know what to do, and how to give appropriate support to a colleague immediately after an incident.

Adaptation to trauma

It is beyond the scope of this book to address post-traumatic stress in detail. Instead we have provided in Figure 7.3 a mapping of a typical process of adaptation to trauma. If you can imagine it being printed on an elastic sheet, the process can be stretched and distorted in many ways according to the experience of the supervisee. Table 7.2 summarises some of the typical reactions experienced by the supervisee at each stage of the process. Necessarily, this is a great simplification; each supervisee's experience will be unique. In particular, while we highlight three very different routes through the trauma, there may be many other possible variations. If the model can be thought of as illustrative rather than prescriptive, however, it can provide a useful template against which to compare and consider the specific reactions and processes experienced by a supervisee.

Supervisory responses to trauma

Supervisory responses to supervisees who have been involved in a potentially traumatic incident can be thought of as being either *mediative*, or

Table 7.2 Explanation of Figure 7.3

Stage	Typical reactions
Shock	Immediately following the incident, the worker may be in a state of shock, numbness and disbelief. They may still have adrenalin pumping through their body, and may not be in a condition to make important decisions.
Reaction	Usually either rage or anguish, but often fluctuating between the two in such a way that it is impossible to find any calm in the middle. Sleep is likely to be disturbed, nightmares and flashbacks may be experienced as sudden and violent. Often the worker looks deadpan, as if wearing a mask.
Blunting and minimisation	The supervisee's reactions may be painful and intolerable. After a while they need to reduce the pain. This might mean changing what they believe to have happened to make it more acceptable, withdrawal from emotional contact with others, drinking to blunt reactions, avoiding anything that may remind them of the incident. They may refuse to acknowledge the extent of their own distress.
Self-doubt	As time goes on, they may begin to feel that they are not the person they once thought that they were. The world can feel hostile, and unsafe. Relationships come under pressure owing to their withdrawal, and there may seem little of value within their life. They may feel that they are 'going crazy'. Often they don't feel anyone else could understand.
Crisis	The turning point. It is no longer possible to continue as if nothing had happened. This is often prompted externally by some other event; e.g. the breakdown of a close relationship, an accident or suspension. This may be the first point at which the worker is prepared to consider professional help.
Route 1 Adaptation and integration	The likelihood of the worker following this route is greatly enhanced if: 1 a thorough debriefing has already been undertaken 2 the worker has an accurate impression of their colleague's reactions to them and the incident 3 they have worked through similar traumas before 4 they have an awareness that their current experience is natural, and transitional 5 they were psychologically stable prior to the incident. Often trauma can happen on the back of another trauma making resolution extremely difficult. The worker stops looking to the past, and recognises that they have to learn anew about themselves and their world. New core beliefs begin to emerge, and these are tested out, and eventually incorporated into a new sense of self.

Table 7.2 (cont.)

Stage	Typical reactions
Route 2 Internalisation of depressive beliefs	Rather than see their self-doubt as a transitional adaptation, the worker believes it is an end point. The new sense of self becomes that of a depressed person, and the worker begins to organise their life as such, avoiding risk and change, and settling for minimal expectations of life. Often a further crisis occurs some years on when they realise how dismal their life has become. Suicide risk is latent, but high.
Route 3 Externalisation and collapse	The worker becomes increasingly prickly, blaming others for everything that is wrong, not only at work, but in the world generally. Their physical health deteriorates, and their isolation increases. Any close relationships are likely to have broken down by now. Although they may have become emotionally distant from others, they often spend long periods crying inconsolably when on their own. Sometimes another crisis will be provoked in order to access the help that they need.

restorative. Mediative responses are those which the supervisor takes within the wider system beyond the confines of the supervision session, while restorative responses refer to those which occur with the supervisee within the supervision session itself.

Although we will suggest particular supervisory responses appropriate to the stage of the trauma, it is important to take a broader overview of these in relation to the specific needs of the supervisee and their context. A further necessary simplification that we have had to make, given that this is a book on supervision rather than trauma, is that we have assumed that the supervisee was in a psychologically healthy state of mind prior to the traumatic incident.

Mediative responses

Immediately after an incident the supervisor will need to take an executive role, ensuring that (in the case of an assault) the supervisee has received appropriate medical treatment and advice, and that the incident is reported and followed through. Practical matters such as covering shifts, cancelling appointments, reallocating cases should be taken care of and not be left to the supervisee. The supervisor might also have an important role as an advocate in dealings with the police, the courts and the press. If this not possible because of a potential conflict of interest, this needs to be carefully explained to the supervisee, and other sources of advocacy arranged. If the supervisee belongs to a trade union or professional association, contact should be encouraged as this may provide an additional source of support and advice.

If the supervisee is to have some time away from work, it is important to stay in regular contact, as false beliefs can quickly develop as to how others see them ('they all think I'm not up to it', 'they think it was my fault', 'they resent having to cover my work' etc.). The contact does not have to be overbearing or intrusive, and often a phone call expressing genuine concern, keeping them up to date and offering any help that may be required will be sufficient.

It is important that colleagues are given a reasonably full factual account of the incident. This can help prevent gossiping and the danger of the story becoming exaggerated. If the story is not aired fully within the team, the supervisee may be left in a position where they have to recall the incident with each member of the team. Sometimes colleagues will try to spare the victim the pain of retelling the story but, in the process, avoid contact with them, and increase their sense of isolation.

The supervisor may also have a role in ensuring that others do not compound the trauma experienced by the supervisee. There was a murder of one young person by another in a residential unit several years ago. A year afterwards, whilst in the process of working with the team, Iain was struck by the huge reservoir of rage that had been attached to a single comment by a senior manager soon after the incident. The manager didn't know the murderer, assumed that the team would be outraged by what he had done, and tried to reassure the team by telling them that he would be put away for a long time. In fact the team felt a loss for both of the young people, and found the comment immensely insensitive.

In the weeks and months following the incident, the supervisor will need to ensure that the supervisee's workload is appropriate, and that they are not unnecessarily forced into situations that may restimulate the trauma. In the worst scenario, where the supervisee is no longer able to continue to work, the supervisor has a responsibility to ensure that alternatives are explored, and that at the very least, the supervisee is treated well by the agency.

Restorative responses

In terms of the future work with the supervisee, the attitude conveyed by the supervisor (and others) toward the supervisee and the incident can be crucial. The supervisee is likely to be in a highly sensitive state and may uncritically internalise even the slightest implication that they have failed, are to blame, or are weak. Even if there is a real possibility that the supervisee behaved unprofessionally, or may have contributed significantly to the incident, their right to good supervision is unaltered.

Different supervisees will have different immediate emotional needs following an incident: some will need to ventilate, others will need to feel that they have regained a measure of control first. The supervisor needs to be sensitive to these differences, and not to prejudge them. How the supervisor responds to, for example, a supervisee who openly expresses (in supervision) their hate or loathing of a service user is likely to determine how far the supervisee will trust the relationship to explore their reactions further.

In the early stages following the incident, the supervisee may still be denying, or not recognising the effect that it has had upon them. Emotional support, together with assistance in problem-solving can help meet some of the immediate demands they are facing. Encouragement to identify and mobilise all the supports and resources available is likely to be another high priority for supervision.

As the supervisee begins to realise that the effects of the incident are persistent, the supervisor will have to find appropriate ways to respond to their needs. Supervision sessions might have to become more frequent to allow this work to be done. Even if the supervisee is on sick leave, supervisory contact should continue. The supervisee may be alarmed, even ashamed at some of their reactions to the incident, and fear that they are breaking down. As a result they may be reluctant to share these with the supervisor. For this reason, it can be helpful to offer information on common and normal reactions to trauma (re-experiencing through flashbacks, nightmares etc.; disturbed arousal such as insomnia, startle responses, hyper-vigilance, panic attacks; avoidance of situations that may act as potential reminders of the incident) and check whether these are being experienced.

Although it is likely that the supervisee will already have given a nuts-and-bolts account of the incident, the full story may remain untold. A full psychological debriefing should be discussed, and if agreed to, carried out as soon as the supervisee feels that they are able. There are strong indications that this may reduce the likelihood of the stress reactions becoming debilitating. If the supervisor does not feel confident enough to carry this out, or the supervisee would prefer to do it with someone else, then it is the supervisor's responsibility to make alternative arrangements. It is important that the supervisor does not take it as a personal insult if the supervisee prefers not to do this with them. The fact that the supervisor can influence their career may inhibit the supervisee too much.

Supervisors should seek out training in psychological debriefing and have recourse to a consultant who is experienced in using debriefing techniques. We believe that this needs to be included in supervision training as a matter of course.

Psychological debriefing is a preventive strategy used to minimise the likelihood of symptoms of post-traumatic stress – flashbacks, nightmares, hyper-vigilance and disturbed arousal, avoidance and phobic reactions, psychogenic amnesia etc. Procedures for debriefing in groups are well documented (e.g. see Parkinson 1993). Individual debriefings can be carried out by the supervisor using the following method:

1 Explain to the supervisee that you will be asking them to talk through the incident in great detail, and that this may be painful at times.
2 Explain that sometimes parts of their story can become buried, only to return in unwanted flashbacks and nightmares. Talking through the incident in great detail can reduce the need to revisit the most painful parts of the experience.
3 Tell them that, if they agree, you will ask them to tell the story from a time before they had any premonition of the incident. They will be asked to tell their story moment by moment, in chronological order, and including all sensations, thoughts, perceptions and feelings that they can

recall. The story will proceed through the incident up to the present, or to a point where they felt the incident was over.

4 If at any point they break down in tears, do not apply pressure, but acknowledge their distress, tell them to take their time and continue when they feel able. It may help to ask them what it was that is making it difficult to proceed, or to put words to their feelings.

5 At each point, ask that they attempt to recall all the noises, smells, tastes, colours, images and sensations within their awareness. The detail is important because it makes the stimuli that may trigger traumatic memories more specific and elaborate. In so doing the likelihood that these memories will be elicited by more generalised stimuli is reduced.

6 Make sure that they talk not only of what actually happened but also what they thought might happen. This may well have been more traumatic than the actual course of events.

7 If they appear to skip part of the story, gently bring them back and help them complete the story chronologically. Often, even small gaps in the story can reveal significant material. Sometimes the gaps are associated with feelings of shame, and may have been shut out; or they may show up an incongruence in their story, and help the supervisee recognise that they may have changed what they believe to have happened to make it more acceptable.

8 At no point ask them to interpret or evaluate their actions, or offer your own perceptions or judgements. At this stage you are not counselling, simply getting the story out as it happened. A review of what can be learnt from the incident should be undertaken separately.

9 Continue right up to the present (with the greatest detail devoted to the incident itself).

10 When it is complete, check how they are feeling and how they have been affected by the session. Help them with their breathing, if need be.

11 Check whether they have experienced any problems since the incident, and normalise any stress reactions. Offer anticipatory guidelines as to typical stress reactions that may follow.

12 Identify and mobilise any supports and resources at home and at work. Clarify immediate plans.

13 Assess whether they would benefit from, and welcome counselling. Refer if appropriate.

14 Summarise the session.

It is essential that the debrief is conducted in a secure and safe environment. Making sufficient time available is also important, as the debrief may take much longer than the incident itself. Normally, the debrief will not be immediately after the incident, but a day or so after. Often, however, the debrief does not happen until much later when the person has reached crisis point, or some other event makes them relive the trauma.

As the supervisee begins to adapt to the trauma, the supervisor can help in a number of different ways:

• helping them map out the effect that the trauma has had on all aspects of their working life

- helping them make sense of these effects
- encouraging them to express their feelings about what has happened to them
- helping them identify what has changed within them and around them
- assisting them in sorting, prioritising and solving the problems facing them
- assisting them in identifying tasks that will help them adapt to their changing circumstances
- offering access to an independent counsellor.

Depending upon the persistence of the stress reactions, it may be that support from the supervisor and the team becomes drained. This is particularly likely if the supervisee has become very withdrawn, depressed, or prickly and blaming. Ideally the supervision relationship will be strong enough for the supervisor to feel able to talk about the situation with the supervisee, and to discuss the options available. This is the crisis point shown in Figure 7.3. It is a crisis in the sense of being a turning point, a point where it is no longer possible to continue in the same way. The crisis for the team might be that they can no longer 'carry' their colleague; for the supervisor, because they have no more help to offer; and for the supervisee, because they must either adapt or sink. Independent professional help needs to be actively considered if it has not been already.

While the depressive and externalised (blaming) routes described earlier occur more often than anyone would wish, it is important to have a sense of balance. Most social workers will adapt to trauma positively provided they receive adequate support, and will not require professional help to do so. The chances of this occurring are naturally much better if they were in a psychologically healthy state prior to the trauma. This provides us with a link back to the first half of the chapter: the best way to reduce the likelihood of a trauma becoming debilitating is to ensure beforehand that the supervisee is not overstressed.

The supervisor's own needs

Although we have made passing references to the supervisor's own needs, these merit further consideration and emphasis. Sometimes the supervisor will already be too stressed even to be able to recognise their supervisee's needs; it may be only when something traumatic happens that this becomes apparent. Inevitably this is too late; this may hold dire consequences for the supervisee, the supervisor, the service users, and the agency. The quality of the supervisor's own supervision is paramount, although as one ascends the organisational hierarchy, the likelihood is that (unfortunately) this will become less and less a forum for having support needs met or practice issues addressed. In recognition of this, several agencies have set up peer and group supervision (see Chapter 9).

It can be helpful for the supervisor to think of their own stress as a barometer for the stress moving through the system. This may allow them to find a way to address the stress experienced by others without denying their own. A related point is that supervisees may find it very difficult to take appropriate care of themselves if they do not see this modelled by their supervisor.

When a worker is assaulted or perhaps has lost control with a service user, the supervisor may be implicated in some way. They can then become the focus of blame from all parts of the system and beyond (particularly if the courts and media are looking for a scapegoat). Support from within a system that may be felt to be pointing the finger may be hard to find or accept. In such cases, independent sources of advice, consultation and support will be needed. We would urge all readers to think hard, now, before they find themselves in such a situation, where they would find those sources.

When the supervisor is less directly affected by the stressors operating on the supervisee, they may, none the less, experience strong feelings of inadequacy and guilt. It may be possible to negotiate more frequent supervision with their own supervisor at such times, or gain access to a consultant.

The reader may feel, having read this chapter, that they are ill-equipped, or perhaps not suited to carry out parts of the work suggested. This need not be a source of guilt, and each of us needs to recognise that we have both talents and limitations. The supervisor does not have to undertake all the supervisory work; indeed if they did, they might rapidly burn out themselves. The important role is in ensuring that all the appropriate supervisory work is undertaken, and this may be done through appropriate delegation and referral. In this respect, the supervisor takes the role analogous to a key worker rather than therapist.

Summary

In this chapter we have identified the various sources of stress that may affect a supervisee, and suggested that good supervision includes regular stress checks. The process of professional burnout has been described, with specific recommendations of both preventive and remedial work. While it is beyond the scope of this book to examine trauma in detail, the essential points have been summarised and indications given as to work that might be undertaken beneficially by the supervisor. Importantly, we have concluded the chapter with a discussion of the supervisor's own needs.

8 Supervision and the team

> We recommend that the primary focus for supervision in any operational unit in field, day or residential social work should be the entire group of staff, not workers as individuals. By 'operational unit'... we refer to any group or team of workers, usually no more than ten, who work within common organisational boundaries, and policies...
>
> *(Payne and Scott 1982: 1)*

The team context of supervision has been alluded to throughout this book so far, but not yet addressed in its own right. We agree with the view expressed in the above quote from Payne and Scott that whilst much supervisory activity may still take place in one-to-one sessions, it needs to be thought of as part of a team approach to the task and to supervision. The latter part of the quote, however, referring to 'common organisational boundaries' needs to take account of the more complex organisational arrangements of social work and particularly community care in the 1990s – a point we return to later.

For supervision to be approached in the team context, the supervisor who is also team manager needs to have a clear view of the kind of team and team ethos that they want to develop. A good understanding of group dynamics is also necessary. The first part of this chapter will therefore summarise some of the key features of teams and groups, and refer those readers who would like to consider these topics in more depth to the relevant literature. Supervision will then be set in the team context, looking at various patterns of supervision arrangements and some of the team and supervision issues that may arise for the supervisor and supervisees. The next chapter will concentrate on group supervision as a method of supervision in its own right, which we think has much to commend it, even though it is not currently widely practised.

For readers wanting to study teams and teamwork in more depth there are several useful publications, most of which were written in the decade following the creation of the post-Seebohm SSDs in the early 1970s. Some of these books give special attention to teams in SSDs that were – and still are – the major employer of social workers and allied staff. Parsloe's book, *Social Services Area Teams* (1981), is one of those based on the extensive research into SSDs undertaken in the late 1970s by Stevenson *et al.* (1978), and it has many useful general points about teams that are applicable in any context. Payne and Scott's *Developing Supervision of Teams in Field and Residential Work* (1982) is a very clear exposition of the team/supervision link, with special attention being given to the residential context, where the supervision issues are in some respects different from those in fieldwork. They also published some exercises for use by staff groups wanting to assess and develop their supervision practice (Payne and Scott 1985). Two other useful publications – both with many exercises on assessing a team and team-building – are Woodcock's *Team Development Manual* (1979) and Dyer's *Team Building* (1977). Hawkins and Shohet's (1989) book *Supervision in the Helping Professions* also has many useful ideas for working in teams.

We need at this point to recognise that supervisors vary in their organisational relationship to the team(s) to which supervisees belong, and this will affect the interplay between one-to-one supervision and team dynamics. In most fieldwork settings, the supervisor is also the team manager, and thus in a direct and powerful relationship with team members, all of whom are likely to be under her or his supervision. By contrast, in some settings (notably many residential units and day centres) managers delegate supervisory responsibilities to other senior staff who are not team managers. The significance for supervision of the differences between having a supervisor who is, or is not, also your team manager will become clearer as the chapter develops. Notwithstanding this variation in supervisors' powers outside supervision, we think it is important for all supervisors to have a good understanding of groups, teams and team dynamics.

What is a team?

The term 'team' is used in several different ways. The main distinction is between those who use it qualitatively to describe a group of people who work together closely as a cohesive group ('working as a team'), and those who use it administratively to describe the membership of an identifiable work unit. We are adopting the latter administrative usage partly because it seems to be the way most people in social work and community care refer to teams, and partly because it is less problematic to define. We also favour thinking of teams as relatively small work units of up to about 12 people.

It is essential that whatever supervision arrangements are made, they are in tune with the varying needs of different kinds of teams and the people in them. Firstly, there are the very significant contextual differences relating to the type of agency, setting, worker, and service user. For example, the team issues in an SSD residential unit for older people are likely to be very different in some respects from those in a small voluntary community agency.

Secondly, there are the internal variations in patterns of team functioning and relationships, and it is to these that we now turn.

Ways of classifying and thinking about teams

Writers about teams have produced a number of different ways of classifying them. One of the best known of these, developed by Webb and Hobdell (1980), is based on the sporting analogy of a continuum including football, tennis and athletics teams. In football teams, members have different roles but share many common skills and are interacting and working together all the time. By contrast, in athletics teams, skills are much more diverse (the sprinter and the shot-putter). Apart from relays, each individual mostly performs independently of team colleagues. Teams in the personal social services similarly vary in the degree of interdependence of members, and of homogeneity of task and skills.

Another model was developed by Parsloe (1981: 41), suggesting a continuum of teams ranging from an individualistic to a collective orientation. She identified some key indicators including: how work is allocated (team manager or team meeting?); how new staff are appointed (are current team members involved or is it all determined centrally?); what social work methods are used; how much team members actually work together; and, most relevantly for us, is supervision undertaken primarily on an individual or group basis?

Building on the ideas of these writers and others, we have identified the *task* and the *process* dimensions of teams as a way of thinking about how any particular team functions.

Task dimensions

Two basic task dimensions are:

• degree of interdependence of team members
• degree of difference in formal power between team members.

For both of these dimensions, three different levels can be identified on a continuum from high to low.

Team member interdependence

Integrated: All team members work together on a common task in such a way that the effectiveness of each team member is dependent on that of their colleagues (e.g. a small residential unit for drug abusers). We refer to this as an *integrated* team.

Collaborative: Each team member carries their own workload, although parts of that workload may be shared with different colleagues. A significant amount of collaboration is involved between members, but this tends to occur in clusters rather than as a whole team (e.g. a child care locality team). We refer to this as a *collaborative* team.

Independent: Team members work individually with little or no collaboration between them. Indeed they may only constitute a team inasmuch as they share the same line manager, attend the same supervision group, or work in the same office. (e.g. volunteers in some counselling agencies). We refer to this as an *independent* team.

Differences in formal power

Hierarchical: Team members vary considerably in their formal position or grade and/or their degree of seniority. ('Seniority' is used here to refer to longevity as a team member, or having some special status). Whilst all are ultimately accountable to the team manager, each staff member is placed in a chain of command. Supervision may be cascaded through several levels (e.g. team leader supervises deputy team leader, deputy team leader supervises senior project workers, senior project workers supervise project workers). We refer to this as a *hierarchical* team.

Deputised: Some differentiation exists between members either by grade, role or seniority, but all are directly accountable to the team manager. There may be a team leader and a deputy, each of whom supervises other team members, but most of the team are of equal status. We refer to this as a *deputised* team.

Flattened: All members are of equal status with no formal differences between them, and all are directly accountable to the same team manager. (e.g. a small team of qualified community workers with the same team leader in a voluntary agency). We refer to this as a *flattened* team.

When combined, these two dimensions produce nine kinds of teams as shown in Table 8.1. Furthermore, by using our classification system, each team can be referred to by type (e.g. a flattened-independent team, a deputised-collaborative team etc.) We give three examples and readers may be interested to consider which of the nine approximates most closely to their own team.

An important third task dimension will be the degree to which, at the one extreme, all team members share a common task (e.g. counselling), or at the other, have different task specialisms (e.g. groupworkers, administrators and ancillary staff in the same team).

Process dimensions

Although more difficult to classify, it is the process dimension that will provide the richness for our understanding of team dynamics. There is inevitably some correlation with the interdependence levels because the more interdependent workers are in carrying out their task, the more likely they are to develop personal ties with each other. Where the roles of team manager and supervisor coincide, we need also to consider the supervisor's own orientation on team process indicators, as this will inevitably affect the supervisory relationship.

Process indicators fall into three clusters:

1 the amount and quality of interaction that occurs between supervisees – and between them and their supervisor – in their work e.g. in team meetings, joint working, training events, and so on
2 the extent to which the team acts as a group in its relations with others. For example, do they send joint letters to senior management, other agencies, the press? Do they attend some meetings and events as a group? When the team acts 'as one' is the supervisor included or excluded?
3 the extent of social and personal relationships between team members. How much social time do team members spend in each others company?

Table 8.1 Types of team classified on two dimensions

		Degree of formal power differences		
		Flattened	Deputised	Hierarchical
Degree of team member inter-dependence	Independent	A fieldwork team who only meet for group supervision. There are no status or role differences, other than that of the supervisor, and each has a discrete individual caseload.		
	Collaborative		A resource centre team, where some supervision is delegated, but most team members are of equal status. Staff work both individually and collectively at different times and in different configurations.	
	Integrated			A residential unit with staff occupying different positions along the hierarchy. All need to work in a highly interdependent way with the resident group.

How much do they share with each other of their personal lives? Are there close friendships in pairs or subgroups? How sexualised are team relationships? And to what extent, if at all, is the supervisor involved in any of these personal/social aspects of team relationships?

Supervision and organisational behaviour are often discussed as though they are all about a rational approach to carrying out the task. In reality, what happens in supervision will be profoundly affected by whether the supervisee and supervisor like each other; whether they have developed a social relationship; the fact that they are sexual beings (see Hearn *et al.* 1989); and by the role relationships the supervisor has, and is known to have, with other supervisees in the team.

The team's external relations

There is one other important dimension by which teams can be differentiated, and that can be a major influence on supervision. That is the extent to which they have an active external relationship with their surrounding community or neighbourhood. Payne's classification (1979: 150, referred to in Parsloe 1981: 35) of 'traditional', 'transitional' and 'community' teams addresses this dimension. Payne (1979) defines the 'traditional' team as having minimum community involvement; the 'transitional' team as active in a network of local agencies and with some contact with the local community; and the 'community' team as when 'social workers are involved in a network which can be described as part of the community support system' (p. 151).

Whilst the 'community' team is a model favoured by some voluntary community groups, Payne's idea was seemingly well ahead of its time, certainly so far as statutory agencies were concerned. However, the recent emphasis on partnership, empowerment and self-advocacy in the Children Act (Department of Health 1989) and the National Health Service and Community Care Act (Department of Health 1990), together with the purchaser–provider split and the emphasis on anti-oppressive ways of working all suggest and probably require a much closer relationship between teams and the community networks of the users of their services.

This community model has far-reaching implications for the approach taken to supervision. It extends the accountability of a team, and of a team manager, beyond individual service users to whole communities, whether geographical (the local neighbourhood) or of common interest (for example a local Vietnamese community). It highlights the tensions between the bureaucratic vertical structure of a large statutory agency and the horizontal alignment with local community interests. It also requires the team members to work together very closely to ensure consistency in their external relationships. For example, when working with individual Vietnamese families, the team needs to have a clear policy on whether, when and how to involve Vietnamese community leaders. If one worker liaises closely with them, and another worker does not, obvious difficulties may result. This has important implications for the content as well as the structure of supervision, and points to the need to set individual supervision arrangements and content in the wider community context.

Multidisciplinary teams

There has been some social worker involvement in multidisciplinary and interagency teams for many years: for example, in health settings (hospitals, child guidance clinics, 'community mental handicap' and mental health teams), and in criminal justice settings (prisons, juvenile justice bureaux). There have also been many situations where although no formalised interagency team exists, it is crucial that the principal workers on a case work closely together as a team.

The lesson from child abuse inquiries is clear: many of the tragedies arose in part because of poor communication between different professionals – within the same agency, and from different agencies – who were working with the same family. Many professionals have much to learn about working with colleagues from other agencies as members of a team – whether or not formally constituted – as distinct from liaising together. Their capacity to do this depends to a considerable degree on the type of relationship established between agencies at senior management level.

The implementation of the NHS and Community Care Act especially, and to some extent the new developments in child care and probation, will mean social workers being involved much more extensively in work groups with colleagues from other disciplines, departments, agencies and professions. This has many implications for new patterns of supervision, and the need for supervisors in the different agencies to be working together closely to establish clear lines of accountability. When more than one supervisor is involved with the same supervisee there is, at best, the potential for confusion and conflict of loyalties; at worst, it can result in destructive splitting and games-playing. In these two-supervisor situations it can be helpful to have an agreement that one is the primary supervisor, rather like the key worker or care manager in social work practice.

Before discussing the significance that team group dynamics can have for supervision agendas, issues and responses, we need to be aware of two important aspects of context. One is the variation in number and type of team meetings. This can vary from the one extreme of teams that only ever meet for periodic administrative purposes, to the other extreme of those that seem to meet virtually all the time to discuss everything conceivably affecting their work together. We are not advocating either of these extremes, but making the point that the agenda for individual supervision sessions will be very different according to what is or is not covered in team meetings, including group supervision (see Chapter 9)

The other aspect, which we shall now consider, is the different kinds of supervision arrangements used.

Different formats for supervision

Several supervision options are possible within the team context, and can be used singly or in combination, thus offering a degree of flexibility and variation.

The one-to-one meeting

This is the traditional model, sometimes referred to as 'tutorial', of the supervisor meeting with the supervisee individually. As discussed in Chapter 5, the frequency, content and approach taken will vary greatly according to the experience and ability of the supervisee.

The one-to-two meeting

There are a range of situations and reasons that may influence a supervisor to decide to meet with two workers together. These may include situations where two supervisors share similar needs, where there may be a collaborative or co-working relationship, or where dictated by the time constraints placed on the supervisor. This could replace one-to-one supervision entirely, or more likely it will complement individual sessions.

Group supervision

The supervisor meets with all or some of the supervisees in a group, with or without concurrent individual meetings (see Chapter 9).

Cross-team supervision

In some circumstances, some aspects of supervision may be arranged with a supervisor other than the designated person. For example, the latter may not have the relevant expertise, say in groupwork or mental health, and may arrange for a colleague who does have it to supervise that part of the supervisee's work. When cross-team or dual supervision occurs everyone needs to be clear – as discussed above – how the agency accountability for that work is held between the two or more supervisors.

Consultation with a consultant

There will be circumstances when arrangements are made for individual team members to have consultation on some aspect of their work and/or personal/professional development with someone external to the agency. The difference between this and cross-team supervision is that agency accountability is not held by the consultant, and the supervisor has to negotiate some way of tying it into supervision. Again, the important thing is to have a clear agreement understood by all involved.

Peer consultation

This could be either in a tandem pair with a colleague, or in a group of colleagues, not necessarily from the same team or even from the same agency. Some experienced workers make their own arrangements to meet for this purpose. The supervision/management issues are whether these meetings are negotiated to be in work time, whether they complement or largely replace line supervision, and how they tie in with agency accountability.

The team as a group, and associated
supervision issues

Teams that do meet, whether more or less frequently, are small groups that have all the well-known features of group dynamics. We shall now discuss some aspects of group structure and group processes as they apply to teams, because they will have a profound influence on both supervision arrangements and efficacy. We have space here only to summarise key points, and readers interested to go deeper into groups and groupwork are referred to that literature (see, for example, Douglas 1983; Heap 1985; Whitaker 1985; Houston 1990b; Mullender and Ward 1991; Brown 1992; Shulman 1992). Although most of these books concentrate on groups for service users, the basic properties are similar whatever the task and membership. In other words, social work and social welfare staff are not significantly different from service users in their group behaviour.

The group as social microcosm

All small groups, and that includes all teams, are a social microcosm of the wider society of which they are a part (Shapiro 1990). As we saw in Chapter 3, this means that the power and status differentials between members are likely to replicate those prevalent in the social systems and institutions external to the group. For example, we know from research (Garvin and Reed 1983; Davis and Proctor 1989) that in mixed male/female groups the tendency is for men to dominate verbally. Also, often quite unconsciously, men may use the presence of women in a group to help them be more expressive in their behaviour. For example, a man may need the role model of a woman freely expressing her feelings before he is able to take what he experiences as the personal risk of attempting to do likewise himself. There may not be a quid pro quo advantage for the woman group member in this situation, which is one of the reasons why men tend to be more enthusiastic than women about mixed sex groups.

We know also that in multiracial groups with a minority black membership, racism is likely to occur, marginalising the black members and their contribution to the group. We are not implying that all mixed sex and multiracial teams will necessarily behave in this way. For example, in teams with a predominantly female or black membership the dynamic is likely to be different. The tendency, however, will always be to replicate the sexism and racism – and similarly the discrimination experienced by other oppressed groups – of the wider society, unless the team manager and the team members work consciously, both in and out of supervision, to ensure they establish a team culture that is empowering for all members (see Brown and Mistry 1994).

We shall now consider some other group characteristics of teams that supervisors need to understand and respond to appropriately.

Team size and composition

Supervisors, and certainly those who are not team managers, will not usually have much direct control over the size and composition of teams. Established team managers may have rather more opportunity to be proactive with senior management and gradually influence these structural factors than will other supervisors. All will have to respond to the dynamic consequences of the size and composition of the teams to which their supervisees belong.

We have deliberately suggested teams as units of not more than about 12 people because when work groups get larger than that they become unwieldy, and cohesion is difficult to achieve and sustain. As size increases, participation becomes uneven with some (more often men) dominant, and others (more often women) finding it difficult to participate actively. Subgrouping is also more likely. Where there is scope to control the size of teams, six to ten members is an optimum range for a good working group. What supervisors need to remember is that some individuals are more likely to become isolated in larger teams and may need extra support in supervision.

Whatever its size, the composition of the membership of a team, as readers will know from their own experience, has a profound effect on group dynamics and group cohesion. The ideal composition will include a good balance of ethnicity, gender, age and experience, with no one too different from at least one other member, and a diverse blend of compatible personalities. In the real world this is unlikely; a team may end up at least for a while with, say, only one black member or only one man. The implication of this for supervision with the 'singleton' team member is to encourage them to share their team experience in supervision, to be alert to the possibility of isolation, stereotyping or scapegoating, and to discuss with them possible external sources of support if they would like it – for example, in a black workers' group and/or from a black consultant. The team manager can also create opportunities for the team as a whole to discuss how they are all relating and working together.

Stages of group/team development

The groupwork literature is replete with various descriptions of the stages of development through which a group may pass, perhaps the best known being Tuckman's linear model of 'forming, storming, norming, performing and adjourning' (Tuckman 1965; Tuckman and Jensen 1977). Another is the 'cyclical' model developed by Schutz (1958), which suggests a rotating preoccupation with inclusion, control and intimacy respectively.

Most of these models refer to closed groups with a set membership that does not change. Work groups/teams do of course have a changing membership: people come and people go, sometimes at frequent intervals, sometimes infrequently. These changes can be either disruptive or strengthening depending on the stage of development a team has reached (see Woodcock 1979), its openness to new ideas, and how the change affects the balance of relationship and power distribution in the group. Either way there is work for the team to do to mourn departing members and integrate new ones.

The team manager-supervisor has a key role to play in helping the team adjust to changes in membership, more so if there are several changes occurring close together, which for a cohesive team can be quite disorientating. It can feel as though something previously experienced as solid and safe suddenly becomes fragile and uncertain. Creating physical and psychological space for new members is necessary, and individual supervision has an important role to play. If however the problem is essentially a team/group problem, as when a long-established team does not fully accept a new member, then this can only be taken so far in supportive supervision with the individual, and needs to be dealt with in team meetings or group supervision.

Henry's paper on open groups (1988) provides a useful framework for thinking about how changes in team membership might be managed. Collective teams, which are strong on mutual interaction and members' concern for one another, are likely to take more responsibility for welcoming and integrating new members than those that are more individualistic in style. In the latter case the burden falls more on the supervisor, and the team will do little for the integration of the newcomer. It is worth noting in passing that this is an example of the potential gains for the supervisor and the supervisee of facilitating peer strength and support in the team.

Team manager-supervisor as group leader

For the team manager-supervisor, there is a fundamental question: 'what kind of supervisory relationship would I like to establish with the team collectively, and with each member individually?' The second question is 'to what extent will team members allow me to be the kind of supervisor I want to be?' In Chapter 3 we examined in some detail the ways in which issues of power, prejudice and identity can have a profound impact on both the collective and individual supervisory relationship. For example, when a new black team manager replaces their white predecessor as supervisor of an all-white team, the fact that they are black will sometimes be a major factor in the initial perceptions and expectations. It may take some time, and some open honest communication from both sides before preconceptions disappear, and she or he becomes valued for their competence and skills as a manager and supervisor, as well as for their personal qualities.

The supervisory relationship in the team context can also be drastically altered by the other roles the supervisor carries, as Illustration 8.1 shows.

Illustration 8.1

One team manager, whilst not fudging his managerial role, had developed a close mutually supportive relationship with the team as a group, and individually with each member, both in and out of supervision. Then a situation arose in which he had to take disciplinary action against one team member. Immediately nearly all the team members sided with their colleague as 'victim' against the team manager who was isolated as 'persecutor'. Overnight his position changed from being viewed as 'one of us' to being 'one of them'. At the same time his identification with his line manager and his other reference group, management, was strengthened as he sought and obtained their support for the disciplinary action. This inevitably changed his supervisory relationship with all team members for some time.

A situation like this can be very painful for all concerned, but it does provide an opportunity for the manager-supervisor to define their role. They have the opportunity to respond in a way that demonstrates that they do not intend to be captured by either senior management or the team. In individual and group supervision – with the person being disciplined, and with the other team members – open and honest expression of feelings about what has happened can be encouraged, avoiding the pressure to become either the ruthless bureaucrat who does not care, or to make inappropriate reparation to the team to try and get close to them again.

The above example touches on the leadership style adopted by the team manager-supervisor, and the distance versus intimacy issue. Supervisors vary from remote figures, clearly not of the group, to those who choose to be very close to team members, virtually denying their distinct role position. Neither of these extremes is satisfactory. Conn's small-scale study (1993) lends some confirmation to the view that women supervisors are more likely to emphasise intimacy, and men to emphasise distance. If this is so, it suggests an agenda for some masculine-orientated (not always the same as male) supervisors of working at getting closer to the team and supervisees individually. For some feminine-orientated (not always the same as female) supervisors it suggests working at maintaining sufficient distance commensurate with their managerial role.

For non-manager-supervisors the distance versus intimacy balance may be more problematic. Whereas the authority role of the manager-supervisor outside supervision is clear, that of the non-manager-supervisor may be much less so. Similarly, the role relationship of the latter with non-supervisee team members may be unclear. This underlines the importance for all concerned of seeking clarification of exactly where they stand.

Roles in the team

We can say with some certainty that in every team, whether or not task roles are differentiated, psychological roles will be. For example, there is sometimes a scapegoat in a team, the one who is regarded as different and who functions, perhaps with their own connivance, as a convenient receptacle into which others can project their 'bad' feelings. The person may or may not be a 'singleton' member (for example, the only black, male, lesbian/gay, or long-serving member of the team), though team members in this situation often attract an exaggerated positive or negative reputation.

When scapegoating does occur in a team, overall work effectiveness is likely to be reduced. The supervisor who is also team leader has a special responsibility – along with the team as a whole – to try to and resolve the issue. The pressure on the supervisor is often either to collude with the rest of the team by reinforcing the scapegoating of the individual, or alternatively getting into a position of protecting that person against the rest. Neither of these positions is likely to be helpful, because they both reinforce rather than resolve that member's isolation and the way they are being used by the group.

There are various strategies that can be adopted to try and resolve scapegoating, and in our view a dual approach combining action in both individual supervision *and* at team meetings is to be preferred. The reason for this dual approach is that whilst the group is the optimum place for resolving what is essentially a group problem, the individuals involved – especially the scapegoated person – face various pressures needing personal attention. Supervision offers the supervisee an opportunity not only to get support and to express their feelings, but also to be helped to look at their own contribution to the dynamic, and what they personally might be able to do about it.

In the team group context, the direct explicit approach of making the scapegoating part of team business for open discussion is often to be preferred. One possible outcome the supervisor needs to be prepared for is the redirecting of the scapegoating towards him or her as an unconscious retaliation for having brought it out in the open and upset the *status quo*. If the supervisor is enmeshed as part of the problem, as distinct from being the receptacle for the feelings of others, there could be a case for the team seeking the assistance of an external facilitator. (See Shulman 1992 and Brown 1992 for a more detailed treatment, within a systems perspective, of dysfunctional individual roles in groups, and suggestions for strategies to try and resolve the group dynamic.)

An interesting and quite common role in groups is that of 'internal leader' (Shulman 1992), the team member who is regarded by others as the one they look to be their leader and perhaps their representative. This role is not to be confused with that of monopoliser, which is dysfunctional for the group. The genuine internal leader can be an asset to a team, especially if the other members are not overreliant on them. This can, however, be a potentially threatening situation for an insecure team manager-supervisor. If the person is really challenging their leadership they may be justified in feeling threatened and seek to do something about it. On the other hand, if the internal leader is a powerful positive influence in the team, empowering rather than diminishing colleagues, the supervisor would be well advised to form an unofficial alliance with him or her. This may include suitable support of that team member's contributions, both in supervision and in team meetings. This is another example of the importance of the supervisor and the team thinking constantly of the sum total of resources they collectively possess for carrying out their task.

As this discussion of team dynamics and the role of the manager-supervisor develops, the importance of establishing an optimum framework for supervision at team level becomes ever-clearer.

Supervisee rivalries

We start this section with a distant but vivid memory for one of us.

Illustration 8.2

Allan remembers one of his own student placements when he and another student colleague – pseudonym Jean – were paired with the same supervisor in a family agency. Supervision was sometimes together, more often separately, and always demanding. At the end of the course, of all the social work students in that year group, Jean, his 'sibling' in the supervisory pair, was the only one who was awarded a distinction for her practice. Allan remembers to this day having had strong irrational feelings of envy that 'father' had favoured his 'sister' and rated her as better than him, even though rationally it was a very appropriate judgement of an extremely able student colleague.

The point of this anecdote is to highlight the competitive feelings (often deriving from childhood experiences and/or social oppressions) that can be generated in team members, by the power and authority – real and imagined – that their shared supervisor has over them. Take the example of a young white woman manager-supervisor who is the mother of two young children, and whose team is multiracial, mixed sex and mixed age. Almost whatever she does, feelings may be generated that she favours white team members or black team members, or men or women, or older or younger team members, and so on. There may be all kinds of fantasies about what happens in other people's supervision and whether they are treated more or less favourably. This is particularly likely in an individualistic, 'athletics' type of team, with all supervision in private one-to-one sessions, very few team meetings, and not much interaction or communication between team members.

The kind of dynamic posited above may occur even with the most fair-handed, warm and able supervisor who works in an equally concerned, committed and anti-oppressive way with all her supervisees. In reality, such paragons are rather rare. Most of us have biases and preferences about different sorts of people; the issue is what we do about it. The young white woman supervisor in the above example will almost inevitably have different levels of empathic feeling for different supervisees. She may perhaps identify most closely with the other young mothers in the team, because of shared experience and struggle. On the other hand, she may actually prefer her supervision sessions with an older member of the team who is very experienced and offers her good support. To prefer being with some supervisees more than others is to be a normal human being, and not a cause for guilt or for overcompensation by giving the favoured ones a hard time. This is the sort of issue on which the supervisor's supervisor may be able to offer consultation – provided, of course, that the same dynamic is not also being replicated in that relationship.

When there is continuing difficulty in a relationship with a particular supervisee, it should not be allowed to drift. Not only will it reduce the benefit of supervision and perhaps the quality of practice, but it is also likely to produce ripples in the team and the other supervision relationships. The dynamics of some typical relationship difficulties are illustrated with examples in Chapter 6, many of them demonstrating that there is a crucial team dimension to both the problem and the resolution.

External influences

The discussion so far has considered relationship issues in the team as though it was a closed unit. In reality, team and supervision dynamics will also be influenced by many external pressures, in particular by the stresses arising from the work with service users. For example, working with abusing men may resonate in stressed male–female relations within the team; a racist incident in the locality may resonate in strained black–white relations in the team; working with people who have severe illnesses and those who are dying may resonate with feelings of impermanence, inclusion/exclusion and loss among team members. In Chapter 6 we included an example of the parallel process that can occur when service users' issues are mirrored in the supervision relationship, and this can extend to the whole team dynamic (see Shulman 1993 for further examples).

As we also suggested in Chapter 6, a systems framework provides a useful basis for trying to disentangle where the source of a problem really lies. Sometimes it will be with both the individual supervisee and the team, and be at least partially imported from other systems such as the agency, the locality, service users, or team members' personal lives. Although the issues will still probably have to be dealt with partially at team level and in supervision, systems under-standing does help to set them in an interactional context.

A team focus for resolving issues

As will be apparent from the perspective taken in this chapter, we favour a collective team approach for both task and relationship reasons. It creates a framework for making the best use of the combined resources of the team; it offers a source of support and strength for stressed team members; and it is a suitable arena for trying to resolve difficulties that may arise. It also frees up individual supervision to concentrate on matters that are properly per-sonal to the supervisee and their work, leaving other matters to be dealt with at team level.

However, the team approach has to be worked at over a period of time to be successful. Much effort and skill is required, particularly from the team leader, to create the necessary climate of trust and confidence. The most difficult situations for the team leader/supervisor to resolve are those in which they personally are integral to the problem. In those circumstances, the help of a consultant external to the team may be needed. A paradox here is that the very circumstances that require external help are often those making it the least likely that it will be sought – and conversely. This brings us to our final topic in this chapter on teams, the need for training in teamwork and team/group leadership.

Training for teamwork

It will be evident from the content and perspective of this chapter that group leadership/facilitation skills are an essential resource for a supervisor who is also the manager. Social work and other qualifying courses vary considerably in the extent to which students are adequately trained in groupwork skills. By 'adequately' we mean not only theoretical understanding of group pro-cesses, but also experiential learning about group membership and group leadership at a personal feelings level, and some experience of working with people in groups. These elements need combining so that thinking and feeling about what is happening in groups/teams occur simultaneously. Although groups may be frightening at times, training should enable supervisors to feel sufficiently comfortable and confident to make full use of the group's rich resources; both for empowering team members, and resolution of difficulties within the team, and with the supervisor themselves.

Supervisors vary greatly in the extent to which their prior training and work experiences will have equipped them with the necessary group skills. We would argue that for those who have not yet developed these skills sufficiently, group training should be regarded as a high priority in any modular training programme. This is not to say that effective teamwork depends solely on having a team manager who is a skilled group facilitator – clearly there is responsibility also on team members to exercise their group skills – but it is a great asset.

There is also a specific need for training in teamwork, and much of this can be done by the team itself, including the team manager. One device is the team away day when the whole team goes to some suitable venue to work together on team tasks and team dynamics. This is also a suitable context for working together on the format and pattern of supervision arrangements, and how they tie in with team-based meetings, management, and other functions.

With careful planning and preparation, do-it-yourself team building can work well (see Hawkins and Shohet 1989 for many useful ideas). However, when the issues are difficult, and particularly if they are about team relationships, a consultant who is outside the 'stuck' system will be needed. Dyer (1977) has some useful checklists for determining whether a team is likely to need an external consultant, one criterion being the extent to which the team leader is central to the problem.

Conclusion

To conclude this chapter on teams, we need to share one of our concerns about the contemporary emphasis on task and outcomes in social work and social welfare. We think that one consequence of this trend is a relegation of the importance of process, resulting in less emphasis being placed on the importance of effective cohesive teamwork in quality service to users. Supervisors need to be skilled in working with groups and sensitive to the systems implications of one-to-one supervision relationships with individual supervisees. The feelings generated when a small group of people are under the formal authority of their shared manager are often strong, and frequently in part irrational, triggered by past experiences of other powerful authority figures. The supervisor needs to be able to understand these processes – and their own part in them – and to work openly with supervisees, both individually, and as a group.

Group supervision

While supervision is most often carried out on an individual basis, the possibilities and the potential for conducting it on a group basis are enormous. Group supervision is largely uncharted territory looking for pioneers. We have no answers, recipes, guides or maps, but hope that you can join us in attempting to discover an approach to supervision that could well become the norm, rather than the exception.

Group supervision is very much an umbrella term used to cover a broad range of activities. It is, however, discrete and different from the other commonly found group or team structures: business meetings, support meetings, planning meetings, training meetings and case review meetings. Group supervision can be defined most straightforwardly as the use of the group setting to implement part or all of the responsibilities of supervision. What this means in practice will become clearer as we go through the chapter.

In the absence of any substantial literature, this chapter rests largely on the experience of five teams involved in a recent study of group supervision over two years, carried out by Iain. We will look at, in turn:

- why each team chose to use group supervision
- how it was introduced
- the choices that they made about boundaries, tasks, structures, roles and facilitation
- the difficulties that they encountered.

The final part of the chapter will reconsider group supervision using the model introduced in Chapter 5, and end with consideration of the qualities of an effective group supervisor and some final thoughts on the advantages and disadvantages of group supervision.

Although much of this chapter is tentative and speculative, we hope that it stimulates your interest.

Why use group supervision?

It is no simple matter determining why one team should use group supervision and another not. As we shall see throughout the chapter, group supervision is both highly context-specific and context-sensitive. We can illustrate this by examining the motivation for introducing group supervision into the teams involved in Iain's study. In each case, while there were multiple reasons for taking this step, we have chosen to highlight only those that represented the decisive factors in their decision. The names given here are not necessarily those by which the actual projects are known.

Park Street Alcohol Advisory Service (AAS) provides a counselling service for people with alcohol- and drug-related problems, their relatives and for people seeking advice on sensible drinking. The counsellors were mostly volunteers, seeing two or three clients each week, while the supervisors were mostly paid staff. With the number of counsellors heavily outnumbering the supervisors, group supervision was the only way in which they could all be seen with sufficient frequency. There was, however, another very important role served by group supervision, and that was to provide the volunteer counsellors with a 'home' group through which they could identify with the project, and which to some degree would lessen their sense of isolation.

The *Moor Community* was a residential project for adults with mental health problems. The project manager was a powerful and charismatic woman, who had been with the team for some time. She felt, and this was echoed within the team, that she had become too central to the project. Introducing group supervision was seen as a means of developing the team, which would eventually flatten the hierarchy and minimise dependency. The staff dependency was also mirrored in the resident group, and it was hoped that by empowering the team, there would be parallel changes throughout the project.

Boarlands Children's Resource Centre (CRC) was developed in response to the 1989 Children Act, and aimed to provide a support to children and families living at home. It served a largely rural and dispersed catchment area. The team consisted of 16 social workers, who would work together in different configurations, at different times, for different purposes. Given this collaborative network arrangement and the size of the team, it was felt that group supervision might help pull it together, foster a sense of identity, provide support and facilitate future working relationships. In many ways this was a pioneering project, and it suited the ethos to be involved in pioneering new ways of providing supervision.

Gladwin Children's Resource Centre (CRC) was similar to the Boarland's team, except that the introduction of group supervision occurred right from the outset when the project was opened. The other difference was that it served a concentrated urban population. They saw that there would be a great need for the team to meet regularly as new programmes were being set up and implemented. Group supervision was, therefore, perceived as a means of facilitating and consolidating change. It was felt that through group discussion of individual cases, not only would an educational function be served, but through a mutual learning process, the team would be developed.

Broadstone Homefinding Team was a collection of senior and experienced social workers who had been moved to a new base, with a new manager, as part of an organisational restructuring. Prior to being brought together into a team, each practitioner worked largely on their own. The manager was an experienced child care practitioner, but not a homefinding specialist. Consequently, although she had responsibility for supervising the homefinders' work, she was not in a position to provide for all of their supervisory needs. Group supervision was seen as a way of maintaining the supervisory role, while using the group's expertise to provide the necessary specialist consultation. It also was seen as a way of addressing a concern that the degree of isolation faced by each worker could lead to an erosion of good practice.

The important point to note in each of the above cases is that group supervision was chosen not because it was felt to be better or worse than individual supervision, but because it addressed specific needs within the team. Indeed, with the exception of Park Street AAS, group supervision existed alongside individual supervision.

Introducing group supervision

If a team decides to introduce group supervision, the first steps will be crucial in shaping its future. In the research study, all team members met to talk about it first, allowing hopes and concerns to be expressed. The sense of ownership at the outset, however, varied considerably.

The *Broadstone Homefinders* saw group supervision as being imposed on them and as a threat, while the Moor Community welcomed it with open arms. The other teams were somewhere between the two extremes. Interestingly, looking across the sample, the more ownership the teams felt for the introduction of group supervision, the less structure was provided for the group sessions at the outset. Thus the Moor Community started with very little structure, while the Broadstone Homefinders had a very detailed agenda to follow. In this section we will review the experience of setting up group supervision and suggest some important issues to consider.

The *Moor Community* was a long-established team and had developed a collection of team meetings: a business meeting, a staff sensitivity meeting, a resident review meeting, handover meetings, plus a range of *ad hoc* meetings. Supervision had hitherto been conducted on an individual basis. This was seen as an anomaly, and was also felt to overemphasise the team's hierarchy. The team manager herself acknowledged this, and hoped that group supervision would both minimise her influence and allow the team to develop and become more autonomous. Group supervision was seen as a democratic and empowering process; initially there was a sense of great hope within the team. In setting up group supervision the team manager sought to be non-directive, and left it to the team to determine how it was to operate. The transition from a dependency on direction to the autonomy allowed by non-direction, however, proved to be too stark. Decisions were made, but these took little account of the prevailing dynamics within the team. Group members had a good sense of what kind of team they would like to be but lacked any plan or strategy for getting there. Given the absence of any one individual to give the group some leadership, a strong initial structure would have provided some of the needed direction. Instead, a minimal structure with minimal leadership was chosen – appropriate as an end point, but perhaps not as a starting point.

Boarlands CRC tackled the problem differently. The manager and deputy worked closely together, and unlike the Moor Community, there were fewer dynamic problems within the team, although certainly differences and tensions existed between members. The dual supervisors, rather than minimising their power and role, attempted to use it to empower the group. Prior to introducing group supervision, they met to work out a suitable strategy for its introduction. They began by using the first session as a workshop to involve the team from the start in determining what group supervision was to be and how it would operate. This was a great success, and mustered significant enthusiasm and hope within the team for the sessions that lay ahead.

At *Gladwin CRC*, group supervision was introduced at the same time as the centre was opened. The supervisor/team leader wanted group supervision to provide an opportunity both to learn about groupwork and to combine as a team around key practice issues; for the most part the team accepted this. Although there had been substantial planning around most areas of service delivery, at the point that group supervision was introduced, none of this had been tried. Working in uncharted territory, there were many immediate and practical needs. These effectively squeezed out opportunities to stand back from their work or to address the team's support needs, at least during the formative stages. The initial structure was largely abandoned and group supervision effectively became an extended planning meeting. Later, when some of the initial pressure receded, a support group was added.

At *Park St AAS*, with group supervision already established, the main issues were around introducing new supervisees into the groups. Meetings with the group supervisor outside the session went some way toward facilitating this process, although the process was largely carried out within the group. Typically the supervisor would welcome the new supervisee to the group, have them introduce themselves, and then each member of the group to them. After that the group would proceed much as before, but with the supervisor paying particular attention to including the new member. Within a small, supportive group, this worked well.

The experience of joining an established supervision group can be bewildering. The new supervisee may not be able see the group through the same filters as other members. On the one hand this allows them to notice aspects of the group that others may have unwittingly screened out. At the same time, however, there will be other aspects that, while internalised and understood by the rest of the supervision group, remain a mystery to the new supervisee. It can be helpful, therefore, if this is acknowledged and specific opportunities are allowed for the new supervisee to share openly both their observations and their puzzles about the group.

The introduction of a new member can also provide an invaluable opportunity for change and growth within a group. At Broadstone Homefinders, the introduction of a new member helped shift the balance from group belief that 'we are very busy social workers, we have no time for group supervision' to 'we are very busy social workers, we need the support from group supervision'. In this case the new member was very experienced and had the confidence to question the prevailing ideology in the group in a direct, open, but non-threatening way. If the new member is not in a position to question the group, then it can be helpful for the supervisor to suspend normal activities, perhaps for a session, and offer a structure that will enable the group to conduct a thorough review. This may not only facilitate the inclusion of the new member but also provide an opportunity to pick up on themes and dynamics rumbling beneath the surface. The management of membership change is a central issue in all open-ended groups. Galinsky and Schopler (1985) and Henry (1988) provide further reading on this subject.

In the Moor Community and Gladwin CRC we can see how easily group supervision can be diverted from its original aims, and how sensitive it is to the influence of team and agency dynamics. Park Street AAS and Broadstone Homefinders show the difficulties and opportunities inherent in introducing new members into the group. Boarlands CRC shows the importance of everyone being included, and the need for a structure to enable this. In the next section we review some of the preliminary questions that need to be addressed.

Choices

From the start, certain decisions need to be thought through. We believe that this is most effectively done by the supervisor providing a structure for the group to address these questions themselves. At Boarlands CRC, the group was divided into smaller subgroups, each with a different series of questions to address. Feedback to the larger group then helped focus further discussion and decision-making. So what might these questions be?

Boundaries

- How long should the group meet for, and how frequently?
- how firmly are time boundaries to be maintained?
- what is the group membership?
- is it open to students on placement, senior managers, administrative staff etc.?
- is attendance voluntary or compulsory?
- what are the rules about confidentiality?
- how is group supervision different from other team meetings and staff structures, for example, business meetings, support and sensitivity meetings, case reviews, planning meetings, team training, individual supervision, staff appraisals etc.?

Tasks

In different contexts, supervision will serve different tasks. It could include any, or all of those outlined below. The clearer the vision that group members have of what group supervision should look like, the more likely they will be able to share responsibility for its development. It can be helpful, therefore, in considering the tasks below, for the group to negotiate the relative weighting given to each:

• providing support to, and developing individual members (the worker dimension)
• providing practice consultation (the practice dimension)
• building and developing the group or team, exploring group issues (the team dimension)
• addressing agency issues, management, organisation, policy, decision-making (the agency dimension).

Structure

Although the structure of the group supervision sessions may well change over time, it is important at least to make some preliminary decisions. A clear negotiated structure can relieve the supervisor of some of the burden of guiding and directing the group while providing some safety for group members. Some choices include:

• use of time
• choice of content
• pattern of participation
• use of activities.

Roles

While the supervisor clearly has an important role within the group, parts of that role may be delegated to other members, including:

• time-keeping
• chairing the agenda, managing the structure
• facilitating the process.

If these are to be shared or delegated, it should be decided how this is to be done. This may be on the basis of interest, skill, seniority, on rotation etc.

Type of facilitation

What is it that is to be facilitated? It is easy to say 'everything', but inevitably people will have different expectations about where they see the relative emphasis of the facilitation. The group should decide if the facilitation is primarily geared toward:

• structure maintenance, e.g. keeping to the agenda, managing time etc.
• clarification of content, e.g. summarising and focusing the discussions etc.
• enabling the process, e.g. including participants, addressing interpersonal difficulties etc.

In terms of process facilitation, it is important to be clear who is supervising what:

- the supervision of individuals within a group/team setting by the supervisor
- the supervision of individuals by the group/team
- the supervision of the group/team as a whole by the supervisor
- the supervision of the group/team by themselves.

Again the choice may be one of relative emphasis, and that emphasis may change through the development of the group.

Methods

Compared to individual supervision, the group forum allows for a much wider use of methods. These may include the use of:

- group discussion
- working in smaller groups, triads, or dyads
- role-playing
- structured exercises and games
- projective exercises (e.g. sculpting, art work etc.)
- listening to audiotaped work
- video.

As we will see, however, in the following section (see group conservatism), unless it is fully clarified *how* these methods are to incorporated into the supervision group sessions and under what circumstances, many of the opportunities may be lost.

Difficulties in group supervision

The principles of good group supervision are no different from the principles of good groupwork generally. The task, power relations and accountability issues, however, give it its unique flavour. How these will be manifested within the supervision group depends on the interaction of the range of practice, worker, team, and agency influences highlighted later in this chapter. For the group supervisor, these influences can become hazardous if they are not anticipated and understood. While not wishing to dwell too much on the difficulties encountered in group supervision, it may be helpful to identify some of those encountered by our five teams. It is important to note, however, that had the teams had prior knowledge of some of these hazards, they might have been avoided.

Dynamics replayed

As we saw earlier with the Moor Community, group supervision can be seen as a means of developing a team. One of the dangers, however, is that the group is unable to break free from its pre-existing dynamics, and ends up simply replaying them within the supervision sessions. This is particularly likely where there is little clear group structure, insufficient direction, or little opportunity to stand back and review the group process. Our experience tells us that groups with a new task must start at the beginning, even if the same collection of people already operate as a group for a different purpose. This means introducing group supervision almost as if everyone is entirely new to groups and to one another. If the group has been working well together at different tasks previously this does not change the natural developmental process; it simply speeds it up.

Erosion of structure and the one-issue group

Having taken heed of the above warning, a group may well decide upon a structure only to abandon it almost instantly. A simple and common form of this is the use of an introductory round robin. At the beginning of the group each member is asked to highlight whatever issues they have for supervision. These are not supposed to be discussed until everyone has made their contribution. The anxiety experienced by the supervisor and group members at this stage of the group can be overwhelming. What if no one has anything to talk about? As a result, the first person to raise an issue is seized upon with some vigour both by the supervisor, who may simply be trying to clarify the issue presented, and by others in the group. The intensity is often such that this is the only issue discussed during the group, regardless of its importance. Afterwards, the person who presented the issue often feels jumped upon, others may feel frustrated, and the supervisor may feel that they lost sight of their role.

If this is an isolated occurrence, there are likely to be few long-term consequences. Should it become a pattern, there is more serious cause for concern. One possible line of inquiry might question whether the supervisor is taking on more roles for the group than is being helpful and is becoming confused in the process. If this is the case, then perhaps another group member could be asked to help maintain the structure, releasing the supervisor to concentrate their efforts on other aspects of the supervision group. Additionally, it may be helpful to clarify the structure as it is introduced, including the expectations held about how group members will use it.

Inverted supervision

Group supervision can be seen as an attempt to democratise the team and empower the staff who may be lower in the hierarchy. However, even when all members ascribe to such ideals, something quite different can occur. Iain observed in his study that while the least senior and experienced staff seemed to be the most in need of supervision, in group supervision it was generally the most experienced and senior staff that were most vocal and rated their involvement highest; in some cases this reached the point of the traditional supervisor–supervisee roles being reversed. Several explanations can be suggested, all of which may have some truth:

- the more senior staff often felt more responsibility for group supervision, and would talk almost to 'rescue it'
- some presented their own issues for supervision so as to model the effective use of supervision to more junior members, only to find themselves caught up in the one-issue groups identified earlier

- as staff become more senior within a team, there is often a reduction in the amount of supervision that they receive; thus group supervision may be seized upon with rather more urgency by them (in compensation for the lack of other supervision opportunities) than more junior team members
- the more experienced staff often had greater confidence in groups, and were therefore less inhibited and able to take risks; conversely junior and less experienced staff were less sure of themselves and how to make use of the group, and had greater fears about being negatively judged.

This is a factor that group supervisors need to take seriously if their best efforts are not to be unintentionally diverted. There are several ways in which this danger can be addressed. The first is through monitoring. At the end of each session all members could be asked to assess their level of involvement/participation, on a simple sliding scale. This would help pick up on any unhelpful trends before they become part of the group culture. Once identified, the next task could be to present the problem to the group, and to encourage them to think through why the pattern was emerging, and how it could be tackled. One way of ensuring the involvement of the more junior, less experienced or less confident members could be to structure the group in such a way that each has some protected time to address their own supervisory needs. If they find it difficult to make use of the space provided, this might be followed up in individual supervision, exploring the difficulties and identifying personal strategies for making effective use of group supervision.

Gender and involvement

While on the subject of involvement, gender issues need to be considered. The research literature consistently suggests that men tend to participate in mixed groups at the expense of women (see Brown and Mistry 1994 for further references and for discussion of some of the issues in mixed groups). Interestingly, in Iain's study, albeit with a very small sample, the trend was reversed; the male group members tended to be quieter and less dominant than female group members. There were, however, a number of factors that throw some light on this apparent anomaly. In the three teams where this was most apparent (Boarlands CRC, the Moor Community, and Broadstone Homefinders) the men were less senior, and all the supervisors were female. At Boarlands CRC and Broadstone Homefinders the men were also very much in the minority (two out of sixteen, and one out of six respectively). There is also some suggestion that the men, across the five teams, tended to be most vocal about content-specific, concrete and practical issues, and least vocal about generalised themes, affective and process issues.

Unfortunately the sample was too limited to make similar observations in relation to other inequalities and differences within the group membership. We think, however, that there will be a real but complex interaction between the power and affiliation dynamics within the group, and those that are prevalent within society. The extent to which the supervisor is able to facilitate the exploration of these dynamics is, therefore, likely to be crucial. One way of doing this might be to incorporate a review at appropriate intervals where group members are encouraged to identify the various differences within the group, and to consider any issues for the group that might arise from them.

Rebound sessions

Another feature of group supervision observed by Iain in his study is what he calls 'rebound sessions'. Often after a good session there is a sense of euphoria, which seems to raise expectations for sessions to follow. It is as if the group has made a significant breakthrough in its development. More often than would be predicted by chance, however, the following session, rather than capitalising on the success, turns out to be very disappointing. The evidence is only suggestive, but it seems that the rebound session tends to be as 'bad' as the previous session was 'good'. Perhaps the expectations were too high, or maybe everyone felt that they no longer had to put the effort into making sessions work. Alternatively, during the 'good' session, members may have felt that they had risked a great deal, and then, unconsciously, needed to hold back during the next session. Whatever the explanation, it is something to watch for, understand and minimise, so that it does not distract from the long-term development of the group.

There are no simple ways of preventing what is quite a common phenomenon in groups of all kinds, although a number of measures may be helpful should a pattern of rebound sessions develop. Bringing the phenomenon to the group's attention is an obvious first step. It might prove useful also to check at the end of each session just how much each member feels that they have risked, and whether their experience is likely to encourage or inhibit further risk taking. A further facilitative step might be to make a deliberate link between sessions, agreeing what had been useful at the end of each session, and clarifying how this might be developed next time. If this is written down and then used as a starting point for the next meeting, it might be possible to foster a sense of continuity.

Group conservatism

There is often a sense of excitement expressed by team members when discussing the introduction of group supervision, in particular about the potential for using and discovering new and creative ways of using the group. Many of the individuals involved in Iain's study were also actively involved in running and participating in all kinds of creative groupwork, both as part of their work, and personally. Indeed, one of the aspects of the study that excited Iain most was the opportunity to follow these groups as they broke new ground and invented new ways of using group supervision. Why was it, then, that over a two-year period covering five teams, there was only one isolated incidence of a group sculpt, with all other sessions being centred purely on discussion? Perhaps the work context makes people feel less safe to take risks, or maybe there is another reason to do with the culture of the team. It is worth noting, however, that whatever the reason, it can lead the group to deny its own creativity and potential.

Explicit agreement within the group contract about the use of a wide range of group methods is important, but by itself it may not be enough. What does have to be negotiated is how those methods are to be introduced, by whom, and under what circumstances. Individual supervision can also be helpful in thinking through how a particular piece of casework (for example) might be presented creatively in group supervision.

Clarity and the persistence of confusion

The importance of having clear ground rules regarding confidentiality, to which all members subscribe, is uncontroversial. There is a point, however, beyond which discussion serves no further direct purpose. This is not because the subject has been exhausted; indeed, one team in Iain's study managed to have such extensive discussions lasting over several two-hour sessions that they almost certainly were beginning to break new ground on the subject. It seems, however, that after such discussions have developed a certain distance, the only question to be answered is whether or not you trust the other people in the group. Further discussion on the subject may become an avoidance, a meaningless substitute activity that can block the group, often ending in exasperation. With the supervisor wishing to promote safety, such issues can feel hard to confront.

Another quest for clarity, usually expressed by someone asking 'what are we supposed to be doing?' featured in all the supervision groups, except Park Street AAS, even a year after the groups had been introduced. This clearly was not a sign of poor conceptual skills, nor poor recall. More likely it was a reflection of the inherent difficulty of differentiating group supervisory activity from activity in other staff groups. This may also help explain the lack of similar confusion at Park Street AAS, where there were no other groups.

In relation to this, it is worth noting that group supervision is often introduced on top of other team structures, almost as an afterthought. For it to find a discrete and clear role, therefore, there needs to be changes within those structures as well. If possible, the introduction of group supervision needs to be linked to a thorough review of all team and supervisory structures.

Vicarious supervision and the fermentation process

One of the principles upon which the effectiveness of group supervision is dependent is the ability of one supervisee to make vicarious use of the experience of another. Early in a group one member might describe a practice issue with which they are struggling, in the hope that others will help them explore it further. Often what happens, however, is that other group members hijack the material and begin to explore how *they* would respond to a similar issue with *their* client. Meanwhile, the member who initiated the discussion seems to take a back seat, apparently detached from the discussion. The interesting observation, however, is that while it may appear that the group has gone off course, time is being allowed for the member's problem to ferment. Often, much later in the group, perhaps well after the discussion

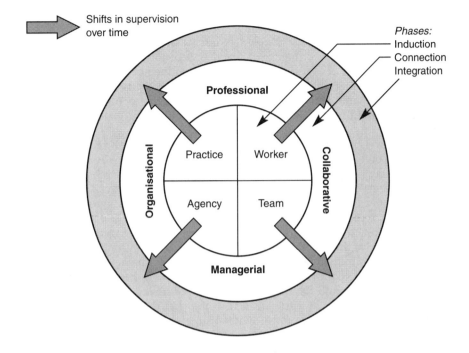

Figure 9.1 A model of supervision

has moved on, the presenter will return from their silence having developed a deeper understanding of the issue that they raised.

Group supervision, much more so than individual supervision, can allow individuals to withdraw, giving space for their ideas to ferment and find realisation. An important group supervisor skill is to be able to distinguish between supervisees who are fermenting, and those who have withdrawn for other reasons.

Influences on group supervision

Earlier we suggested that group supervision is highly context-specific and context-sensitive. It might be helpful if we now develop this theme further by considering how each of the major dimensions (worker, practice, team, agency) influence group supervision. We repeat here (Figure 9.1) the model of supervision discussed in Chapter 5.

Worker

If we start by considering homogeneous groups (i.e. where all supervisees are at the same or similar developmental level), we notice that in the induction phase, the importance of group supervision is at least twofold. The first is supportive, in the sense that through hearing the struggles of others and sharing their own, supervisees may feel less isolated and more able to gain a more balanced view of their own practice. Secondly, the group can act as a secondary source of experience, enabling group members to learn from the experience of others, thereby accelerating their own professional development. At the same time the new worker can begin to bridge the divide between their immediate concrete experiences and the general principles involved.

At this level, however, group supervision cannot meet all of the supervisor's or supervisee's needs. The supervisee's confidence may be very fragile, and they may not yet feel sufficiently confident to engage wholeheartedly in group supervision. Staff in the induction phase often have very specific and immediate needs that they may not find space to address in a group. Equally, the supervisor may not yet have sufficient knowledge of or confidence in the supervisee's practice. For both, there is an urgency to talk together about immediate practice that cannot be satisfied entirely within group sessions. It is likely that both individual and group supervision will be needed in tandem.

By the time the connection phase has been reached, the immediate supervisory concerns should have been thoroughly addressed. Assuming that the supervisee's practice is at least satisfactory and that their anxiety has abated, there becomes less urgency for individual supervisory meetings. During this phase, the supervisee will be making all kinds of connections between different parts of their practice: between practice and theory; between their experience, their practice, the team, and the agency. This can be a very exciting time; the supervisee may have a strong need to share their discoveries, and, unlike those in the induction phase, may also have the confidence to do so. Group supervision may overtake individual supervision in its relevance as the supervisee learns how to have their needs met. Unless group supervision is provided, there is a danger of individual supervision becoming stale and unchallenging. During this phase, individual supervision will serve several functions. The role of the supervisor will be akin to that of 'keyworker' – maintaining an overview of the supervisee, connecting them to sources of advice, consultation and support. It will also continue to be the venue for annual appraisals and performance reviews.

In the integration phase, we might expect the supervisees to be thinking about becoming supervisors or trainers themselves. During the early stages of this process they are likely to want to go back to individual supervision, both because they want unique advice on this process and because they can observe the supervisor, not as a model practitioner, but as a model supervisor. At the same time, group supervision can become a place to test personal theories and try out new roles to see how comfortable they are. For the group supervisor, this can be experienced as a challenge and a threat unless they understand the developmental processes involved.

The above scenarios, however, are oversimplified. Most supervision groups have a mixed membership, with some in each phase of development. This can lead to a phenomenon that we have called 'Inverted Supervision', whereby those people within the group that gain the most benefit are the most experienced and most senior, and those that gain the least are the least experienced and least senior. While there is no doubt that in individual supervision the supervisor's own interests can override the supervisee's needs, in groups the dynamic is quite different. This is discussed further later in the chapter.

Practice

Some of the key issues here are those of *isomorphism, parallelism,* and the choice of a supervision contract that includes the *use of immediacy.*

Isomorphism refers to a matching between the form of supervision and the form of practice. If the supervisee works mostly in groups, then there is a strong argument for being supervised in a group. This may not only sensitise the supervisee to the experience of being a group member, but also offer opportunities to observe and perhaps model the supervisor's behaviour. Likewise if they work individually, individual supervision offers similar opportunities.

The similarity in structure also allows direct *parallels* to be drawn between the experience in supervision and in practice, consciously or otherwise. This can work in three different ways. The first is when something that happens in group supervision resonates with a supervisee's own groupwork practice, and in so doing opens up a whole new arena for exploration and understanding.

Illustration 9.1

Ben comments that in the supervision group he gets very irritated when others give long rambling accounts of their cases. Mary asks if he is referring to her, which he acknowledges. This is pursued for a while, until the supervisor asks if there is anyone else that makes him feel like that. Ben then pauses, and says 'actually Usha's [a young client] mother talks endlessly about all kinds of trivia in family sessions, and I often end up shouting her down.' This provided a springboard for exploring that relationship further.

A second way is when talking about an example of groupwork practice acts as a metaphor for the group supervision process.

Illustration 9.2

Julie has been talking about some work with a group of young offenders. She describes herself as feeling left out and peripheral. She is concerned that the kids are beginning to compete for who had committed the worst offence. A further concern is that the group lacks safety because it is going too fast without having prepared its ground. Another member of the supervision group comments that 'it sounds rather like you're talking about us'. Earlier in this session some members, who had been absent the previous session, talked of feeling punished by the rest of the group and wondered whose crime was worse, theirs, or that of the punishers (competition for the worse crime). The punishment in this case was withholding information about what had been discussed in the previous session ('left out'). A further parallel was in relation to the group moving too fast. Previous group supervision sessions had been characterised by overcaution, and hence little movement. In this session the supervisor actively pressed the group to move on. Here the offenders group in an indirect way voices a fear that pushing ahead could mean the supervision going out of control.

The third way occurs when dynamics originating in the practice arena are unconsciously mimicked within the supervision group, most often by supervisees taking on the role of individuals in the practice group and arguing their case.

Illustration 9.3

Ade presented a group for supervision that he felt was dominated by two very vocal members at the expense of the other three, who were always silent. In turn, in the supervision group two members took up the theme with some gusto, to the exclusion of the rest of the group. After some time Ade noticed and commented that exactly the same was happening in the supervision group. This opened it out, and allowed the issue to be researched directly within the supervision group. The two vocal members owned that they had picked up that Ade was feeling very anxious and that they talked because they sensed he was uncomfortable with silence. The silent members were all silent for very different reasons, which challenged Ade's assumption that they had no space. Further discussion of the supervision group then led Ade to reconsider his ideas about the practice group.

The extent to which this source of information can be used directly will depend upon how explicitly *the use of immediacy* (drawing upon the immediate experience within the supervision session as a source of material for exploration) has been agreed in the supervision contract; the use of immediacy is more relevant where the supervisee's practice requires a deeper understanding of interpersonal processes.

Team

Teams can be described as either independent, collaborative, or integrated (i.e. having low, medium or high levels of interdependence; see Chapter 8). It could be argued that for integrated teams, such as those found in residential care, group supervision would be the method of choice. In such teams most of the work is shared, and it clearly makes sense for this work to be supervised together. As the team is the principal vehicle for service delivery, the importance of team development is heightened, and the relevance of group supervision becomes all the more apparent.

The force of such arguments, however, must be toned down because the similarity between the group supervision process and the team dynamic process can confuse the issue as well as throw light upon it. The Moor Community (residential) is a case in point. This was a highly integrated team for which the potential advantages of group supervision were obvious. There were opportunities for team building, addressing team dynamics, collaborative case work, collective decision making, giving and receiving support, learning about groupwork, and skills and knowledge sharing. Group supervision was potentially a panacea. Unfortunately, rather than resolving the difficulties within the team, it simply repeated them. The indecision, dependency and lack of adventure that were plaguing the team were played out repeatedly within the supervision group; group members mostly waited for someone else to take the lead; dominant members dominated, quieter members remained silent; when frustration led to action, the momentum was lost between sessions; experimentation in terms of using alternative group methods was often expressed, but never followed through; attendance was highly variable, even though compulsory. In addition, confusion reigned between the purpose, task and practice of group supervision, and the tasks and processes of other team meetings. Group supervision, in effect, became part of the problem rather than part of the solution.

Paradoxically, among the five teams in the study, there was an inverse relationship between the success of group supervision and the degree of team interdependence. The counselling service team had the fewest problems with group supervision, the residential team the most. The sample is much too small to generalise from, but perhaps we could speculate that there is an optimum gain that one could expect from group supervision; and that in attempting to realise too many of its potential advantages, there is a danger of realising none.

Agency

As we have already mentioned, in at least one of the teams (Park Street AAS), group supervision was dictated by the agency primarily on logistical grounds. The agency culture also plays a key role. Despite attempts to flatten hierarchies and reduce bureaucracy in social service departments, their size, accountability to the public, the legislative system and the government often works against this. One resource centre worker who had previously worked in statutory child care commented that she felt guilty when she attended group supervision – as if somehow the agency might catch her 'navel-gazing'. Indeed, such was the agency paranoia that in this team group supervision was divided into two parts; one for specific work issues, the other for more emotional personal and team issues. Both parts were meant to be included in the study, but the feeling was so strong that the agency might not approve, that only the 'safer' first part was audiotaped for the research.

In contrast, the voluntary agencies seemed much more group-orientated, and saw group supervision less as a luxury to feel embarrassed about and more as a necessary way of working. This was not only a reflection of the more democratic culture existing within these organisations, but also of the fact that they were less susceptible to public scrutiny.

The skilled group supervisor

Skilled group supervision does not come about by chance. It requires imagination, effort and skill in equal quantities, within a planned collaborative effort. The role of the group supervisor is complex and demanding, and primarily involves harnessing the power of the group to achieve its aims. If this is done successfully many of the advantages outlined earlier in the chapter may be realised. In this section we identify what we believe makes for a good group supervisor, and in doing so, are aware that we run the risk of setting up an unattainable ideal. We start by identifying those qualities and attributes that we see almost as preconditions for the group supervisor, and then identify those which turn a good group supervisor into an excellent one.

Essential qualities and attributes

The most significant precondition for the group supervisor is their own belief system. Unless they carry a personally felt conviction in the positive power and potential of groups then their efforts will be at best limited, and at worst destructive. A significant part of this conviction is the belief that group members have the capacity within them to change and develop, and that this is enabled through interaction with one another. The supervisor needs to enjoy being in groups, at least after some of the initial anxiety has abated, and feel excited and challenged by them; and to be able to model that within the group. All this adds up to a strong sense of commitment to group supervision, which needs to be backed up by a willingness to devote time for both planning and reviewing group sessions.

Supervisors must have trust and confidence in themselves and be able to invite the same in others. This involves demonstrating honesty and openness, together with warmth, empathy and a strong sense of fairness. Group supervision is only likely to be of benefit as long as it is purposeful, and that requires that the supervisor can maintain an overview of the purpose served by the various discussions and activities engaged in by the group. This does not mean that the supervisor must understand what is going on at every moment, which is clearly impossible. Rather, having clarified how the group is supposed to operate, and why, there will be times when it is difficult to determine whether the group is following a fruitful path or not. At such times, the important skill is to voice one's own confusion directly in order that the group can achieve this clarification for itself.

The good supervisor understands and accepts their own limitations. Rather than punishing themselves for not being perfect, they need to be able to delegate effectively within the group, and make good use of the many talents within it. Without the ability to do this, all the qualities and attributes that we have listed as desirable below suddenly become essential.

Desirable qualities and attributes

While we believe that all of these listed qualities are essential for good group supervision, as long as the supervisor can make good use of the resources within the group, it is not essential that they possess them all themselves. These include:

- taking both an individual and collective perspective, and relating each to the other
- attending to both process and content, and being able to link process with task
- keeping in mind the history of the group, and its developmental stage
- making appropriate and skilled interventions to facilitate exploration
- enabling the group to identify both what can be learnt generally from specific problems, and how general discussions can inform specific problems
- knowledge of, and ability to use appropriately, a wide range of group methods
- good boundary management (time, structure, supervisory task and purpose, focus and agenda etc.)
- an awareness of oneself, and of the dynamics operating within groups
- ensuring that all group members have equal opportunity to participate fully
- the ability to confront unhelpful or destructive behaviours, including those discriminatory or offensive to group members.

Advantages and disadvantages: an interim conclusion

The jury is still out on the merits of group supervision. While there are promising signs, the picture is rather more complicated than much of the existing literature suggests. In all probability it is neither better nor worse that individual supervision, simply different. In Table 9.1, we have gone as far as we can to identify the relative advantages and disadvantages of group supervision. It might be helpful to think through and weigh up these in relation to your own team, giving thought to how to foster advantages while reducing the effect of disadvantages.

Sales and Navarre (1970), is the most-quoted research comparing individual and group supervision – although their interest was in the fieldwork instruction of social work students. They found little difference in the overall effectiveness of the two methods, although those that had experienced group supervision were better at generalising learning and had a greater contextual awareness, while those experiencing individual supervision were better at case work with specific service users. They did, however, note that, all other things being equal, group supervision shows significant savings in supervisor's time.

We suspect that this time-economy argument may only hold true for settings, such as at Park Street, or in colleges, where the supervisors are vastly outnumbered by the supervisees. Elsewhere the argument becomes more complicated. Often, as we noted earlier, group supervision supplements rather than replaces individual supervision. This may, in effect, result in increased pressure on the supervisor's time. Furthermore, the demands of facilitating

Table 9.1 Advantages and disadvantages of group supervision

Advantages	Disadvantages
1 The opportunity to make use of a wider variety of learning experiences	1 To maintain relevance of discussions to the widest numbers, specific and urgent needs are often only discussed in generalised terms
2 The opportunity for supervisees to share their experiences	2 The group may stimulate sibling rivalry and peer competition that hinder the supervisory process
3 Emotional support from peers	
4 Safety in numbers	
5 Opportunity to compare and contrast own experiences and practices with others	3 It is more difficult to incorporate a new appointee into a supervisory group than to provide them with individual supervision
6 Can help foster team or group cohesion and identity	4 It is easier to hide and opt out of the responsibility to engage in exploration, problem-solving and decision-making
7 Opportunity for supervisor to see supervisees in a different kind of relationship	
8 Opportunity for supervisor to become aware of potential problems that derive from and relate to the unit/project/team	5 Greater opportunities for critical feedback, which can be inhibiting if confidence is lacking
9 Allows for responsibilities, functions and roles of the supervisory process to be separated and delegated among a number of people	6 The supervisor is more exposed and requires greater self-assurance than in individual supervision
10 Peer influence may make modification of behaviour more likely	7 Communications and interventions that assist one member may create problems for others
11 Supervisees can observe and learn from the supervisor, both directly and as a role model	8 While encouraging autonomy, the supervisor may find it more difficult to restore the focus should the group follow a non-productive route
12 Development of confidence and skills in groups may be transferable to work with service users	9 Supervisors will have to acquire or refresh their knowledge of group interaction, group dynamics, and individual behaviour in the group context
13 Allows a gradual step from dependence on the supervisor, through a lesser dependence on peers, to self-dependence	10 The supervisor must focus both on the individual and the group
14 Allows greater empowerment through lateral teaching, learning and support of peers	11 In highly cohesive groups, the pressure to conform to group thinking and attitudes can become counterproductive

the group, while ensuring the supervisory needs of individuals, can require substantially more time devoted to planning, preparing and reviewing sessions.

While we would strongly encourage the use of group supervision on a wider basis, we believe that the decision to do so should be based on a balanced consideration of all the advantages and disadvantages for a given setting, and not simply economy.

Conclusion

Group supervision is an approach with enormous potential and one that may become increasingly common in the future. For that potential to be harnessed and realised, however, its complexities demand careful consideration. As we hope we have shown, provided the supervisor is aware of some of the dangers, the complexities can be effectively managed. As more and more supervisors take the plunge, models will hopefully emerge to inform practice. For the time being, however, we are in pioneering territory.

Training and development

Introduction

By this stage of the book, some readers may understandably be comparing our emphasis on supervision as a highly skilled priority activity with a different reality they find in their agency. We are aware that in some settings supervision is given little importance, few resources, and an inadequate training and development infrastructure. We hope that this is not the norm, but think that it is not the exception either. However, the social work and community care scene is changing rapidly, and we believe that the trends point to supervision becoming more central in agencies in the contract culture. It is in our view essential that the supervision offered in this changing context is of the high quality we have proposed throughout the book. Let us first take stock of the current situation.

The world of social work, probation, social and community care is being transformed in the 1990s. Perhaps the greatest change is in the division between purchasers and providers of services, and the emphasis on needs-led assessment and user empowerment. The implications of these developments for supervision are profound. The former brings supervision into the arena of negotiation for provision and purchase of services. In this respect staff supervision is increasingly being used as a hallmark of quality service; purchasers will be looking for proof that such statements carry meaning. Meanwhile the changing emphasis towards user-led services will require reorientation of staff into new ways of approaching their task.

The second major feature of the changing work culture is the emphasis on quality assurance, staff appraisal and work competencies, epitomised in the rising prominence of NVQ assessments and qualifications. However, we believe that this development, particularly the centrality of staff appraisal systems, points to supervision as a pivotal function of increasing importance in both statutory and independent sector agencies in the future. There are many aspects of these contextual developments that are to be warmly welcomed.

We also have some anxieties that in a world dominated by competencies and outputs, the whole is in danger of being reduced to the sum of its parts. This makes it crucial that the matching infrastructure for the training and development of supervisors includes space for the feelings and relationship aspects that have been emphasised throughout this book.

Unfortunately the trends, which all point towards putting supervision in the centre of things in the coming years, are for the most part not being matched by the supportive infrastructure of training and development referred to above:

- there is no formal route or qualifications for the role of supervisor, unlike the quite recently introduced system of formal accreditation for agency practice teachers who supervise students (see below for more comment on this)
- relatively few agencies have clearly articulated detailed policies on supervision
- the typical training pattern is a series of *ad hoc*, free-standing short workshops or training events, which are not part of a comprehensive and coherent plan, and which a cynical supervisor might describe as a token gesture.

The aim of this chapter is to outline the elements of a comprehensive plan and programme for the adequate preparation of supervisors. Throughout this book we have had in mind particularly the needs of the recently appointed first-time supervisor, although set in the context of a developmental approach (see Chapter 2 and especially Chapter 5) that reflects on the supervisor's changing needs and changing response as they move through different phases in their career development.

This chapter is aimed particularly at three categories of staff:

- senior agency managers and policy makers, because these are the people with the position and power to give training for supervision the status and resources needed
- the trainers of supervisors, who carry responsibility for ensuring that high-quality comprehensive training and development programmes are provided
- supervisors themselves, whatever their career stage may be.

Some staff will be in all three categories. One of the fascinating things about supervision is that all supervisors are – or at least should be – also supervisees, which offers a very powerful and sobering source of user involvement when thinking about supervision and the necessary ingredients of training.

The remainder of the chapter has several major sections:

- agency policy on supervision and supervision training as a precondition for good practice
- a developmental career stage approach to supervision training
- the components of good quality training programmes for supervisors, both generic and specialist features.

Agency policy: preconditions for effective supervision

We cannot overstate the value of having a comprehensive agency policy on supervision. This section outlines the cornerstones of an effective policy – and provision.

A facilitative anti-oppressive agency culture

Agency culture is in some ways a more difficult concept to define than more tangible factors like organisational trees, competencies, output targets, resources and so on. It refers to atmosphere, attitudes, relationships, how people treat each other, what they feel about their work and how it is regarded by others. The most significant influence on culture is likely to be how power differences are regarded and managed in the agency. As outlined in Chapter 3, we are referring here to both power differences that derive from relative positions in a hierarchical organisation, and those which derive from different forms of social oppression.

It is ironic that at the very time that much official emphasis is being placed on concepts like anti-discrimination, equal opportunities and empowerment, many staff in agencies are feeling more disempowered than ever before. For supervision to be effective, not only does the supervision process itself have to be empowering, but equally the whole approach taken by the agency to its staff – at all levels – needs to be enabling, facilitative, confidence-building and anti-oppressive. Staff are not units of resource in the marketplace, they are human beings working in an organisation whose mission is to reduce suffering and disadvantage among human beings. Power differences there will be, but abuse of managerial and other forms of power is not only unacceptable, it will inevitably generate an agency culture of fear, disillusionment and often despair. It is indeed difficult for supervision to be effective in such a climate.

By contrast, an agency in which there is genuine equality of opportunity, in which discrimination and oppression are unacceptable, and in which the reality of managerial and supervisory power is used to strengthen staff and the quality of the work they do, is one in which supervision can fulfil all the functions outlined in Chapter 1 and throughout the book. Moreover it will be based on the values framework we also outlined in the first chapter. Readers interested in pursuing ideas about organisational culture in more depth are referred to the work of McLean and Marshall (1988) and Hawkins and Miller (1994).

A system of supervision integral to agency functioning and organisation

All agencies need to have clear and committed policies on staff supervision at all levels. This means that every member of staff, whatever their level in the organisation, is both entitled and required to receive regular good quality supervision. Naturally, the frequency and approach taken will vary considerably according to the task and the level of competence and experience of the person concerned.

Realistically, supervision will only occupy a central position in an agency if it has built into it certain required elements. This means, for example, having the qualitative aspects of the supervisor's work monitored regularly as part of the agency arrangements for accountability and quality control. An important way of getting information about quality would be to ask the supervisee to evaluate their own supervision service. In other words, it would no longer be possible to treat supervision only quantitatively. This means applying the same consumer-orientated principles to supervision that are now widely applied to service delivery.

Identified supervision competencies

If we are to talk about 'good' and 'effective' supervision, we need to be able to articulate what precisely that means, as we have attempted to do throughout this book. However, supervisors themselves and their trainers – not to mention the supervisees – are also entitled to know exactly what their agency expects from them. This means compiling a list of key competencies and the associated indicators regarded as the essential skills of the supervisor.

One useful attempt at compiling a 'checklist of supervision competencies, with performance indicators' is that developed by Richards *et al.* (1990: 93–102). Although written with a focus on staff supervision in child protection work, their framework is easily adaptable to supervision of work with other service user groups. They identify the three main functions as: ensuring that staff members can function, learn and develop; ensuring that the work process is supervised; and mediating between staff, higher management, outside agencies and the community being served. For each of these they list the relevant competencies and suggest indicators of those competencies. Feltham and Dryden (1994: 140–5, from Borders and Leddick 1987) have reproduced a list of competencies for counsellor supervision that are divided into three categories: conceptual skills and knowledge, direct intervention skills, and human skills. A combination of these lists would produce a fairly balanced expression of supervision competence to meet the needs of most readers.

We suggest that every supervisor be given, and have the opportunity to discuss, a list of the competencies and indicators they are expected to demonstrate, and which will be focused on in their training courses (see below).

Staff development policies

In all social service agencies, staff are likely to be the most valuable resource. A dynamic workforce who enjoy high levels of job satisfaction are likely to produce higher quality work, and certainly will have much lower absentee rates than dissatisfied, highly stressed staff (Pritchard 1986). It is, therefore, in the agency's interest as much as that of the staff themselves that the agency invests in a comprehensive staff development programme. Supervision has a central role to play in this process.

Quality assurance and staff appraisal should be as much about staff development as about monitoring staff performance. The two go hand in hand, but it is often the negative connotations of the latter that undermine confidence in the former.

The desirability of staff development is uncontroversial. The problems come when appraisal meetings in particular, and 'normal' supervision generally, identify learning needs of the supervisee that the agency is then not able to meet. Expectations may be raised only to be dashed. A staff development policy, therefore, needs to be linked to a well-resourced training programme with a range of in-house and external training events. This programme should be responsive to the needs and wishes of staff, so that both supervisees and supervisors can be proactive about what kind of provision is needed and not just reactive to the plans of others.

Although we have said that staff development and training needs to be well resourced, there is often scope for creative thinking about how to make the best use of the expertise that already resides in the agency.

Student supervision and the accreditation of practice teachers

As mentioned in Chapter 2 and elsewhere, many staff supervisors first experience being a supervisor when they work as practice teachers with students. The standard and status of practice-teaching has improved significantly with the advent of comprehensive training programmes for practice-teacher accreditation. Notwithstanding the crucial differences between staff and student supervision, the latter provides an excellent grounding in many of the skills of supervision outlined in this book. Thus there is a double gain for the agency in giving a high priority to student supervision: firstly it is an investment in well-qualified practitioners for the future, and secondly it provides excellent preparation for future staff supervision.

There is, however, one problem in this argument we see looming in the distance. Many agencies are finding the most efficient use of accredited practice teachers is to treat them as specialist practice teachers who take several students, with perhaps half their time allocated to this task. While there is much sense in this, it does mean that student supervision is concentrated on specialist staff who may or may not become staff supervisors in the future. Thus there may be a discontinuity in the training/expertise continuum we are suggesting. We do not have an easy answer to this potential problem, but it underlines once again the need to view supervision strategies in the wider agency context.

Innovation and creative use of resources

Agency policy on supervision needs to be based on a much wider vision than one-to-one meetings between supervisor and supervisee. That may be fine for certain bureaucratic organisations, but not for the professional staff of social work/social welfare agencies. There are various other complementary resources available to enrich supervision and staff development.

In Chapter 9 we discussed some of the potential advantages that different forms of group supervision can offer both supervisor and supervisee. This same peer learning dimension can be taken a stage further when peer consultancy groups of experienced workers are encouraged as a basis for professional development and improved quality of service delivery. We have talked about the need for supervisors to be supervised on their own supervisory practice. Given the limitations of traditional supervision structures for senior staff, group supervision for supervisors in larger agencies can be both an effective and empowering opportunity.

Another option of which we have some experience is inter-team supervision/consultancy when two teams – perhaps the staff of two hostels with a similar clientele – meet together to offer advice and learn from each other's experience. Specialist consultancy is a further option that may arise when the supervisor does not have a particular expertise, or when a supervisee would benefit from support from a colleague who experiences the same oppression e.g. as in Illustration 3 in Chapter 6.

Small agencies

We are aware that much of this section on agency policies has assumed that agencies are quite large organisations. Whilst this is true of most statutory agencies, it will not be true of many of the smaller voluntary and independent agencies that may be providers of services on contract to social services or probation departments. These small agencies also need clear policies on supervision and staff development. They need to be realistic about what training provision they can offer in-house, and what may need to be provided externally. Apart from the intrinsic importance of good quality supervision and training programmes, what is on offer may also be a crucial determinant of whether an agency gets contracts to provide specialist services. It is also likely to be a significant factor in the agency's ability to attract well-qualified staff, for whom supervision and opportunities for professional development may be key issues in whether or not they apply for the post.

A developmental approach to supervisor training

A comprehensive agency strategy and programme for supervision training requires a developmental approach. A career development continuum can be considered as having five distinct stages.

1 Student supervision

The CCETSW policy on the accreditation of practice teachers is having a major impact on the quality of student supervision in Britain. Two alternative routes are offered: the basic training, and the portfolio route. The former is a comprehensive 150-hours programme spread over a period of about six months, the key components of which are: supervised supervision of a student on a major placement; periods of theoretical and skills training; and required academic study. Space does not allow a detailed account of this training, and we suggest that interested readers could approach their regional practice learning centre for more information. The relevance to staff supervision is twofold: much of the training is excellent preparation for staff supervision at a later stage, and the training format offers pointers to staff supervision training programmes.

The portfolio route is a bridging arrangement for experienced student supervisors to gain accreditation on the basis of an evaluation of their previous student supervision work, plus some additional requirements. The analogy here is that when a comprehensive training programme is introduced for new supervisors, parallel arrangements need to be made for experienced supervisors who have had very little formal training for the task.

2 Pre-appointment training

New supervisors are usually appointed only a month or two before they take up the post. If it is part of a promotion to team manager, the person is making a major job change virtually overnight, quite possibly with no advance training or preparation. This highlights the need to have pre-appointment courses for experienced staff who are approaching the point when they are likely to assume supervisory responsibilities. It is in the agency's own interests to maximise the proportion of people going on these courses who will actually become a supervisor. For this reason, agencies are increasingly using staff appraisal evaluations to approve – formally or informally – someone as potentially suitable for a supervisor post. This then determines those who may go on pre-appointment courses.

While training courses at this stage cannot, by definition, include the course member's own experience as a staff supervisor, they can include several other important linked experiences. These include:

- for those who have experience of student supervision, an opportunity to reflect on and learn from perceived strengths and weaknesses as a practice teacher
- current experience as supervisee, reviewing what is found helpful and unhelpful, including the possibility of renegotiating the existing supervision contract
- conceptualising a core theoretical model for supervision (of the kind developed in Chapter 5)
- an examination of the transferability of the worker's current skills as a practitioner.

3 Training of new supervisors

Preparation of new supervisors is the central concern of this book, and in the next section we identify the key elements that need to be included in any training programme. Perhaps the most important task for a new supervisor is learning to take on the new role, and for this reason we think training is best organised in relatively homogeneous groups with others taking up similar roles. By this we mean not only training with other new supervisors, but also being with those doing comparable work, e.g. new supervisors of child care locality teams training together; new supervisors of staff in day centres for adults with learning disabilities training together; similarly for managers of hostels for offenders, and so on.

If training is being taken seriously, it will inevitably be a major call on the new supervisor's time during their first year in post. This requires agency management to ensure that suitable allowance is made in their workload. As we write this, we can imagine some senior managers rejecting our proposal as unrealistic. Yet, if supervision is to be a mainstream highly skilled activity, an infrastructure of support is essential. On the 150-hours training courses for practice teacher accreditation, a common complaint by practice teachers is that inadequate allowance is made by their agency for the time they need to undertake the course. We can understand – though not concur with – those agencies that do not regard student training as a high priority for their resources. However, we hope most would agree that a rigorous well-resourced training programme for new staff supervisors needs to be a high priority.

4 Training of established supervisors

Until major training programmes are available for all new supervisors, the training needs of established supervisors will depend in part on what sort of training they experienced when they first took on a supervisory role. They have the great advantage of being able to draw on their substantial hands-on experience, but the corresponding disadvantage is that supervisory habits die hard, and there may be some unlearning to do.

We think the experienced supervisor can benefit from a combination of specialist and generic training. The former enables the specifics of supervising particular activities to be taken to a more sophisticated level (for example, supervision of child abuse investigations), and the latter offers the opportunity to broaden horizons through learning with supervisors from across a wide spectrum of activity, including interagency training events. Peer learning is likely to be the core of training activity at this level. The possibilities for change may lie in the capacity of the training events to motivate the experienced supervisor to see change as building on existing strengths, rather than implying that they have been doing it all wrong over many years.

5 Training the trainers

If supervision is to become increasingly important as a means of ensuring quality within organisations, then there will be a need not only for more training but also for more trainers. In social service departments, the probation service and the larger voluntary organisations, this has been traditionally provided by their own training sections. At the time of writing, however, a rather different picture is unfolding. Many of these training sections are being cut back, with the residue restricted largely to a training management and purchasing role. Indeed, often even these responsibilities have been handed back to operational managers. This has always been the case for the smaller voluntary organisations who have had to buy in training from independent trainers or training agencies. There are certainly advantages to this arrangement, providing the training needs can be adequately identified, good trainers and consultants found and the costs realistically assessed. Many of the trainers and consultants, however, who are now successfully working independently learned their trade within an organisational training section. With that apprenticeship avenue rapidly closing up, it does pose a question about where the trainers for the future will come from.

At present, trainers who wish to specialise in supervision training have several *ad hoc* options. They can attend training courses or workshops led by acknowledged experts in the field, take notes, quiz the trainer, and repackage the material to suit their own style and purposes. Whilst this strategy is not exactly plagiarism, we would suggest that it is best approached as an open agenda with the trainer when applying for the course. It may also be possible to negotiate the possibility of an individual consultation. Alternatively there are some publications (e.g. Hawkins and Shohet 1989; Richards *et al.* 1990; Morrison 1993; and this one) that can be drawn on for ideas, though they cannot provide a ready-made training course package to suit a particular purpose. All the above options do of course assume that the would-be trainer already has an in-depth knowledge of supervision and general experience of a range of training methods.

The present arrangements for training social work supervisors are mostly unsatisfactory and inadequate. The problem is not so much finding trainers willing to provide supervision courses, but rather finding ways of ensuring quality control of what they have to offer. We hope that before long some positive developments will emerge, perhaps through one of the national bodies, the colleges, or regional consortia established to address the problem.

The elements of good training

There are a number of *generic* aspects that apply to training programmes for all supervisors. There are also some *specialist* aspects, deriving from the type of work and service users, the context and the particular social work methods being practised. We shall first consider some of the generic elements, and then illustrate the specialist elements with a few examples.

Generic elements

An anti-discriminatory/anti-oppressive approach

We have tried throughout this book – and especially in Chapter 3 – to establish a firm value base for supervision. We have made the point that the supervisor in supervision needs to role model the same standard of anti-oppressive practice that is expected of the practitioner in their work with service users. Similarly, training programmes for supervisors need to address anti-discrimination issues in supervision, and to model good practice through how the training programmes are organised and run.

The starting point, however, is at least one step further back, and a management issue. It is about developing an anti-oppressive culture in the agency, and providing genuinely equal non-discriminatory opportunities for staff to gain promotion to supervisory and managerial posts. This approach then needs to be carried forward into the training programme itself. Indicators will include the composition of the course membership (including the staff group); the ground rules and how they are arrived at; the illustrative material; the ways in which power issues are managed; how any discriminatory or oppressive behaviour is responded to; the recommended literature; domestic issues like type of food available, disability access; and so on.

Many training agencies now have clearly defined policy guidelines for anti-discriminatory practice on all training courses. These include statements about use of language, course content and the response to any form of discrimination – whether by course staff or members – during the training programme.

Skills/laboratory training

In our own training experience, we have found that practising skills is frequently both the most initially resisted and the most positively evaluated part of courses. There are two approaches that can be used, each of which has its own merits: supervising other course members 'for real', and using role play. The first option is when one course member 'supervises' another on some current work they are doing that is in some way problematic, and on which they would like some help. A third person takes the role of observer, and offers feedback and support. Roles in the triad are then exchanged so that each course member experiences the supervisor role. This approach has the great advantage that the trainee supervisor is working with a real current situation. The authenticity is not of course complete because the 'supervisor' does not have the real-life authority of the actual supervisor. They are thus practising consultancy not supervision skills, unless it is agreed that there is a role play element of behaving as if having supervisor role authority.

Role play in this context has its advantages and disadvantages. The advantages include being able to choose particular scenarios that may not be in the current experience of other course members, for example because they are not now practitioners. The parameters and options can be controlled more precisely. On the other hand, role play has all the familiar difficulties of acting, authenticity and conviction; trainers are referred to Burnard (1989) for some helpful guidance. We have found that the nearer the role play is to the real thing (including re-enactments of situations experienced in the past by course members), the more productive it tends to be. Whatever approach is taken to this skills training, it is useful to film some of it on video to help trainees evaluate their own style and method.

Audio and videotaping actual supervision sessions

This is another use of video or audio recording that can be an even richer learning experience. It can also be quite a threatening prospect, perhaps particularly for the experienced supervisor. The agreement of the supervisee is obviously needed, and this can be extended to a mutual viewing and discussion of a supervision session. The supervisee can also learn about their own style and skills directly from this scrutiny of supervision sessions, and through the mutual learning experience become sensitised to the existence of, for example, parallel processes. We would recommend that several supervision sessions are taped, as this takes some of the heat out of the exercise, and makes it more likely that authentic work is illustrated for comment. If supervisees agree, taping can be used for group as well as individual learning purposes. (A further use of video tapes is the use of 'triggers', a visual version of scenarios like those in Chapter 6.)

Peer exchange

If the most highly rated activity on the course evaluation form is not skills training, then it is likely to be the opportunity to meet with course colleagues who are peers and share similar tasks and experiences. This argues for a high proportion of the time to be spent in small learning groups, both facilitated and unfacilitated. It also highlights the value of having course staff who either still are – or have recently been – supervisors of a similar supervisee population.

The value of peer exchange is also of course at the heart of group supervision (see Chapter 9), and the use of small groups on supervisor training courses can model the potential benefits of supervision undertaken in a group. In fact if several supervisors who share the same line manager are on the same course, they could have a group supervision session of their own to learn about some of the issues and benefits.

The team context and supervisee feedback

Another recurring theme throughout the book has been the centrality of the team context, and this raises the issue of how the team dimension might be brought into the supervisor's training programme. Some team members may be apprehensive about whether they will be used as guinea pigs by their retrained supervisor, and they may have legitimate concerns about confidentiality. Team members can be fully included in trying out and evaluating particular approaches to supervision during the middle section of a sandwich course. They can also be involved directly in the course programme in some way, such as having a joint one-day workshop on supervision issues of mutual interest.

Supervisee feedback should be integral to the supervisor's own learning about their supervisory style and skills. However, as discussed earlier, the power differential often makes it difficult for the supervisee to give honest feedback to their supervisor. The course can help with this issue, for example by making it a requirement for supervisors to come with their supervisees' evaluation of their approach to supervision. With new supervisors, there may not yet be very much experience of their supervisory practice; for course learning purposes their supervisees can also be asked for their hopes and expectations of supervision. One spin-off may be that the external influence of the course frees up supervisor and supervisees to communicate more easily about aspects of supervision that might otherwise have been left unsaid.

Another team issue with which training can help is in developing a structural model for the organisation of supervision and team meetings of various kinds. In Chapters 8 and 9 we referred to the importance of viewing supervision as part of the team dynamic, and of the need for the supervisor to be aware of possible processes, such as sibling rivalry between supervisees.

Concepts, theories, models, research – literature to inform practice

Supervisors need to have some grounding in the relevant literature to inform their supervision practice. Many, if not most of them, are first-line managers, one of the most demanding tasks in the personal social services. Their time is, therefore, very precious, and if they are to do the necessary reading they will appreciate guidance on where to find, in palatable form, the information they require. Trainers can play a vital role in providing this guidance – as distinct from direction – as part of the courses. Some new supervisors will prefer to 'do' first and then read; others will want to read first before embarking on supervision. In this book, we have referred to most of the existing literature and tried to indicate what it offers.

The study priorities for different supervisors will vary considerably; one of the most helpful things a course trainer can do is to help each individual to work out their own personal study priorities. We think that any checklist should include reading on:

- anti-oppression/anti-discrimination (Chapter 3)
- group processes (Chapters 8 and 9)
- interviewing and communication skills (Chapter 6)
- relationship skills (Chapter 6)
- adult learning (Chapter 2)
- general supervision (all, especially Chapter 1)
- specialist supervision (this Chapter)
- stress (Chapter 7)
- self-management (throughout)
- management (throughout)
- contracting (Chapter 4)
- systems (throughout)
- models of supervision (Chapter 5)
- developmental stages of supervision (Chapter 5)

In-course consultation on current supervisory dilemmas

This can be an invaluable resource for course members. It can be offered individually by course staff, though this can be very time-consuming if there is a high take-up rate. Other alternatives rely more on trainees working with each other, with help: for example, in tandem pairs or group consultation, the latter being a particularly useful way of exploring group approaches to supervision. Actual situations can be reviewed in role-play with different people trying different ways of responding to the same situation. In much of this work there will be confidentiality and boundary issues to be cleared with line managers and supervisees, but if the agency has a committed learning ethos, this consultation can be viewed as a valuable additional resource.

Specialist elements

We have selected four examples to illustrate specialist training aspects. Two are based on service user groups (child protection, and probation work with offenders); one on context (residential); and one to illustrate method (groupwork).

Child protection

There are several aspects of child protection work that put particular pressures on supervisors. Whilst not necessarily unique to child protection – some of them are replicated in mental health work, for example – they do require specific attention in training programmes for supervisors in this specialism. The pressures stem from the high public profile of the work, and most of all from the deep feelings evoked when children are abused.

We suggest the following areas as some of those needing special attention in child protection supervisor training:

- how to manage the major personal impact of serious cases of child abuse, especially sexual abuse, on both the supervisee and the supervisor, without losing sight of the task
- how not to let one or two high profile cases (perhaps where the media are also involved) to so dominate the supervision agenda that the needs of other children and families get sidelined
- how to balance the attention given in supervision to procedures and process, respectively. Child protection work necessarily involves extensive procedures, and there is a danger that the 'therapeutic' work with children and families gets low priority in supervision
- how to ensure that the supervisors themselves get good supervision and support for their stressful work.

Creating space on the training course for supervisors to express their fears and anxieties about their awesome responsibilities, and to have these fears legitimised, may be as important as the formalised aspects of training.

Readers interested in going more deeply into supervision in child protection are referred to the book by Margaret Richards and colleagues (1990).

Probation work with offenders

Although supervision has always been considered an essential professional activity in the probation service, it has not hitherto been a statutory requirement. However, this changed in April 1995 with a new Home Office directive requiring all staff to have regular 'performance appraisals' focused on competency-based work descriptions. We regard this as 'good news and bad news'. The 'good news' is that, as we have anticipated, supervision-related activity will have a higher profile in the future, providing the opportunity to implement good practice. The 'bad news' is that this is not necessarily because of renewed interest in supervision as a professional process; it can be viewed as a control and monitoring device, which may later become linked to rates of pay.

One of the features of probation work that distinguishes it from many other social work contexts is the question 'who is the client?'. The far-reaching changes in recent years are pushing the probation service increasingly into a social control 'corrections' agency in which the client is the criminal justice system, rather than the offender. Probation supervisors have mostly been social work trained, yet as we write, there are Home Office proposals to unhinge probation from social work, by taking most if not all probation training out of universities.

The above trends may mean that the training of probation supervisors – most of whom are senior probation officers – also gets separated entirely from that of supervisors in other social work agencies. The implications of all this change for the probation supervisor training course curriculum are considerable. There is the likelihood of pressure to concentrate on procedures and monitoring of national standards. In our view, the professional, political and values issues affecting supervision cannot be separated. This needs to be recognised and given priority space on the probation training programme agenda.

Residential work

The scope of residential work is enormous and it is not possible to do it justice here. Several points, however, are essential concerning the training of supervisors working in residential settings. The first is the fact that, unlike in much of fieldwork, the supervisor and supervisee often work alongside one another. On the plus side, this allows for some informal supervision to take place whilst actually carrying out the work. It also allows the supervisor to have a much clearer impression of the work that becomes the focus of supervision. On the negative side, it can lead to a blurring of boundaries and roles to such an extent that the whole supervision process loses focus and direction. The negotiation and management of both roles and boundaries, therefore, needs to be a central theme in any training.

Allied to this is the collaborative nature of residential work. While individual workers may be assigned keyworker roles in relation to particular residents, the nature of group living and shift patterns demand the involvement of the whole team and, indeed, other residents. Consequently, the primary forum for casework discussion is more often in team meetings and group supervision than in individual supervision. Indeed, much of what gets discussed in individual supervision will, in any case, eventually have to be shared with the team.

Supervision can feel like a minefield, where every session holds implications for other parts of the residential system. Typical dilemmas include: how much support can be offered through individual supervision before it begins to undermine the importance of the team as a source of support; and how appropriate is it for the supervisee to talk about other team members within supervision, and at what point does this begin to hinder more direct communication within the team.

Training will need to help supervisors to develop a good appreciation of systems theory, group dynamics and teamwork to carry out the task effectively.

The other important consideration is the diversity of the residential worker's task. In just one shift this can change from writing a report, to cooking a meal, counselling a resident, running an art group, balancing the petty cash and confronting a resident's behaviour – to mention a few. As a result, there are often major problems facing both supervisor and supervisee in deciding what most merits exploration in supervision. The identification and monitoring of appropriate content becomes a key issue for both supervision and supervision training. Training can help by making models like those in Chapter 5 accessible and usable in everyday practice. In this way the supervisor is assisted in developing a clearer picture of the supervisory process, and can identify when and where the focus of supervision becomes unbalanced.

Groupwork

There are at least three particular issues that arise when considering supervision of groupwork, that need to be given special attention in the training of groupwork supervisors:

- accountability
- the skills repertoire of the supervisor
- the complexities arising from co-working arrangements.

Accountability is more complex than in casework because groups are often composed of members with different keyworkers who have different line managers. There are various possible models of accountability for supervisors to consider in training (see Manor 1989 for a useful discussion of these), the crucial point being the need for them to clarify which model is being used in each situation. Groupwork supervision highlights the model developed in Chapter 5, which views supervision after the induction phase as concentrating on the various connections between the worker, team, agency and practice systems.

The second issue concerns the skills of the supervisor in supervising groupworkers. This is an issue that arises for supervisors of any specialist method of social work. In our view, if they are to supervise groupwork being undertaken by their supervisees, supervisors need to have well-developed groupwork skills themselves. However, this is not always the case, and one of the things training can assist with is reassuring supervisors that they are not expected to be omnicompetent. It is more important to recognise gaps and either to seek appropriate training and/or to make arrangements for supervisees to get the assistance they need from other sources.

Groupwork in Britain often involves a co-working relationship in which the two workers will have different supervisors, and yet need shared groupwork supervision. This is really an extension of the previous two points, because the supervisor in training needs to think about accountability systems and the special skills involved in supervising a pair of co-workers together.

In the chapter on group supervision we explored the many aspects of group dynamics that can influence the success or otherwise of group approaches to supervision, including the possibility of unwittingly mirroring work with groups of service users. The discussion underlined the importance of supervisors understanding these various group processes, and the extent to which context influences behaviour in the group. This is a core area for work in supervisor training sessions, with the outside perspectives of trainers and other supervisors potentially providing the key to unlock the dynamics of problematic or 'stuck' group supervision.

Readers interested in going deeper into groupwork supervision/consultation issues are referred to an article by Allan on models and methods of consultation (Brown 1988).

Conclusion

In this chapter on training and development, we started with the contemporary agency context, which is increasingly emphasising the importance of staff appraisal and task competencies. We think these trends reinforce the importance of supervision and the role of supervisor, making it essential that training is comprehensive, integrated and linked to defined supervisor competencies. However, this whole book has stressed the importance of the supervision relationship and the qualitative dimension, which in turn requires a creative and holistic approach to training. Learning is more profound when training encompasses and integrates theoretical, experiential and reflective aspects.

Core themes in a time of change

11

Summary

Supervision is about people working with people

Throughout we have emphasised the centrality of the relationship between the supervisor and the supervisee. The relationship is the bedrock on which the work relies: if it is problematic or ineffectual, then the agency goals of enabling and ensuring high standards of social work practice are unlikely to be achieved. As with the practitioner, the supervisor has to rely heavily on their use of self as their principal working tool.

The supervisor and the supervisee each bring to supervision not only their current work concerns, but their respective personal and professional histories. These will include an internalised model informed by previous experiences and preconceptions of supervision. These past experiences will affect the initial supervision relationship, and the perspectives brought to it by each participant.

Issues of power and oppression are central to supervision

By definition, the supervisor has formal power over the supervisee, and this power inequality permeates and complicates all aspects of the supervision relationship. However, there are other kinds of power that enter the supervision equation, stemming from the unequal way in which people are treated in the wider society. Different groups in the population are oppressed because of their personal characteristics such as skin colour, sex, class, age, (dis)ability and sexual orientation. Supervisors and supervisees are not exempt from these processes, which are both imported into the social microcosm of the supervisory relationship and intertwined with the inequalities of formal power. If these power dimensions of supervision are not openly recognised and tackled, not only will the relationship be adversely affected and oppressive, but any proclaimed anti-oppressive value base for work with service users will be seriously undermined.

Supervision is a highly skilled creative activity

There is a danger that supervision can become a mechanistic bureaucratic activity concerned mainly with monitoring performance, the rigid implementation of agency policy and the exercise of control. At its best, it can be a very skilled, flexible and imaginative activity, which empowers supervisees and enables them to work more effectively and less stressfully. It can be organised as a one-to-one, tandem pair and/or group activity; it can rely solely on discussion, or include a range of other ways of learning like role-play, video, sculpting or computer programmes; it can be highly structured or free-flowing; it can be supervisor-led or based on mutual participation. Skilled creative approaches need managerial support made tangible by investment of resources in comprehensive good quality training.

Social work is a very stressful activity

Supervision of a demanding complex and stressful occupation like social work is itself a stressful occupation. Supervisors need special skills in helping workers to cope with the stress of the job and sometimes with traumatic experiences. They have to do this whilst trying to cope with their own stress, often exacerbated by the knowledge that they are held accountable for the work of their supervisees. The supervisor in turn needs skilled help from their supervisor in managing these processes in ways that strive to disentangle their own needs from those of supervisees.

Supervision is part of wider socio-political and organisational systems

Readers will be only too well aware just how much their work is being affected by contextual pressures and constraints. Many of these derive from governmental attitudes and policies often experienced as unsympathetic and sometimes openly hostile to social work and social workers. There seems to be a constant process of change with more work expected from reduced resources. The application of the market ethos to personal social services is viewed by many as the antithesis of the person-centred profession they thought they had joined.

Another contextual target for dissatisfaction and concern is the agency organisation itself, and the senior managers who make the decisions. Some of this may be wholly justified, some may be a projection of what the workers feel to be the frustrating and stressful pressures of the job. Working daily with people who are impoverished, disadvantaged, disabled and oppressed, often due to structural forces beyond their control or that of their social worker, takes its toll.

The team or work group is the immediate context of supervision, and this may be an empowering source of strength and support from which to face the wider pressures and frustrations of the job. Alternatively, if the team is fragmented, conflicted or worse, this will have immediate adverse effects on supervision – and on practice.

Much of the book has focused at the micro level on the supervision relationship itself, while frequently drawing on the systems model to emphasise the importance of wider influences on the supervision process. Our basic model comprises agency, team, practice and worker. The corollary of this systems perspective is the recognition that part of the responsibility of the supervisor is to try to influence the context positively to create a facilitating environment for supervision. This is both feasible and essential at team level, highly desirable at agency organisation level, and sometimes possible to a degree in the wider systems that impinge on the agency.

Finally, there is the context of the service users. Their ethnic origin, community background, the area they live in, the kinds of needs and problems they have, will all impinge on supervision. They may, as we have seen, have a direct impact through the parallel process phenomenon.

Looking ahead

All one can say with some confidence about the future of social work is that further changes are both inevitable and unpredictable. If present trends continue, social work will be almost unrecognisable when compared with how it was 25 years ago. At the time of writing, this transformation is under way with the purchaser–provider split, quality assurance, the rapid growth of a private sector in welfare, an emphasis on competencies and outcomes rather than process, and a radical revision of social work training. At the risk of being portrayed as dinosaurs, our view is that these trends make it even more important to retain the person-centred focus on relationship that we have maintained throughout the text.

If as seems likely, the focus of social welfare supervision becomes more and more concentrated on quality assurance, staff appraisal and other quasi-managerial functions, it may become necessary – if regrettable – to separate out the consultative and developmental components of supervision, and purchase them from consultants. If statutory agencies are prepared to put resources into purchasing consultancy – and this is a big if – this kind of separation could have some advantages. The main one would be the removal of the ensure/enable duality of the supervisor's role, which as we have seen, can sometimes lead to mistrust and suspicion of the supervisor, making it difficult for them to fulfil the enabling role.

One disadvantage of splitting off the consultancy function of supervision is that the supervisor would still have to know enough about the supervisee's work to carry out their agency accountability responsibilities. Another is that where the supervisor is also team manager, this split would profoundly change the nature of the team as a professional group, not least because the facilitative role of the supervisor would be removed.

If macro policies are thought to be changing rapidly, new information technology developments are occurring at an exponential rate and will have a major impact on supervision – as on everything else. Distance learning interactive techniques may become technologically possible for all kinds of off-site work in the near future. Computer boards will no doubt grow, allowing social workers access to immediate and expert consultation and advice on a world-wide basis. Potential advantages are obvious, and will no doubt change our views about how we think about supervision in the future. However, we cannot and do not wish to envisage a situation that minimises the value of face-to-face supervision: in our view this needs always to be the primary means of addressing the more complex support and developmental needs of the worker.

We would like to see group approaches to supervision becoming much more the norm. Groups have the potential for a quality of empowerment that, by definition, is not possible in a one-to-one relationship where one person has much power over the other. We fear that group approaches may be selected sometimes because they are thought to be cheaper: we doubt this is true, and think they need to be chosen on grounds of merit not economy.

To bring an end to this speculation, it might be prudent to listen to the words of Charles Handy (1989): 'We are entering an Age of Unreason, when what we used to take for granted may no longer hold true, a time when the only prediction that will hold is that no predictions will hold.'

References

Ahmad, B. (1990) *Advanced Award for Supervisors: Implications for Black Supervisors*. London: CCETSW.

Allan, M., Bhavnani, R. and French, K. (1992) *Promoting Women: Management, Development and Training for Women in Social Services Departments*. London: HMSO.

Bamford, T. (1982) *Managing Social Work*. London: Tavistock.

Bandler, R. and Grinder, J. (1979) *Frogs into Princes*. Moab, UT: Real People Press.

Blocher, D.H. (1983) Toward a cognitive developmental approach to counseling supervision, *The Counseling Psychologist*, 11(1): 27–34.

Borders, L.D. and Leddick, G.R. (1987) *Handbook of Counseling Supervision*. Alexandria, VA: Association for Counselor Education and Supervision.

Bourne, I. (1996) 'Groupwork Approaches to Social Work Supervision', unpublished PhD thesis. Bristol University.

Brent Borough Council (1985) *A Child in Trust* (Beckford Inquiry Report). London: Brent Borough Council.

Brown, A. (1984) *Consultation*. London: Heinemann.

Brown, A. (1988) Consultation for groupworkers: models and methods, *Social Work with Groups*, 11(1/2): 145–63.

Brown, A. (1992) *Groupwork* (3rd edn). Aldershot: Ashgate Publishing.

Brown, A. and Mistry, T. (1994) Groupwork with 'mixed membership' groups: issues of race and gender, *Social Work with Groups*, 17(3): 5–21.

Burgess, H. (1992) *Problem-Led Learning for Social Work*. London: Whiting and Birch.

Burgess, R.M., Crosskill, D. and LaRose-Jones, L. (1992) *The Black Students' Voice: Report of the Black Students' Conference 1992*. London: ABPO/ABSWAP/CCETSW.

Burnard, P. (1989) *Teaching Interpersonal Skills: A Handbook of Experiential Learning for Health Professionals* (Therapy and Practice 10). London: Chapman and Hall.

Butler, B. and Elliott, D. (1985) *Teaching and Learning for Practice*. Aldershot: Gower.

Carby, H. (1982) White women listen! Black feminism and the boundaries of sisterhood, in Centre for Contemporary Studies (eds) *The Empire Strikes Back*. London: Hutchinson.

CCETSW (Central Council for the Education and Training of Social Workers) (1989) *Regulations and Guidelines for the Approval of Agencies and the Accreditation and Training of Practice Teachers* (Paper 26.3). London: CCETSW.

CCETSW (1991a) *Rules and Requirements for the Diploma in Social Work* (Paper 30, 2nd edn). London: CCETSW.

CCETSW (1991b) *One Small Step Towards Racial Justice*. London: CCETSW.

CCETSW (1991c) *Setting the Context for Change.* London: CCETSW.

CCETSW (1992a) *Improving Practice with Children and Families.* London: CCETSW.

CCETSW (1992b) *Improving Practice with Elders.* London: CCETSW.

CCETSW (1993) *Improving Mental Health Practice.* London: CCETSW.

Conn, J.D. (1993) Delicate liaisons: the impact of gender differences on the supervisory relationship within social services, *Journal of Social Work Practice,* 7(1): 41–53.

Corrigan, P. and Leonard, P. (1978) *Social Work Practice under Capitalism: A Marxist Approach.* London: Macmillan.

Coulshed, V. (1990) *Management in Social Work.* London: Macmillan.

Cross, D.G. and Brown, D. (1983) Counselor supervision as a function of trainee experience: analysis of specific behaviors, *Counselor Education and Supervision,* 22: 333–341.

Dale, P. (1986) *Dangerous Families: Assessment and Treatment of Child Abuse.* London: Tavistock.

Danbury, H. (1986) *Teaching Practical Social Work* (2nd edn). Aldershot: Gower.

Davenport, J.A. and Davenport, J. (1988) Individualizing student supervision: the use of androgogical-pedagogical orientation questionnaires, *Journal of Teaching in Social Work,* 2(2): 83–97.

Davies, M. (1988) *Staff Supervision in the Probation Service.* Aldershot: Gower.

Davis, L. and Proctor, E. (1989) *Race, Gender and Class: Guidelines for Individuals, Families and Groups.* Englewood Cliffs, NJ: Prentice Hall.

Day, L. (1992) Women and oppression: race, class and gender, in M. Langan and L. Day (eds) *Women, Oppression and Social Work,* pp. 12–31. London: Routledge.

de Gale, H., Hanlon, P., Hubbard, M. and Morgan, S. (1993) *Improving Practice in the Criminal Justice System.* London: CCETSW.

de Souza, P. (1991) A review of the experiences of black students in social work training, in CCETSW (1991b) *One Small Step Towards Racial Justice.* London: CCETSW.

Department of Health (1989) *Children Act.* London: HMSO.

Department of Health (1990) *National Health Service and Community Care Act.* London: HMSO.

DHSS (1985) *Social Work Decisions in Child Care. Recent Research Findings and their Implications.* London: HMSO.

DHSS/SSI (1986) *Inspection of Supervision of Social Workers in the Assessment and Monitoring of Cases when Children, Subject to a Care Order, have been Returned Home.* London: SSI.

Divine, D. (1989) Unpublished report for West Midlands Probation Service.

Divine, D. (1991) Towards real communication: a study of confirmation procedures in the West Midlands Probation Service, in CCETSW (1991b) *One Small Step Towards Racial Justice.* London: CCETSW.

Dixon, D.N. and Glover, J.A. (1984) *Counselling: A Problem-Solving Approach.* New York: Wiley.

Doehrmann, M.J.G. (1976) Parallel processes in supervision and psychotherapy, *Bulletin of Meninger Clinic,* 40(1): 1–104.

Dominelli, L. (1988) *Anti-Racist Social Work.* London: Macmillan.

Douglas, T. (1983) *Groups: Understanding People Gathered Together.* London: Tavistock.

Dryden, W. and Thorne, B. (eds) (1991) *Training and Supervision for Counselling in Action.* London: Sage.

Dyer, W.G. (1977) *Team Building.* London: Addison-Wesley.

Edelwich, J. and Brodsky, A. (1980) *Burn-out.* New York: Human Sciences.

England, H. (1986) *Social Work as Art.* London: Allen and Unwin.

Feltham, C. and Dryden, W. (1994) *Developing Counsellor Supervision.* London: Sage.

Ferns, P. (1987) The dangerous illusion, *Community Care,* 8 January.

Finkel, K.C. (1987) Sexual abuse of children: an update, *Canadian Medical Association Journal,* 136: 245–52.

Fisher, B.L. (1989) Differences between supervision of beginning and advanced therapists: Hogan's hypothesis empirically revisited, *The Clinical Supervisor*, 7: 57–74.

Ford, K. and Jones, A. (1987) *Student Supervision*. London: Macmillan.

French, J.R.P. and Raven, B. (1967) The bases of social power, in D. Cartwright (ed.) *Studies in Social Power*. Ann Arbor, MI: Institute for Social Research.

Freudenberger, H. (1980) *Burn-out*. New York: Anchor Press.

Galinsky, M.J. and Schopler, J.H. (1985) Patterns of entry and exit in open-ended groups, *Social Work with Groups*, 8(2): 67–80.

Gallessich, J. (1982) *The Profession and Practice of Consultation*. New York: Jossey-Bass.

Gardiner, D. (1989) *The Anatomy of Supervision*. Milton Keynes: Open University Press.

Garvin, C. and Reed, B. (eds) (1983) Groupwork with Women/Groupwork with Men (special issue), *Social Work with Groups*, 6(3/4).

Goldstein, H. (1973) *Social Work Practice: A Unitary Approach*. Columbia, SC: University of South Carolina Press.

Grimwood, C. and Popplestone, R. (1993) *Women, Management and Care*. London: Macmillan.

Handy, C. (1989) *The Age of Unreason*. London: Hutchinson.

Handy, C. (1991) *The God of Management: The Changing World of Organisations* (3rd edn). London: Business Books.

Hanmer, J. and Statham, D. (1988) *Women and Social Work: Towards a Woman-Centred Practice*. London: Macmillan.

Hawkins, P. (1982) Mapping it out, *Community Care*, 22 July, 17–19.

Hawkins, P. and Shohet, R. (1989) *Supervision in the Helping Professions*. Milton Keynes: Open University Press.

Hawkins, P. and Miller, E. (1994) Psychotherapy in and with organisations, in M. Pokorny and P. Clarkson (eds) (1994) *Handbook of Psychotherapy*. London: Routledge.

Heap, K. (1985) *The Practice of Social Work with Groups*. London: George, Allen and Unwin.

Hearn, J., Sheppard, D.L., Tancred-Sheriff, P. and Burrell, G. (eds) (1989) *The Sexuality of Organisations*. London: Sage.

Henry, M. (1988) Revisiting open groups, *Groupwork*, 1(3): 215–28.

Heppner, P.P. and Roehlike, H.J. (1984) Differences among supervisees at different levels of training: implications for a developmental model of supervision, *Journal of Counseling Psychology*, 30: 252–62.

Hess, A.K. (1987) Psychotherapy supervision: stages, Buber, and a theory of relationship, *Professional Psychology: Research and Practice*, 18: 251–59.

Hollis, F. and Woods, M.E. (1981) *Casework: A Psychosocial Therapy*. New York: Random House.

Holloway, E.L. (1987) Developmental models of supervision, *Professional Psychology: Research and Practice*, 18: 209–16.

Home Office (1991) *The Criminal Justice Act*. London: HMSO.

Home Office (1992) *National Standards for the Supervision of Offenders in the Community*. London: HMSO.

Home Office (1993) *The Criminal Justice Act*. London: HMSO.

Houston, G. (1990a) *Supervision and Counselling*. London: The Rochester Foundation.

Houston, G. (1990b) *The Red Book of Groups*. London: The Rochester Foundation.

Humphries, B., Pankhania-Wimmer, H., Seale, A. and Stokes, I. (1993) *Improving Practice Teaching and Learning*. Leeds: CCETSW.

Jayaratne S., Brabson, H.V., Grant, L.M., Nagda, B.A., Singh, A.K. and Chess, W.A. (1992) African-American practitioners' perceptions of their supervisor's emotional support, social undermining and criticism, *Administration in Social Work*, 16(2): 27–43.

Kadushin, A. (1968) Games people play in supervision, *Social Work*, 13(3): 23–32.

Kadushin, A. (1974) Supervisor–supervisee: a survey, *Social Work*, 19: 288–98.

Kadushin, A. (1977) *Consultation in Social Work*. New York: Columbia University Press.

Kadushin, A. (1992) *Supervision in Social Work* (3rd edn). New York: Columbia University Press.

Kolb, D.A. and Fry, R. (1975) Towards an applied theory of experiential learning, in C.I. Cooper (ed.) (1975) *Theories of Group Process*. London: Wiley.

Krause, A.A. and Allen, G.J. (1988) Perceptions of counselor supervision, *Journal of Counseling Psychology*, 35: 77–80.

Lambeth Borough Council (1987) *Whose Child?* (the Tyra Henry inquiry report). London: Lambeth Borough Council.

Langan, M. and Day, L. (eds) (1992) *Women, Oppression and Social Work*. London: Routledge.

Loganbill, C., Hardy, E. and Delworth, U. (1982) Supervision: a conceptual model, *The Counseling Psychologist*, 10(1): 3–42.

Manor, O. (1989) Organising accountability for social groupwork: more choices, *Groupwork*, 2(2): 108–22.

Marton, F. and Saljo, R. (1976) On qualitative differences in learning: I Outcome and process; II Outcome as a function of the learner's conception of the task, both in *British Journal of Educational Psychology*, 46: 4–11 and 46: 115–27 respectively.

Mattinson, J. (1975) *The Reflective Process in Casework Supervision*. London: Institute for Marital Studies.

McLean, A. and Marshall, J. (1988) *Cultures at Work: How to Identify and Understand Them*. Luton: Local Government Training Board.

Mearns, D. (1991) On being a supervisor, in W. Dryden and B. Thorne (eds) *Training and Supervision for Counselling in Action*. London: Sage.

Morrison, T. (1993) *Staff Supervision in Social Care*. London: Longman.

Mullender, A. and Ward, D. (1991) *Self-Directed Groupwork: Users Take Action for Empowerment*. London: Whiting and Birch.

NALGO (National Association of Local Government Officers) (1989) *Social Work in Crisis: A Study of Conditions in Six Local Authorities*. London: NALGO.

Nelson, L.N. and Holloway, E.L. (1990) Relation of gender to power and involvement in supervision, *Journal of Counseling Psychology*, 37(4): 473–81.

Nicholson, N. and West, M. (1988) *Management Job Change: Men and Women in Transition*. Cambridge University Press.

Oliver, M. (1983) *Social Work with Disabled People*. London: Macmillan.

Oliver, M. (ed.) (1991) *Social Work: Disabled People and Disabling Environments*. London: Jessica Kingsley.

Orme, J. and Glastonbury, B. (1993) *Care Management*. London: Macmillan.

Parkinson, F. (1993) *Post Trauma Stress*. London: Sheldon Press.

Parsloe, P. (1981) *Social Services Area Teams*. London: Allen and Unwin.

Parsloe, P. (1991) What is probation? *Social Work Education*, 10(2): 50–9.

Payne, C. and Scott, T. (1982) *Developing Supervision of Teams in Field and Residential Social Work, Part One*. London: National Institute for Social Work No. 12.

Payne, C. and Scott, T. (1985) *Developing Supervision, Part Two*. London: National Institute for Social Work.

Payne, M. (1979) *Power, Authority and Responsibility in Social Services*. London: Macmillan.

Pettes, D. (1979) *Staff and Student Supervision*. London: George, Allen and Unwin.

Philipson, J. (1992) *Practising Equality: Women, Men and Social Work*. London: CCETSW.

Pritchard, C. (1986) *Maintaining Morale Through Staff Training and Development*, University of East Anglia Monograph. Norwich: University of East Anglia.

Pritchard, J. (ed.) (1994) *Good Practice in Supervision*. London: Jessica Kingsley.

Proctor, B. (1978) *Counselling Shop*. London: Burnett Books.

Reisling, G.N. and Daniels, M.H. (1983) A study of Hogan's model of counselor development and supervision, *Journal of Counseling Psychology*, 30: 235–44.

Richards, M., Payne, C. and Shepperd, A. (1990) *Staff Supervision in Child Protection Work*. London: National Institute for Social Work.

Rogers, C. (1961) *On Becoming a Person: A Therapist's View of Psychotherapy.* London: Constable.

Ronnestad, M.H. and Skovholt, T.M. (1993) Supervision of beginning, and advanced graduate students of counseling and psychotherapy, *Journal of Counseling and Development,* 71: 396–405.

Ronnestad, M.H., Winje, D. and Linder, H.C. (1984) *Methods and Focus in the Supervision of Psychotherapy.* Unpublished manuscript cited in Ronnestad and Skovholt (1993).

Sales, E. and Navarre, E. (1970) *Individual and Group Supervision in Field Instruction: A Research Report.* Ann Arbor, MI: School of Social Work, University of Michigan.

Satyamurti, C. (1981) *Occupational Survival.* Oxford: Basil Blackwell.

Schutz, W.C. (1958) *FIRO. A Three-Dimensional Theory of Interpersonal Behaviour.* New York: Rinehart.

Shapiro, B.Z. (1990) The social work group as social microcosm: 'frames of reference' revisited, *Social Work with Groups,* 13(2): 5–21.

Shulman, L. (1992) *The Skills of Helping: Individuals, Families and Groups* (3rd edn). Itasca, IL: Peacock.

Shulman, L. (1993) *Interactional Supervision.* Washington, DC: NASW Press.

Specht, H. and Vickery, A. (eds) (1977) *Integrating Social Work Methods.* London: Allen and Unwin.

Stevens, A. (1991) *Disability Issues: Developing Anti-discriminatory Practice.* London: CCETSW.

Stevenson, O., Parsloe, P., Browne, E., Hill, M., Hallett, C., Rowlings, C. and Strachan, S. (1978) *Social Services Teams: The Practitioners' View.* London: HMSO.

Stevenson, O. and Parsloe, P. (1993) *Community Care and Empowerment.* York: Joseph Rowntree Foundation.

Stoltenberg, C. (1981) Approaching supervision from a developmental perspective: the counselor complexity model, *Journal of Counseling Psychology,* 28: 59–65.

Thompson, N. (1993) *Anti-Discriminatory Practice.* London: BASW/Macmillan.

Tuckman, B.W. (1965) Developmental sequence in small groups, *Psychological Bulletin,* 63(6): 384–99.

Tuckman, B.W. and Jensen, M. (1977) Stages of small-group development revisited, *Group and Organisational Studies,* 2(4): 419–27.

Vickery, A. (1977) *Caseload Management.* London: National Institute for Social Work.

von Bertalanffy, L. (1971) *General Systems Theory: Foundations, Development, Application.* London: Allen Lane.

Webb, A. and Hobdell, M. (1980) Coordination and teamwork in the health and personal social services, in S. Lonsdale, A. Webb and T. Briggs (eds) *Teamwork in the Personal Social Services and Health Care.* London: Croom Helm.

Westheimer, I.J. (1977) *The Practice of Supervision in Social Work.* London: Ward Lock Educational.

Whitaker, D. (1985) *Using Groups to Help People.* London: Routledge and Kegan Paul.

Williams, W. (1987) A black and white issue, *Community Care,* 15 October.

Wilson, M. (1987) Child sexual abuse histories among professionals, *Child Abuse Review,* 1(7): 4–5.

Woodcock, M. (1979) *Team Development Manual,* London: Gower Press.

Worthington, E.L. (1984) An empirical investigation of supervision of counselors as they gain experience, *Journal of Counseling Psychology,* 31: 63–5.

Worthington, E.L. and Roehlike, H.J. (1979) Effective supervision as perceived by beginning counselors in training, *Journal of Counseling Psychology,* 26: 64–73.

York, R.O., Moran, J.R. and Denton, R.T. (1989) Are social workers sexually biased in their evaluations of supervisors? *Administration in Social Work,* 13(1): 45–57.

Index